The Salad Oil King

M.G. Crisci

Orca Publishing Company   San Diego   2016

Published by Orca Publishing Company

Illustrations by M.G. Crisci
Edited by Mathew J. Crisci, Robin Friedheim
Design by Good World Media

Library of Congress
No. 1-2304072401

ISBN 978-0-9914773-5-7

Manufactured in the United States of America

First Edition

Also by M.G. Crisci

ACE 44
Call Sign, White Lily
Indiscretion
Mary Jackson Peale
Now & Then
Papa Cado
Papa Cado's Book of Wisdom
Save the Last Dance
Seven Days in Russia
This Little Piggy

Learn more at
mgcrisci.com
speaker.mgcrisci.com
presskit.mgcrisci.com
ace44movie.com
twitter.com/worldofmgcrisci
YouTube.com/worldofmgcrisci
Facebook.com/worldofmgcrisci

This book is dedicated to my son Matt,
my editor, my inspiration, my collaborator, my friend

Author's Note

The Salad Oil King is a work of fiction inspired by true events. The protagonist did exist during the approximate time frame of this story. Many of the historical circumstances are real, as are some elements of the protagonist's business dealings. However, all the other characters, names, and events are fictional.

During a Chinese famine of the 1870's, a Hong Kong merchant sold

 a sardine can filled with mud to an other merchant,

 who sold it at a profit to a third merchant,

 who sold it at a profit to a fourth.

 When merchant No. 5 opened the can he discovered the fraud and complained. No. 4 replied, "Why did you open the can?

-Anonymous

Part One
Becoming Fonso

Chapter 1

———

July, 1963
Bayonne, NJ

It was almost dusk at the tank farm. An endless maze of huge red and green storage tanks connected to hundreds of pipes, huffed and puffed against a vibrant blue canvas.

The day shift was gone. All that remained was a guard sipping a bottle of 7-UP in the wooden shack at the entrance. And a skeleton maintenance crew on a dinner break in a nearby repair shed who were devouring Benuti's daily deli special — a crusty Italian hero stuffed with Genoa salami, Parma prosciutto, provolone and roasted red peppers.

Two men, one built like a pick-up truck, the other like a toothpick, pulled up to the guard shack. They were driving an unmarked 1961 Ford Grand Torino station wagon. "We're from Global Express (GLOBEX). Mr. Gravenese suggested this was a good time to do the usual inventory verification." The guard looked in the car, waved them through.

Pick-Up truck's driver was veteran FBI agent Fred Norman, 56, who ran the Bureau's North Jersey field office. Toothpick was his protégé, Jim Edwards, 29, a charter member of the new breed of college-educated, science-based agents.

The tank farm was situated on a piece of unattractive industrial wasteland at the end of the Bayonne Peninsula.

To the West was the bustling transportation complex of Port Elizabeth. From there, trains were dispatched across America, and huge container ships visited international ports of call from Europe to China.

To the East was a picture perfect view of the lower Manhattan skyline, the Statue of Liberty, and Fonso Gravenese's home away from home — Wall Street. In the background was the incessant hum of traffic from America's busiest, and perhaps ugliest thoroughfare, the New Jersey Turnpike.

Norman pulled to the far corner of the parking lot, out of the guard's view. He popped the trunk and removed a lightweight plastic extension pole. He fiddled with it for a few minutes to make sure the sections opened and closed properly.

"Let me guess," teased Edwards, "your snitch sells the Bureau information and poles?"

"Junior, let's get to it," smirked Norman. "IT" was a cluster of tanks on the edge, not visible to the guard.

The men trudged through a muddy patch of earth littered with Tootsie Roll wrappers, Coke bottles, Wise Potato Chip bags, and half-eaten Devil Dogs "Over here," shouted Norman, who stood at the base of a 120-rung steel ladder bolted to the side of a tank. "You first," he said, tapping the lower rungs.

Edwards looked straight up. "You must be kidding. I'm acrophobic."

"Wasn't in your profile," commented Norman. "Start climbing."

Edwards took a deep breath before he began his journey. A third of the way up, he stopped to catch his breath. Norman — in great shape for a man his age — grew impatient. "You should be ashamed. A guy almost twice your age, and carrying a pole no less, is whipping your ass to the top of Mount Grain."

Minutes later, the two men climbed over the three-foot high wrought iron railing bolted to the top of the tank. "Let's take five," said Edwards, perspiring like a pig.

"No rush," said Norman. "Cause we're not leaving till we find that damn trap door. According to my source, GLOBEX always took Gravenese's representations at face value." At the time, GLOBEX was one of the world's most trusted banking institutions.

"Boss, surely you jest," said Edwards. "One-point-eight-billion-dollars *($13.9 billion today's dollars)* in misrepresentations? Impossible."

Norman shrugged. "Maybe the Global auditors didn't want to dirty their fancy English suits."

The men circled the perimeter of the tank in opposite directions. "Here," said an excited Edwards, sounding like Columbus discovering America. "But it's bolted shut, and, I don't have anything to open it."

"Scientists," smiled Norman, as he pulled a flat adjustable wrench out of his jacket. "Maybe there's still room for a few dinosaurs."

A few formidable grunts and groans later, the trap door sprung open like a Jack-in-the-Box. Norman poked his head inside. The tank appeared to be filled to the legal limit with light, golden vegetable oil. In the middle of the tank was a guide hole for testing liquid inventories.

The usual process was to place a measuring rod, similar to an extra-long automotive dipstick, down the guide hole until it reached the bottom. When the stick was removed, it indicated how many feet of oil were actually in the tank. Every Global warehousing inspection had certified inventories were exactly as represented by International Grain management.

Norman followed the prescribed process and obtained the same results. "I don't get it Snitch seemed absolutely, positively certain."

"People make mistakes," consoled Edwards.

"Not when they're part of the inner circle."

A frustrated Norman paced the tank perimeter a few times. He came to an abrupt halt. "Einstein was right. Doing the same thing over and over, expecting different results is insane." He pulled the stick out. "Let's try the test a little differently."

Edwards watched.

"This time I'm going to drop the goddamn pole outside the test hole and stir it around." Norman directed. "Start snaking, I'll guide it." The two men lifted the pole, dropped it into the outer ring, and let gravity take over. Seconds later the pole came to an abrupt halt. Norman tried to wiggle it free. "I think we just hit a Long Beach Island sand bar."

"Jim, give the pole a few slow twists. I think we finally got Little Big Man." The men carefully hoisted the freed pole, and laid it on the roof of the tank. The majority was covered in a slimy, brown sludge.

"I'm not sure I'd put that on my salad," smiled Norman.

Edwards was incredulous at the obvious scam. "Amazing. Right in the middle of New York Harbor?"

"That's the answer to question number two," said Norman. "The first question is, how much did the bastard actually skim?"

Edwards shrugged his shoulders.

"Let's start checking the other tanks," said Norman.

"Boss, think about what you're suggesting. There have got to be over a hundred tanks here. If we want a hard tally, we'd need a separate pole for each tank to be admissible evidence." Norman concurred. White-collar crooks and their expensive defense attorneys were getting smarter. Cases frequently had to be dismissed based on technical violations of client Fourth-Amendment search-and-seizure rights.

"Well, at least we've got exhibit number one," said Norman.

"Maybe," cautioned Edwards. "It's not like we had a search warrant."

The men closed the tank, and headed down the steps. Suddenly there was the rumble of thunder, a few bolts of lighting, and the heavens opened. The pole slipped out of Norman's hand and tumbled fifty or so feet to the muddy ground. By the time the two men reached terra firma, they were completely drenched.

Norman slammed the pole against the tank in frustration. "If I didn't know better, I'd say that little grease ball just made a deal with the devil to give us the shaft."

Chapter 2

June, 1906
Porto Empedocle, Sicily

Dominic Pasquale Gravenese was born in the tiny seaside town of Porto Empedocle in southern Sicily. Dominic barely finished grammar school.

According to some very sketchy records, the place had 6,000 residents, one coffee bar, and a hall of records where births, marriages and deaths were registered. Most of the men worked in some aspect of the local fishing industry.

Dominic, 15, would have none of that fishing stuff. Too many hard hours, too little cash. He decided he would become a successful business-person. After thinking about it for a while, Dominic decided to invest his modest savings in a traveling retail store: wooden horse cart lined with straw and hay that carried a half dozen pieces of genuine Deruta ceramic.

As every Italian knew, Deruta dishes and plates, made at the family's centuries-old factory in Central Umbria — about 650 miles north of Empedocle — were Italy's finest and most expensive. Every family aspired to own a few pieces, if only to pass them from one generation to the next.

Six days a week, Dominic would travel to different area markets, and set up shop. He would artfully display his pieces on the bed of straw. To attract shoppers, he tied a large red, green and white sign to the rear of the cart that proudly proclaimed, "Deruta for Less."

When the shoppers gathered, he would explain, he had made a deal with the Deruta family. They sold him some of their best pieces that had small, virtually invisible blemishes. "The Deruta's want local Italian families to own at big discount, rather than sell them to greedy, wealthy tourists."

Dominic was charming and persuasive. Most shoppers wanted to buy then and there. He explained that was not the way the family wanted the process to work. "To protect the Deruta reputation, you select and pay in advance. Dominic will come back three to four weeks later with your order."

"How I know you don't steal my money?" demanded a skeptical woman. Dominic's response was vintage medicine man. "Dominic steal? Signora, I have a family. A reputation. Name one person who says I steal?"

$

There was a reason it took three to four weeks for Dominic to deliver the ceramics. Dominic had made an exclusive deal with his cousin Bruno Salerno of Partimico, another tiny Sicilian town about 30 kilometers away, to copy and produce quality Deruta ceramic knockoffs.

Bruno had exacting standards. Each piece had to be good enough to fool the Deruta family. That kind of craftsmanship took time. From time to time, the men would argue about the importance of volume and speed over quality. "We can sell much more, make more money," Dominic would argue. Bruno would counter, "When you steal, it must so good nobody complain." Bruno always prevailed.

In time, Dominic made Bruno his equal partner. For the next three years, business boomed. One day Bruno discovered he wasn't that equal. Dominic had manipulated their records. Best Bruno could determine, he actually received about 25 percent of the profits.

Shortly thereafter, the Provincial Polizia received an anonymous tip about Dominic's knockoff business. Fortunately, one of the local Polizia that Dominic bribed was able to alert him the night before the Polizia planned to make a surprise appearance.

Dominic stuffed a small bag with cash and a change of clothes, and disappeared into the night. Days later he boarded a passenger ship in the Port of Naples. He was off to America to make a new life. A life filled with good fortune, good health, and a woman to love.

As he stood on the ship's deck with the salt air filling his nostrils, he had time to reflect on his first business venture. He concluded the snitch could have only been Bruno.

He vowed to never again completely trust anyone in business. Only he would know what he was doing, and how and why he was doing it.

Chapter 3

April, 1910
Little Italy, NYC

The 18-year old Dominic arrived at Ellis Island in the Spring of 1910, and was quickly drawn to Little Italy, the home of many Italian immigrants.

As Dominic would tell friends later, Little Italy "was our kind...in the beginning." The neighborhood stretched east from the Bowery to Old Broadway, and north from Canal to Houston Street.

$

Dominic settled in a one-bedroom tenement flat at 80 Spring Street. To local residents, Dominic appeared to be a charming, hardworking entrepreneur with a little working capital and a lot of big dreams. After walking the neighborhood and observing what and how people bought, he decided to go into the retail fish business. He would sell directly to local residents from a big red cart with large wooden wheels.

Six days a week, he would leave his tiny flat at 2 a.m. and travel to the wholesale markets near Fulton Street. There he would select what he thought was the best fish at the best price. He'd then pile his inventory on a bed of glistening chopped ice and return to Little Italy.

Each day he moved his red cart to a different location until he was confident he identified those with the best sales potential. To mark his arrival, he would shout in a deep, confident voice, "Come and get it. Dominic here with the freshest fish this side of heaven. Look out the window ladies, see for yourself."

$

One sunny Tuesday in August, Philomena Bonniello, a beautiful young woman with a soft olive complexion, long brown curls and a straw hat, joined her mother, Concetta, on what had become a daily negotiation with Dominic.

Concetta, friendly, weathered, short and squatty, had migrated to New York with her husband and daughter from the agricultural village of Benevento, outside of Rome, about eight years before. When Concetta bought anything, she never took the first price. She knew it and Dominic knew it.

"I say Mrs. Bonniello, 15 cents a pound for fresh cod like stealing from the poor."

"Too much."

"But look in his eyes. They so clear. They saying, Mrs. Bonniello take me home. Make me family."

"Ten cents, my best and last offer," said Concetta firmly.

Philomena smiled at the exchange. Dominic looked into her dark brown eyes and melted. "Because you have the most beautiful daughter in all of Little Italy I give you your price this day, one condition."

"And what is that?" replied Mrs. Bonniello, not expecting the answer she heard.

"You invite Dominic to dinner. I even give you the extra cod to cook…absolutely free."

Philomena demurely rolled her eyes. Momma looked at her. She nodded. That was that. Their first official date was cappuccino and two chocolate chip cannolis at Ferrara's pastry shop. Coffee quickly became lunch. Lunch became dinner. And dinner became a marriage proposal in front of Vincent's Clam Bar on the corner of Hester and Mott.

On May 21, 1915 — ten months after they married — a son, Alfonso, arrived via a difficult, premature birth. Born under the astrological sign Taurus the Bull, he gestated in his mother's womb for just seven months and two weeks.

The doctor explained, "The good news, you are the parents of a healthy young boy. But, because he was born so premature, he may be smaller than the average as an adult."

Neither Dominic nor Philomena took mind. They were elated mother and baby were healthy. Dominic made it his business to play with Fonso at the end of each business day. By the time Fonso was three, the father-son routine was in full bloom. When Fonso woke from his afternoon nap, he would sit on the floor, legs crossed, waiting for his father, who arrived home about 4 p.m.

"Where is my little King?" Dominic would ask with arms outstretched. The men would then play games until Philomena announced dinner was ready.

As events unfolded, Philomena was unable to have any additional children, and Dominic did not want to adopt. "I am not raising a child who is not my blood," he roared whenever Philomena raised the subject.

It also turned out the doctor was right about Alfonso. He was diminutive compared to the other neighborhood kids his age. He also had a squeaky, high-pitched voice. That was only the half of it. By the time Alfonso — now nicknamed *Fonso* – was five years old, he had developed a chronic vision problem called amblyopia, caused by an acute misalignment of the left eye. When Fonso stared straight ahead, one eye was normal while the other moved uncontrollably from side to side. The only known solutions at the time were frequent visits to an ophthalmologist, experimental eyes drops from Europe, individually supervised ocular physical therapy sessions, and specially formulated glasses. The sum total was quite a bit of money. Consequently, Dominic knew had to find a way to increase his income. His first instinct was to sell more types of fish. The change in strategy helped a bit, but was still not enough to provide the lifestyle he wanted for himself and his family. Despite their difficult times, Philomena never complained.

$

One evening after dinner, Dominic sat quietly in the corner, reading his newspaper and sipping a glass of grappa. Grappa is a popular, bitter Italian digestive made by distilling skins, pulp, seeds and stems in grain alcohol. The clear liquid is reminiscent of paint thinner.

Dominic noticed an interesting success story in the business section of the popular New York *Journal American* newspaper. The CEO of Mobil Mystery Oil talked about how he had increased company profitability by developing supplemental income streams. In other words, motor oil remained his primary product line, but he now also manufactured related automotive products such as carburetor cleaners and fuel additives, using his existing production machinery and distribution channels.

That story became the basis for a distinctly Dominic supplemental income stream of revenue. Every time a customer bought fish, he would stuff about four ounces of ice — approximately one handful — in its mouth *before* he weighted it. Once the price was agreed, he would distract the customer with a charming casual comment. He would quickly pop the ice out then wrap the fish.

He estimated his new income stream increased his net income by 25 percent. The scheme worked like a charm — the money started rolling in. Before long, all the doctor bills were current, new pieces of furniture dotted the apartment, and a brand new Philco radio with shiny big black dials sat in the far corner of the living room.

Philomena couldn't help but notice the sudden success. Dominic said nothing, and Philomena chose not to ask.

$

Fonso, never a great student to begin with, volunteered to help his father after school. Initially, Philomena resisted. She wanted her son to get a good education. "Education gives people opportunity," she said.

Fonso had a more persuasive argument for his father. "Papa, why pay a perfect stranger? I'll do for less. And we'll keep the money in the family."

At first Fonso just cleaned the cart at the end of each day. Dominic assumed Fonso had no idea about his little scheme until the day...

One of his regular customers, Mrs. Benuto, approached Dominic's cart. Mrs. Benuto was a brute of a woman who looked as if she could carry a thousand raviolis in one hand. She prowled the neighborhood with a scowl on her face that could make a wild lion flee in fear.

Mrs. Benuto had just ordered about ten pounds of codfish from Dominic for the Sunday family dinner. "These over here are the best," she pointed. Dominic turned his back to his customer, picked up the fish, and quickly stuffed some crushed ice in its mouth. Fonso's eyes bugged out of his head.

"Dominic, what's taking so long," said Mrs. Benuto. "Patience, Mrs. Benuto. I am taking the fin off before I weight. I do that for good customers."

She smiled, not realizing how close she'd come to discovery.

Fonso realized interruptions could seriously derail Papa's narrow time-to-stuff window. He decided to help by creating an entertaining diversion for Mrs. Benuto and the other women standing in line.

"Ladies and gentlemen," he barked. "Today I would like to show you my latest yo-yo trick." He took his hat off and tossed it to the ground. "First, I will fully extend my string, then make Charlie — I call my yo-yo Charlie — dance along the sidewalk to the song *Whistle a Happy Tune*. When he's finished dancing he will rest in the hat."

A smiling Mrs. Benuto turned to watch. "You take care of me, Dominic, I want to watch your little boy." She melted as Fonso charmed the crowd with his song-and-dance routine. Papa jammed more ice into the fish, weighed and wrapped it in newspaper, and marked the price with a big black crayon.

When Fonso finished, he bowed, and bent over to pick up his hat. A smiling Ms. Benuto placed a quarter in the hat. "Nice boy." The others followed suit. Fonso was genuinely surprised.

"That is very nice of you, but I can't take…"

"Sometimes," said Mrs. Benuto, "when you ask little, you get more." Fonso would remember that lesson years later. Fonso smiled. Mrs. Benuto had done just the opposite. She paid a 30 percent premium for the fish, not including Fonso's tip.

After Mrs. Benuto left, Dominic proudly put his arm around Fonso, "I think you're now a partner."

The more hours Fonso worked, the more songs he added to his little show, songs like *East Side-West Side* and in the *Good Old Summer Time*.

Chapter 4

———

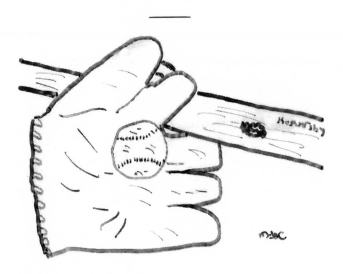

June, 1927
Little Italy, NYC

$

Dominic foolishly assumed Philomena was like the other neighborhood women. He never discussed his business, kept all the records, and made all the bank deposits and withdrawals...until that night after dinner. "Fonso, go play in your room. Mama and your Daddy want to talk."

It was almost 9 p.m. Dominic was listening to the evening news in front of the radio. "Want a grappa?" interrupted Philomena.

Fonso, now twelve, was doing homework in his room. He decided to place his ear on his bedroom keyhole."

Dominic knew something was up. Philomena never got Dominic a grappa. She felt grappa was a man's drink, so a man could get it for himself.

"What you want to talk about?" asked Dominic. "I want to talk about *OUR* fish business. I reviewed our bank balances yesterday. Our fish business is doing much better than before."

Dominic became flustered. "You did what? How you...."

"And I think I know why. You are lucky to have Fonso as such a good worker."

Dominic popped out of his chair in horror. "You tell no one, *Capische?*"

"Don't you mind," reassured Philomena with a gentle smile and a touch of reassurance. "Not to worry. Mums the word." Philomena wasn't finished. "I want you to do something for me."

"And, that is?" asked Dominic, eyebrows raised.

"When the time comes, I want a house. No more apartment. It will be good for us and good for Fonso."

"Fair enough," said Dominic. I love you like crazy. You have your house as soon as we have most of the money. No big mortgage like Americans."

"Deal," said Philomena, sticking her hand out to shake.

"I shake you alright but not in hand," laughed Dominic as he picked his wife and carried her into the bedroom.

$

Fonso overheard the entire discussion. He figured this might also be his moment to make a request or two. "Papa, I'd like to talk man-to-man," said Fonso the following evening after dinner.

Dominic smiled. "Come sit." The two men sat in the living room while Mama cleaned up.

"You know I love baseball."

Dominic nodded.

"But we both know I'm a little short to play many positions."

"Sooo?" said Dominic.

"I have found the answer," Fonso confidently. "My best position is second base. I can be like Rogers Hornsby, Eddie Collins and Frankie Frisch."

"Good solution," replied Dominic. "In America no dream is too large."

"Papa I agree. But to be the best in baseball, Fonso should have the best equipment. Right?" From a very young age, when Fonso wanted to emphasize something, he developed an odd habit of referring to himself in the third person.

"I see," smiled Dominic.

Fonso continued to weave his web. "You know Fonso stopped by Mariucci Sporting Goods today. He showed me the new Roger Hornsby glove. The one that has a deep pocket to make you catch better. But those prices, mama mia. He realized it would take two, maybe three seasons to save enough. So Fonso stops and thinks. Finally, the solution arrives."

Philomena, listening in the kitchen, had all she could do not to bust out laughing.

"Papa, you buy me the glove now. I give you an I.O.U. for the full amount. You take it out of my salary for two, maybe three months."

"Deal." Papa extended his hand.

"Of course, in the meantime, you put the I.O.U. money aside. If you like the way I work, you give me a bonus equal to the I.O.U."

Like father like son, thought Philomena.

Papa again extended his hand.... Fonso wasn't quite finished. "Papa, I learned something else on the trip to Mariucci's. Saving for anything good, costs more and more money. To be fair, most of my friends who work after school make three times more per hour."

"What friends?" challenged Dominic.

"Not right to talk about friends behind their back. Let's agree on double."

$

Dominic went to the park with his new glove on Sunday morning hoping to get into a pick-up game. Usually the two best players would act as managers and pick their other teammates for a seven-inning game. When the game was over, the kids would spend the afternoon with their families.

This day the two managers were Ricco Cicolo and Pino Mariucci, both 17. Only eighteen kids showed up, so Fonso knew, despite being the youngest and least athletic, he had to be picked. Reluctantly, Ricco made Fonso his last pick. Ricco couldn't help but notice Fonso had a new glove with a deep pocket which should make it easier for him to catch. And he couldn't make too many mistakes at second base because he was surrounded by a very good first baseman and shortstop.

Fonso and his black horned-rim glasses went to bat three times and struck out three times. He also made errors on the two balls that were hit directly to him. His team lost by one run. A despondent Fonso stood in the corner under a tree, tears welling in his eyes.

Pino made it his business to come over and mock Fonso publicly. Then he stomped on his Fonso's new glove. "You little putz, you ain't ever gonna be good at nothing," laughed Pino. The strapping, broad-shouldered Ricco was furious. He wasn't particularly school smart but he had a fierce pride in his heritage. The way he saw things, Italians didn't treat other Italians that way. You saved that crap for the Chinese up Canal Street and the Jews on the Bowery.

Ricco then demonstrated why he had been expelled from three different schools by the age of thirteen for a variety of offenses — included punching out a teacher because he didn't like his grade in Catechism class. Ricco punched Pino so hard, he bounced off the nearby tree. Blood started to spurt from his mouth. Ricco moved forward to inflict more damage. Pino ran like hell.

$

As a thank you, Fonso bought Ricco a chocolate milkshake at Esposito's candy store with an extra scoop of the ice cream of his choice.

A few days later Fonso was alone cleaning up the fish cart. Pino appeared out of nowhere. Fonso picked up a fish knife and screeched "back off."

Pino sneered and kept coming. Rico again appeared out of nowhere. The mere sight of him sent Pino fleeing.

A few milkshakes later the men created the Hornsby Agreement. Ricco promised, as long as he knew Fonso, he would always have his back. In exchange, Fonso, convinced he would be a successful businessman, promised Ricco he would always share his good fortune.

Neither realized their new friendship would last a lifetime.

Chapter 5

May, 1930
Lower Manhattan, NYC

Fifteen-year-old Fonso decided it was his job to help Mama get her house. His plan was simple — the Gravenese's would own or control lots of fish carts, and have many people working for him.

While his father worked the ice scam, Fonso recruited other neighborhood fish vendors to join their team. "Giovanni, work with us. We will show you how to make more money selling your fish. Maybe 30 percent more right away. Guaranteed. You keep part, and we keep part."

Once a cart seller agreed to join the Gravenese cooperative, Fonso and Dominic provided the initial training to make sure their scam was executed flawlessly. Fonso also provided tips on how to make the shopping experience more entertaining for shoppers while they were being scammed.

Before long, branded Gravenese fish carts collected a share of virtually every fish sold in Little Italy. And neighborhood shoppers loved the idea of poking fish and being entertained while they negotiated what they thought was the best price.

$

As the business expanded, Dominic quickly learned enough would never be enough for his enterprising son.

Fonso decided the family business need a new advertising campaign to drive more traffic to the carts. He created a slogan he thought would attract attention: "Gravenese Means Fresh Fish at Fair Prices." Then hired some grammar-school kids to place posters in virtually every retail store window. They were paid a quarter for every poster. Initially, Papa protested about selling fish on a price strategy. "Fonso, makes no sense. We make less on every fish."

"Papa, you are looking at it all wrong. Think about how much money we make in total. The more carts we control, the more fish we sell, the more money we make. But it's also important we give everybody a taste. We just make sure nobody knows what the other gets. That way we always come out way ahead."

$

Despite the exploding cash flow, Dominic had another concern. "Fonso, how we do know all our people are honest? We cannot watch everybody, all the time."

"Good question, Papa," said the confident young man, strutting around like Napoléon.

"That's why we need to hire somebody who always knows who sells how much."

"Suppose, we find people steal?"

"Papa, you have to realize, when it comes to money, everybody steals. We just have to tell them don't steal like a greedy pig."

"How do we do that?" wondered Dominic.

"Leave that to me," said Fonso.

$

Fonso called Ricco. Together, they created an unwritten business agreement.

Ricco would handle all future cart placement and relocations. For services rendered, Ricco received a one-time initiation fee of fifty dollars per cart location or relocation and an ongoing maintenance fee of ten dollars per cart per week.

Fonso would keep and monitor the books. Should it appear a vendor was shortchanging the Graveneses, Ricco would act as the collections department, and receive 10 percent of what he collected.

Fonso became the first customer of what would eventually become the Cicolo Security Services Company.

$

Over the next two years, the Gravenese fish cart business boomed. Fonso also learned some important lessons.

1. Successful business partnerships were ultimately all about trust.

2. Getting others to always play by your rules required periodic intimidation. (But it was best not to know much more than that.)

3. When Ricco messed up someone, it was important the messed-up person spread the word. There was no substitute for personal testimonials.
4. Women shoppers prefer to buy from good people, people who give back to their community.
5. From a donor perspective, the best give-back programs were those that generated the most visible publicity for the least amount of money.

Chapter 6

———

August, 1932
Battery Park, NYC

Despite his early business successes, Fonso had low self-esteem. He was well aware his stocky appearance and general lack of athleticism left him at a distinct disadvantage when it came to girls. As result, he bought himself a colorful bike with whitewall tires.

On Sundays he would ride down to Battery Park at the tip of Manhattan Island, said hello to the Statue of Liberty, and watch the ships come and go at the Staten Island Ferry terminal.

One Sunday, he treated himself to a hotdog at the stand near the main ticket booth. A cute 16 or 17-year old girl smiled at the homely figure. He smiled back and then froze. He didn't know what to do next. The girl made it easy. She walked over. "Hi, my name is Cindy. What's yours?"

"Fonso."

"That's a cool bike, Fonso. But, where's your girlfriend?"

"She didn't come…I mean I don't have one."

"My goodness, are you really a virgin?"

An embarrassed Fonso remained silent.

"Got any money?"

"You want a hot dog, ice-cream, or something?" asked Fonso.

"Sounds like you've got some real money."

"Let's just say, I run a good business."

Cindy suggested the unexpected.

"I want the something." You know, for two dollars you can get a lot of something."

Fonso finally got the hint. He returned the quip. "Fonso isn't sure. You know Fonso never buys at the full retail price."

Cindy laughed confidently. "Would you tell Fonso that Cindy is giving him her best price. But because he's such a gentleman, she will give a one-time discount."

Fonso nodded.

"Good. Now that that is settled, would you mind telling Fonso that Cindy has reserved a private spot in the bushes where nobody can see anything."

$

He was certain his close friendship with Cindy happened because he owned a cool bike

$

After the Cindy affair, Fonso decided bicycles would become his way to give back to the community. But not just any bicycles. Fonso decided to donate a portion of his earnings to buy

24 top-of-the-line German-made Schwinn model B607's bikes for the St. Patrick's Parish Boys Club. The bikes were hand-painted with whitewall tires, shiny chrome handlebars, bright enamel bodies, a cantilevered frame, and a special built-in kickstand. Fonso also had a custom made wrought iron bike rack built by Gino the blacksmith, so the bikes wouldn't walk away when not in use.

Father Don, St. Patrick's Pastor, publically praised Fonso's largesse as a model for Little Italy's young men. "God recognizes Fonso Genovese's work ethic and generosity," said the Pastor from his Sunday pulpit. "God also recognizes the fruit does not fall far from the tree. So we would also like to recognize Dominic Genovese for being an outstanding role model for his son."

Father Don even invested a portion of his meager priestly earnings into a forged brass plate, engraved with Fonso's name that was permanently affixed to the bike rack.

"I think our boys should never forget the name of their generous benefactor," said Father Don at the dedication.

$

Father Don and the boys were not the only recipients of Fonso's largesse.

Fonso's bike supplier, Franklin Donato, was a most happy fella. Franklin's usual inventory was comprised of low-cost everyday household items such as pots and pans, toasters, and hand beaters that fell off the trucks. Typically, he remarketed his merchandise one unit at a time.

When Fonso offered to buy the 24 Schwinn's and pay cash up front, Franklin thought manna had dropped from heaven. Not surprisingly, Franklin gave Fonso a substantial discount off the wholesale price — a favor Fonso would remember years later. As Fonso said, "If you're a friend of Fonso's, you are a friend for life."

Chapter 7

October, 1932
North Bronx, NYC

One evening after dinner, Dominic announced, "Philomena, I find the perfect house to for us to live, build a new business and Fonso finish high school." Fonso hated classes, homework, teachers, and being told what to do.

He handed Philomena a picture of a narrow brick house at 1812 Haight Avenue in the Williamsbridge section of the North Bronx. It was three stories high with a well-maintained backyard, and a small front porch overlooking the park across the way. Philomena gasped, "Can we afford such a grand place?"

"No worries. Thanks to Fonso's ideas, we make more than enough. I decide to retire from fresh fish. More money in meat."

"Wonderful. When are you thinking we move?"

"Next week," said Dominic.

"Why so soon?" wondered Philomena.

Dominic's response sounded lame, "With all the new expenses, it is getting harder and harder to make a fair living."

Philomena sensed there was more. But she also realized when it came to business, sometimes it was not worth knowing more.

The reality was that Pino Mariucci was now a made man in the Garafolo Family. He had gotten wind of the success of the Gravenese fish cooperative. One evening, over a glass of wine at La Mela Restaurant on Mulberry, Pino explained to Dominic that he had to pay 25 percent of profits to his organization for weekly operating insurance.

Dominic protested meekly. "We already share with Ricco."

Pino smirked. "You can never have too much insurance. But we are also friends, so you don't have to start payments until next week."

Fonso said nothing.

Dominic told Fonso what happened when he returned home.

Fonso telephoned Ricco later that night and told him about the Pino shakedown. "He is trying to squeeze you and me." Ricco was furious. He recalled his most recent run in with Pino's territorial greed just six months ago.

Ricco's security services company had grown from its humble beginnings with Fonso. They were now a member of the Moretti family, the exclusive protection agents for all the zeppole and sausage stand vendors at the annual Feast of San Gennaro on Mulberry Street.

The feast had grown dramatically over the past decade — there were now more revelers, more stands, and more revenues to protect. The Garafolo family wanted a piece of the action. In a brokered deal, the Garafolos, in the person of Pino, were given all the vendors on the east side of the street from Canal to Houston in exchange for certain prostitution concessions in other parts of Manhattan. The deal lasted one festival. Pino decided the west side of the street had the bigger vendors who paid more for protection insurance.

The Morettis complained to the Garafolos about the broken trust. The agreement was unstated but clear. If Pino disrespected boundaries again, the Moretti Group in the person of Ricco and friends could do as they pleased. There would be no reprisals.

$

An intimidated Dominic went to the bank the following Monday, and made the first week's premium payment to Pino. The next day he sent Philomena to withdraw all the remaining cash in a shopping bag.

With the cash at home and bags packed, Dominic explained the exit plan to Fonso. Early the next morning, the Gravenese family left their fully furnished apartment, slipped into a waiting cab, and fled to the North Bronx.

Before they put the key in the door at their new home, Dominic stopped at Williamsbridge Saving & Loan on the corner of Morris Park Avenue and Williamsbridge Road. There, he opened a bank account, and rented a large safety deposit box.

$

A few days later Ricco and Fonso spoke on the phone.

Ricco explained that no more premiums were due from the Gravenese family. Fonso probed. All Ricco would say was that "the matter was closed." And he was looking forward to working with Fonso again in some capacity. Fonso probed one more time.

"You know what makes smart people smart?" asked Ricco. "They know what they don't know."

The next sound Fonso heard was a dial tone.

About two months later the *Daily News* reported an unidentified man was fished out of the East River around the base of the Manhattan Bridge.

Fonso had learned his first lesson in honor among thieves.

$

The early Williamsbridge Road days were busy ones for the Gravenese family.

Dominic searched for the right location for his new butcher shop on busy Morris Park Avenue. Mama furnished and decorated her first house. And Fonso, now seventeen, began the junior year of high school at Cardinal Hayes, just off the Grand Concourse and 152nd Street.

The local real estate agents suggested Dominic look for a location east of Williamsbridge Road. They told him the neighborhood's predominantly middle-class residents did not have a popular-priced butcher shop. Ultimately, Dominic decided on a site at the corner of Lurting and Morris Park Avenues, next to the busy Venice Pizzeria, and directly across from the well-regarded Cisco Fruit and Vegetable emporium.

Dominic's bottom line — the area was highly trafficked, the lease was fairly priced, the store didn't require many leasehold improvements.

The afternoon hours before he signed the lease, Dominic took a walk after lunch. He decided to stop at a small park a few blocks west of Kingsbridge Road. He noticed an unassuming four-store shopping strip. There was a candy store, a dry cleaner, and a huge pharmacy called Salardi's, which proudly proclaimed it was the oldest full-service pharmacy in the North Bronx. Adjacent to Salardi's was an empty store with no signs in the windows.

Dominic decided to check the place out. As he walked the aisles, he couldn't help but notice the store was well stocked, creatively merchandised and attractively lit.

A tall, distinguished man with gray hair, approached, "Can I help you find something sir?"

"Not really, I just moved into the neighborhood with my family."

The man stuck out his hand and smiled, "Eugene Salardi welcomes you to the neighborhood."

"Are you the Salardi on the sign?"

"If you mean am I the owner, the answer is yes. I have been on this corner since my father came from the old country 20 years ago."

"A Pisano?" asked Dominic.

"Yes, a Pisano," he nodded. "But a very Italian-American Pisano."

"You speak perfect English."

"Why shouldn't I?" commented Salardi. "English is my first language?"

"May I be personal?" asked Dominic.

"Depends."

"Everything seems to cost a little more. And, you're far away from the main section of Morris Park Avenue."

"So?" said Salardi.

"You make money?" asked Dominic.

"Let me answer this way. I have made enough money to send my three daughters to some of America's finest Colleges — Harvard, Colgate and Dartmouth," replied the smiling Salardi.

"How you do it? I don't understand."

"It's not complicated to imagine, but it is hard to execute," explained Salardi. "I decided I would open the best pharmacy in the area, offer home delivery. Then I spent the money to make my store the best shopping experience in the area. You can even have a free cup of coffee at Salardi's, whether you buy something or not. All those little things allow me to charge a premium price for all my regular products. Nobody complains."

The proud Salardi continued. "In fact, customers now come from other neighborhoods to shop and chat with friends, and catch up on the latest gossip. Plus, everybody knows they can depend on Salardi's to deliver important medicines, all day every day."

"Thank you very much. You give me an idea. How do I find the real estate agent for the empty stores?"

"You are looking at him," smiled Mr. Salardi. "Actually, I own all the stores. I found real estate a good place to invest profits in America."

Thirty days later, Salardi and Dominic had agreed on the terms of a lease. Dominic had decided to open a different kind of butcher shop. It would be called Dominic's Fine Meats. He bought a specific refrigerator to dry-age better cuts of meat, and interviewed the best wholesale distributor he could find, Aldo Locatelli. Aldo's pitch was simple. "If you can find better meat at a better price in the North Bronx, Aldo will give you his first child." (Aldo never married.)

Aldo became Dominic's exclusive product supplier. He also introduced Dominic to his cousin, Frankie Locatelli. "Hiring Frankie will make more money." Aldo was correct. Frankie — an expert meat trimmer — increased the amount of thick slab bacon, pork ribs, rib roasts and prime New York strip steaks from hog and cattle sides by 20 to 25 percent.

$

Dominic also remembered fondly what Fonso had done to promote his fish carts in Little Italy. So after school, Fonso visited every store on the east side of Morris Park Avenue and offered a free prime aged steak to every merchant who placed a Dominic Fine Meats poster in his window.

Dominic also picked up other merchandising tips from Mr. Salardi. He stacked piles of bright shiny red meat in the refrigerator cabinet with clear labels and price tags. He covered the floor with shaved hickory chips so the store had a pleasant aroma. And he gave Mr. Salardi an endless supply of prime meat in exchange for an endless flow of referrals.

Dominic also used the sales skilled he honed on the streets of Little Italy. He created THE Gravenese Guarantee. "If you find better tasting meat, I return the full purchase price. No questions."

Dominic also made it almost impossible for shoppers to protest the premium prices by bribing them with free espresso, cappuccino and pastries, and fun little gifts for the kids, including pieces of Double Bubble chewing gum with cartoons and Dick Tracy comic books.

Dominic learned one additional customer retention trick from Mr. Salardi — the House Account. Customers loved the idea of walking in, buying their meat, and signing an I.O.U. It made them feel important, that somebody trusted them. "House accounts are for my best customers," Dominic would pitch. Once a month, Philomena would send bills to the home of the house account holder. When they stopped by to pay their bill, they would inevitably be lured into making another purchase.

Fonso suggested a little additional twist to insure his father was paid promptly. They prominently displayed a poster that thanked Dominic's best customers for their house accounts. If someone didn't pay as agreed, a big black line went through their name. Nobody wanted a line.

House accounts taught Fonso another lesson in consumer psychology. Customers with house accounts always bought more, but if you weren't careful they would carry large unpaid balances. So he mastered the art of friendly persuasion. "Mrs. Bello, my Papa gives you the best meat whenever you want. Because you pay so late our employees and their families go hungry."

After nine months, the business was in the black. After eighteen months, Dominic had earned more money than he ever made with his fish carts. Best of all, his profits were all legit. There were no Pinos, no Garafolos…and no stuffed-ice scams.

Chapter 8

April, 1933
South Bronx, NYC

Philomena, now 37, and still extraordinarily striking, was like a kid in a candy store when it came to furnishing their new home.

She saw a large Labor Day sale ad in the *New York Daily News* for the popular Hearn's Department Store on Third Avenue and 149th Street, about 40 minutes from Haight Avenue. She boarded the bus on Morris Park, a few blocks from her house. Got off at the 180th Street train station and took the elevated subway to 149th Street. Along the way, she was able to stare directly into the shabby African American apartments that dotted the El. She thought to herself, what self-respecting white family would want to live among jungle people?

Hearn's was everything Philomena hoped and more. Seven stories of attractively displayed housewares, furniture, and clothing that rivaled the more famous, and more expensive, Macy's at Herald Square in Manhattan. And Hearn's was happy to deliver purchases right to your door...at no additional charge. They even took the furniture and appliances out of the shipping crates and placed them precisely where you wanted.

Philomena, quite orderly by nature, knew she couldn't afford to tackle every room at once. She developed a Philomena priority list. The master bedroom was first. As she joked to Hearn's prudish sales clerk — "sex comes first; family second." Fonso's room was next — "so he didn't bother mom and dad at night." In true Italian fashion, she was always concerned that her men's stomachs were satisfied, so the kitchen came next

Months into the process Philomena got around to the living room. One evening a tired Dominic came home from a long day's work at his market.

"I have a surprise for my husband."

He looked at her smile. "You bright face can light the sky. Love you very much." In the corner of the living room sat a big English style wing chair. "My king's new throne. Fonso, get Papa's newspaper, while I finish making dinner. I'll call when we're ready." Within a matter of minutes Dominic's eyes closed. As he fell fast asleep, his head comfortably came to rest on one of the upper chair wings.

Philomena's frequent trips to Hearn's created a routine. After shopping she would walk up a small hill to Woody's luncheonette on the corner of 152nd Street. She loved the 35-cent lunch special — a juicy hamburger, accompanied by a choice of Mozzarella or American cheese, a mixed salad and a cup of coffee. After lunch she would stop at the Church of the Immaculate Conception on 150st Street and Melrose Avenue. There she would say a few prayers before re-boarding the Third Avenue El.

Philomena loved the Church, a hidden gem of Gothic architecture with a two-story grand Kimball organ in a rear balcony. She thanked God for her family, her friends, her good fortune, and for allowing such a splendid Church to be part of her life.

$

When Philomena was finished inside the house, her thoughts turned to the 60-foot long x 20-foot wide backyard. She identified a sunny patch in the rear as the ideal location for a small tomato garden to grow juicy beefsteak tomatoes during the summer, surrounded by a border of colorful yellow and white zinnias. Dominic loved beefsteak tomatoes and buffalo mozzarella. But he was not crazy about all the manual labor. He made a Dominic-style deal with Philomena. "You like, you do." But Philomena wanted what she wanted — so she prepared the soil and added fertilizer for the summer harvest.

The second wish was a bit more complicated. Philomena wanted a large wood table in the yard with benches for family meals and two Adirondack chairs, so she and Dominic could sit and read. But she also wanted the table to sit under a pergola covered in red-skinned grape vines that provided shade on sunny summer days.

Dominic liked her ideas. But he didn't have a clue how to measure and cut the wood properly or cast concrete forms.

Fortunately, Philomena had something most of the women she met did not have — unlimited access to the Gravenese savings accounts and safe-deposit box. She hired a small local home improvement firm, the Scaramuzzo Brothers, to build the pergola to her precise specs. They even built a charming canvas roof on the top of Dominic's chair on the off chance that he might doze off while reading. Philomena called the chair, "*His* Summer Throne."

Dominic was so impressed by the old-world craftsmanship and attention to detail that he gave the brothers ten 1 ½-inch thick, prime-aged strip steaks as a tip.

The unintended consequence of Dominick's generosity? The Scaramuzzos told every one of their family and friends about Dominic's "best-anywhere" butcher shop.

Chapter 9

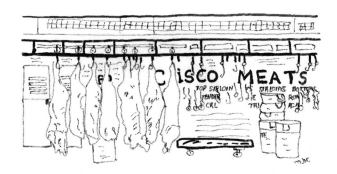

June, 1933
North Bronx, NYC

The success of Dominic's growing retail operation finally caught Fonso's eye. He was very unhappy at school. The Christian Brothers were stern teachers. And the classes too hard. The fact that he had been demoted one grade to catch up did not sit well.

Fonso also missed the action of being in business. One night over dinner he unfolded his new plan though the back door.

"Mama, great supper like always." Fonso never complimented his mother on her meals. Philomena knew something was up.

"Mama and Papa, it's no secret Fonso is not doing well in school."

"We did notice the first reports," said Philomena.

"They very, very bad." scowled Dominic.

"Maybe Cardinal Hayes is simply the wrong school," suggested Philomena.

"Perhaps school in general is the wrong place for Fonso," said Fonso.

"Young man," said Philomena, we want you to be successful, take advantage of all that America has to offer. That's why a good education is so important."

"Does that mean anyone who doesn't graduate from high school or go to college is a failure?" asked Fonso. "Look at Papa."

"What are you suggesting?" said Philomena.

"I've watched Frankie Locatelli trim the steaks, the bacon and the roasts. I would like to work as his assistant. In time, I can take over trimming all the meat."

"What about Frankie?"

"Papa, don't you always say, "La Familia comes first?"

$

Fonso learned the business of meat quickly, thanks to Frankie's tutelage.

He even experimented with some new trimming technique that yielded more saleable meat from every slab of beef and pork. "Papa, we now make 20 percent more money on every sale because of the way I trim. Imagine if we can buy our meat for less, we'll make even more money."

"Fonso, you do good so far. However, Aldo very fair. We get good prices and good service. What more can we ask?"

"Better prices and good service...just leave it to me, Papa."

Fonso knew the key to lowering his cost of goods was to eliminate the middleman and buy direct from the source. One morning after Aldo had taken his weekly order from Dominic, Fonso decided to follow him on his rounds. After visits a few additional North Bronx butcher shops, Aldo took the subway to the 125th Street station and began to walk west.

A few minutes later, he was standing at the edge of a bustling wholesale meat market under the West Side Highway that extended from 125th to 129th Street. Each purveyor had a big company sign. Metal awnings bolted to the walls held giant hooks with massive sides of beef and pork waiting to be sized and packed. The smell of sweet fat drippings filled the air and seeped into the sidewalks. Refrigerated trucks filled with boxes of choice and prime cuts of meat spewed black clouds of burnt oil as they pulled in and out of the curbs.

Locatelli entered one of the larger buildings, Cisco's Wholesale Meat Packing Company. Fonso waited until Locatelli left then went inside. The place hummed with activity. There was an assembly line of butchers with butcher blocks, trimming piece after piece of meat, and tossing the waste into large tin pails.

"Kid," said a gruff, heavyset man with a stubby black beard, "what do ya want?"

"My father and I own a market. We heard Mr. Cisco sells very high-quality meat," said Fonso politely. "I was wondering if I might speak to him."

"Kid, we don't do one-offs. Get yourself a middle man."

"Would it make a difference if I told you I actually represent a group of North Bronx butchers?" said Fonso, making it up as he went.

"How many?"

"Maybe forty."

"Wait here."

The man shouted at a desk to the rear of the busy floor. "Matty, there's a customer that wants to talk to you."

A heavyset man about six-foot-three, with powerful arms and a big smile on his round face, lumbered over.

"Kid, I forgot to ask. What's your name?"

"Fonso. Fonso Gravenese."

"Matty, meet Fonso Gravenese," said the man who then walked away.

"My father owns a market in the North Bronx. We want to buy direct."

"Why?"

"Make more money."

"I'm sure my brother Tony told you, we don't sell direct. Too much trouble."

"Suppose I said, if you treat Fonso right, he will deliver forty retail markets."

Cisco stared down at the confident little man. "What do you mean by treat you right?"

"The way I understand the process, the wholesale distributor adds a 20 percent commission to your price. So suppose you sell to me at your price and I split the wholesale mark-up with you. I get a lower price and you make more per pound."

"Kid, if you can deliver on that promise you've made a friend for life."

"I need just one more thing from you."

"And what's that?"

"Locatelli's customer list."

Cisco paused, "I have never…"

"Like Papa always says, "Never say never."

Cisco loved the kid's big brass ones.

$

Cisco delivered his first order direct. Fonso fired a surprised Aldo Locatelli. Three days later Fonso also fired Frankie and hired an experienced butcher whom he schooled in his new trimming techniques.

Cisco started to become impatient about other orders from the other customers. Fonso paid a visit every one of Aldo's customers personally. He decided to share his portion of the Cisco rebate, and make up the difference on new volume. His pitch was always the same. "Same meat, same service at 5 percent less. But that's not all. We trim to order, so you have lower people costs."

Two-thirds of the butchers agreed immediately. The other third required some additional persuasion. Fonso decided to engage Ricco Cicolo again. Two weeks later, all 60 customers had switched from Locatelli to Fonso.

When the dust settled, Cisco was quite satisfied that Fonso delivered as promised. Fonso and Dominic reinvested half of their new found profits in a few additional trimmers and put the other half in the bank.

Fonso now owed Ricco a like-kind favor to be called in at some point in the future.

Chapter 10

———

Thanksgiving, 1933
North Bronx, NYC

"Dominic, I love our new neighborhood. I've made so many friends," said Philomena after dinner one evening.

"We even got an invitation from our next store neighbors, Jim and Theresa Cafora, to join their family for Thanksgiving dinner."

"They are very nice people," said Dominic.

Thanksgiving at the was truly a family affair. Jim's brother, Tom, and his wife Gloria, as well as Theresa's sister Margaret and her husband Johnny Tucci greeted the Graveneses warmly.

During introductions, Dominic and Philomena learned Tucci was a security guard at the Yale Lock Company in Yonkers and Tom was a delivery supervisor at Continental Baking in the South Bronx. The jovial Johnny joked, "this working for a living is not what it's cracked up. That's why I'm calling it quits in another 27 years."

For three hours, fifteen people sat around the table, sharing a four-course feast. It began with Margaret's signature lasagna and Gloria's escarole salad with mozzarella, roasted red peppers, fresh tomatoes, and green olives.

Once the prelims were finished, Jim brought out a perfected roasted 25-pound turkey with all the trimmings. "Ta-ta," announced Margaret. Dessert — compliments of the Graveneses — was a mountain of zeppoles and a ricotta cheesecake stuffed with candied fruit.

As was tradition, after dinner the men sat around with a gigantic dish of fruits, nuts, finocchio, a sweet Italian after dinner celery, and a bottle of alcohol-based liquid digestives including Grappa, Limoncello and Cynar.

"Can I stay, Papa?" Fonso asked.

Dominic looked at his new friends. "Okay with you?"

They all nodded.

"Good, my son almost a man."

"So Tip-Top, what's new? said Jim.

"What's a Tip-Top?" wondered Dominic.

"I'm sorry," said Jim, I forgot, you're new to our family. My brother Jim's company makes Tip-Top bread. Ever hear the slogan, "Builds Bodies Eight Ways?"

"Why, sure."

"Because he supervises all the delivery trucks, the kids decided to call him, Uncle Tip-Top.

The four men chuckled heartily.

"Jim," said Tip-Top, "I do have a little employee dispute brewing. You know Roberto Moretti?"

"Sad, I heard. Heart attack after dinner," said Johnny.

"Well, he was one of my top guys. Trusted him like a brother — he never once tried to rip me off. Anyway, the other day, that Moulinyou — a derogatory Italian slang that means black eggplant — Javonne Davis tells me he's been a Continental route driver for ten years, and is next in line for Roberto's spot."

Johnny started to laugh. "First a bread truck supervisor. Then what? A Moulinyou President."

Fonso was interested in racial slurs. "Does the route make a lot of money," asked Fonso. Dominic's eyes popped in fear.

"Why," smiled Tip-Top. "You want the job?"

"No sir, I was just asking."

"Let me put it this way kid, I've got 37 trucks running bread and numbers. Moretti's route was Number One five years running."

"So," said Johnny, "you need help?"

"Maybe. If Davis doesn't go away quietly."

"Just let me know. Family helps family. I know some people who can make Javonne disappear. Capische?"

$

Fonso would never forget that first Thanksgiving.

About two weeks later, Johnny Tucci was found with three shots in his head in an empty lot in about three miles from the Yale Lock Company in Yonkers. There was no motive and no clues. Just a grief-stricken wife, who remarried six months later, and relocated to wherever.

The FBI crashed Uncle Tip-Top's numbers racket, and he was sentenced to ten years at Attica Prison outside of Buffalo. Not a dime of his numbers earnings was ever recovered.

Chapter 11

June, 1935
North Bronx, NYC

For the next 18 months, Dominic's Fine Meats continued to grow, although the long hours were starting to take its toll on Dominic. One day he complained he was not feeling just right. A few hours later, the family's physician, Dr. Richard Cafora, another cousin of Jim Cafora, examined the pale-looking Dominic.

"Dominic, you've developed an irregular heartbeat. The medical term is atrial fibrillation."

"It may be age, the extra 30 extra pounds you've added — the five foot, seven-inch Dominic, now weighed 250 pounds— or the stress of your long business hours. Most likely, it is a combination of all three. I am going to give you a prescription for Quinidine. Just take one a day, and make a few lifestyle changes. You should be fine."

Three months later, Dominic rested in his custom Adirondack chair after planting a few highly-durable Labrusca grapevines. He fell fast asleep. His head tilted to the right and came to rest on the brace that held the canvas top.

Philomena smiled from the window. "Fonso, see Papa rest. Papa works hard and long. You are now a man, please help him in the business as much as you can. Go wake him up, dinner is ready."

Fonso shook his motionless father. He shook him again. He had never seen death up close, but he knew. His friend, mentor, protector was gone. He was filled with a sense of loneliness he had never experienced before. Telling Mama was the most difficult thing he ever had to do. They hugged silently on the little back porch for what seemed like an eternity.

$

Dominic's premature death shook the neighborhood. At 39, his friendly smiling face had become a fixture at Carlo's bakery, where a few of his buddies from the old country hung out on Sunday mornings after Church. The men talked mostly about American baseball and Italian football. Dominic never understood why soccer wasn't popular in his new homeland.

Dominic's eulogy was personally passionate because Father Acampora, the pastor of Our Lady of Solace Church on Morris Park Avenue, had become a friend and close confidant. Dominic confessed his many mistakes in private so Father

Acampora took solace in the fact that Dominic had died at peace with the world.

He spoke that Sunday from the pulpit, "Sometimes God decides to take early. In Dominic's case, perhaps one might argue too early. God has a plan for all of us. Dominic and I spoke many times about many things, so I can tell you he was a man at peace. He loved his family and he loved America. As he said so many times, 'America is the land of dreams, if you dream hard.'"

Dormi & Sons Funeral Parlor, near the corner of Morris Park and Williamsbridge Road, was filled with prayers and final wishes for two days. Philomena did her best to control her emotions. Sitting in front of Dominic's open casket was difficult. But she would have it no other way.

"Mama, take a break," Fonso suggested, as the tears rolled down Philomena's cheeks.

"No. Papa and I did everything together. He was more than a husband. He was my best friend."

"Mama," said Fonso meaning it, "now I'm your best friend. I will love and honor you. I will always take care of you. Nothing to worry about." Fonso would keep that promise to his momma for 32 years until September, 1964.

Philomena beamed. "I'm a lucky mother. You are a good man. I hope you find a woman like your Papa found me. Life is lonely. Everybody needs someone."

"Mama, everything will turn out just fine for your son. Like Father said in Church, God has a plan for all of us."

$

Dominic's sudden death had an immediate impact on Fonso's business career — for the better.

Fonso decided he had no interest in spending his entire life as a pair of hands behind a butcher counter. He would sell the business. He hired a professional business broker to handle the matter. Fonso knew the business did fairly well, but Dominic never shared the specifics. The broker's conclusion took Fonso by surprise. "Your Dad kept very professional books and records and the cash flow is very attractive." Within a matter of months, the broker then sold Dominic's Fine Meats for a handsome profit.

Fonso took his newfound wad of cash into the family safety deposit box at Williamsbridge Savings & Loan. Never a big fan of banks, Fonso figured the boxes were a more anonymous location until he made some decisions.

He was greeted by another surprise at the Williamsburg S&L. There were two safety deposit boxes, not one. And both boxes were stuffed with so much cash, he had to rent a third box.

Fonso now had almost $200,000 in cash. One hell of a sum of money for a man his age. His past work experience had also given him future direction. He wanted to acquire an existing wholesale business in the meat industry. Perhaps one in distress that he could rebuild.

Chapter 12

October, 1935
Metz Meat Company, Demarest, NJ

After talking to people who knew people, Fonso locked and loaded on the venerable Adolph Metz Meat Packing Company headquartered in Demarest, New Jersey. The company, founded in 1891 by an industrious German immigrant, Adolph Metz, made a single variety of fresh sausages. By the time old man Metz died in 1926, the company had morphed into America's largest manufacturer and processor of a wide variety of premium pork and beef products.

The word on the street was that his lazy heirs had made a mess of the company, and sold it at a bargain-basement price to a group of bankers who knew absolutely nothing about the meat business.

$

The new CEO was Thomas Pinkerton III, a Yale MBA with absolutely no meat experience graduate. He in turn hired Manhattan's leading consulting firm, the Arthur Little Company, which also knew absolutely nothing about the meat business. They decided Metz's first priority was to modernize the inefficient production facility.

Consequently, Pinkerton hired a prominent mid-west executive search firm to find an experienced candidate in the heart of the Midwest meat belt. Somehow they found Fonso, who after one phone conversation agreed to interview for the position of production manager.

The more Fonso learned about the company's situation during the interview process, the more he smelled opportunity. So he made Pinkerton an out-of-the-box offer. He said he would agree to rebuild the operation if he could buy 10 percent of the company at the prevailing book value.

Pinkerton accepted on the spot. He loved the fact that Fonso was ready, willing and able to put his money where his mouth was. He also liked Fonso's extensive retail experience.

At 20 years old Fonso became one of the meat industry's youngest production manager, with a staff of almost 200 butchers.

As a first step, he retrained every butcher on how to generate significantly more yield from every slab of beef and pork. Then he organized all the butchers into ten separate teams, each responsible for trimming only certain portions of the meat. Fonso's trimming techniques and assembly line efficiencies generated increased cash flows of 20 percent with no increase in costs. The entrepreneurial Fonso also found a way to turn the fat trimmings Metz previously paid to be carted away into a personal cash machine.

He changed the waste management company from Vonage Services in Demarest to Pinto

Services in South Lodi, officially own by Ricco Cicolo — Fonso was a 51 percent silent partner with the only vote.

Fonso's pitch to the Board was simple. "Pinto has agreed to the same job for 10 percent less." Mr. Cicolo also offered to provide Metz with a weekly haul-away report — a Fonso idea which reinforced exceptional value for money from Pinto Services. Nobody in management really cared about the change. To them garbage was garbage — reducing expenses was all that mattered.

Each day, Pinto trucks collected the daily fat trimmings, compressed them into 60-gallon drums in grossly unsanitary conditions. The drums were then shipped to the Armorene Food Company in the thriving Kansas City meat-processing stockyards known as West Bottoms. There, the edible fat was reprocessed into a popular form of cooking lard and sold it to a variety of retail food outlets. In order to secure the Armorene business, Ricco sucked up an executive vice president, Tommy O'Toole, who agreed to waive the cumbersome requirement for U.S. Department of Agriculture inspection certificates. In exchange for a waiver, Ricco wired a monthly supplemental processing fee to an O'Toole bank account specifically established for this and other such vendor payments.

In order to keep his side business private, Fonso gave cash bonuses to those loyal employees who worked overtime off the books. This business-within-a-business enterprise taught Fonso a valuable lesson he would employ many times over the years — money properly placed bought loyalty.

$

During the next two years, the by-the-book Pinkerton and his senior management team stumbled and fumbled, overheads ballooned, and cash flows shrunk. As a 10-percent owner he was a member of the Board, and privy to all the current and impending problems.

Late one afternoon, Pinkerton called an emergency Board meeting. He announced he had a solution to all the Metz business issues — the acquisition of another Jersey-based processed-meat firm called Kadesh. His McKinsey advisors said their due diligence had shown them to have an excellent brand name and an efficient production facility. The idea was to shut down Metz production, and make Kadesh and Metz products in their facility. "We'll double sales, and reduce overheads, which should allow us to pay off the acquisition debt and improve overall cash flow."

Fonso sat silently as the suits weaved their pitch. The nine-person Board voted for the acquisition. Fonso was the sole descending vote. He knew Kadesh was kosher, and both brands could not coexist in the same production facility. He also knew that Hebrew National, another high-quality kosher brand, was about to expand its activities. He figured the whole plan would quickly backfire, and the Metz brand would become available at fire-sale prices. He would then sell Kadesh to Hebrew National, which would be a likely suitor, particularly at a bargain basement price.

As Fonso watched from the sidelines, the profits from his Metz unsanitary fats business and his share of Pinto waste removal contracts piled up. Six months later, he had socked away another $200,000 in safe- deposit boxes at the Manufacturers Hanover Trust Bank on Route 9 in Englewood, New Jersey, ten miles from Metz headquarters.

Chapter 13

MANUFACTURERS M HANOVER TRUST M

June 1938
Manufacturers Hanover Bank, Englewood, NJ

Two-plus years later Metz collapsed and was forced to declare bankruptcy. Fonso had since moved to Englewood to be closer to work. But he made it a point to speak to his mother everyday on the phone. He also had consolidated all of his assets — now about $400,000 — in declared accounts and safe-deposit boxes at Manufacturers. His activity did not go unnoticed by Branch Manager Aemon O'Brien, who made it a point to greet Fonso personally when he came into the bank. "If you need anything at all, come see me."

Ignorant about bankruptcy proceedings, Fonso decided to take O'Brien at his word. The men sat in O'Brien's office as Fonso explained the Metz situation. O'Brien outlined general bankruptcy procedure, the role of the courts, and desires of creditors, etc. "It all starts with having an attorney who specializes in bankruptcy matters. Otherwise your team has no quarterback."

"Suggestions?" asked Fonso.

"Our friends at Stafford & Wilson. They are one of New York City's finest, and we work well with them. All plusses, in your case."

"Can you set up an introductory meeting?"

"Consider it done," said O'Brien.

"How will I know what to offer for Metz?"

"Actually you are not buying anything from Metz. You will be buying the company from the courts with the agreement of the creditors. Besides setting up a preliminary meeting with S&W," said O'Brien, "we should start the loan process. Identify the size and terms of a business loan based on your assets and Metz's projected cash flows."

"Maybe I can save a few dollars on legal fees by getting a jump start on the term sheet," smiled O'Brien. "You will be amazed how quickly billable hours pile up." The more O'Brien spoke, the more Fonso realized he knew little about conventional business practices.

$

After the first S&W meeting, the senior partners were not sure they wanted the ill-informed Fonso as a client. S&W quickly learned that despite Fonso's gruff, unpolished demeanor, he had resources, was an exceptional listener, and one hell of a negotiator. They met again with different results.

Fonso met with O'Brien after the second S&W meeting. O'Brien explained, "I've met with our loan committee. Assuming you put $300,000 in first monies, Manufacturers Hanover is willing to extend a loan of $1.7 million to buy Metz. The rates will be our best customer terms with no prepayment penalty, in exchange for a significant minority positon in Metz."

Two days later the loan papers were signed and Fonso made the courts an attractive sealed-bid offer.

During the proceedings he asked to make a few comments. "Not the norm," said the judge. Fonso explained he understood that but there was something that needed to be said. The judge allowed him three minutes.

"I'm certain our offer of 70 cents on the dollar rewards creditors for their patience. But equally important, I want to be on record that it is our intention to retain all existing employees. I have learned over the years that treating employees with respect and dignity benefits, them, their families, and the community in which they live."

The judge was impressed. After reviewing the bids, and conferring with staff, the Honorable Judge Julian Rutherman awarded the Metz Company to Fonso.

At the age of 23 years and nine months, the unassuming, diminutive Fonso, dressed in his signature baggy black suit and thick horn-rimmed eyeglasses became the principal stockholder, CEO and President of Metz. He also had absolute veto voting power.

Three days later, Fonso threw a celebration party for his new employees with Judge Rutherman and Aemon O'Brien in attendance. The surprise guest of the evening was Jake Rutherman, the popular and eloquent U.S. Congressman from North Bergen who was a first cousin of the Judge Rutherman.

The Congressman — seeking a fourth term nine months hence — toasted Fonso's rise to influence in glowing terms. "The pain of the Depression, while finally behind us, still rings in our ears — good people wandering aimlessly with no jobs for no good reason, other than the shameless greed of a few on Wall Street. Thanks to the boldness and daring of Fonso Gravenese, 500 jobs will stay in our district where they belong."

Rutherman raised his glass. "So I would like to toast Fonso personally and pledge this Congressman's support to Metz's future needs."

Two months later, Rutherman appointed Fonso head of his fund-raising committee. Fonso was now an emerging New Jersey business leader and a soon-to-be political fixture.

$

Shortly after the party, Fonso made his first management hire — Ricco.

To outsiders, Fonso's first management hire would have appeared strange. But Fonso knew there were rough seas ahead, he just didn't know when and where. And, other than Ricco, he wasn't sure who he would be able to trust.

"Ricco," said Fonso in the back room of Pinto Services, "want to work full time?"

"Fonso, I ain't never worked a regular job. Like my father once said, 'I'm unemployable.'"

"I don't disagree. But this job might just meet your requirements. We'll make it up as we go and there is a hug pot of gold at the end of the rainbow."

"Me and my family have always had your back, why change now?" said Ricco.

Chapter 14

September, 1938
Metz Meat Company, Demarest, NJ

The Great Depression left millions of Americans —
particularly schoolchildren — with nutritionally deficient
meals well into the 1930's, despite enormous agricultural
surpluses. The Roosevelt Administration empowered the
Department of Agriculture (DOA) to create a
bureaucratic maze of agencies, committees, and task forces,
which generated enormous media buzz. But, they did little
to solve the underlying issues of supply, demand, and
pricing. The problem was particularly acute with certain
livestock. Farmers destroyed and buried millions of hogs
rather than lose money processing them into hamburgers,
frankfurters, bacon, etc.

In June 1940, the DOA consolidated these disparate
agencies into the Federal Surplus Commodities
Corporation, more commonly known as the Surplus
Marketing Administration (SMA).

Their mandate: appoint reliable processed meat suppliers in to deliver federally-inspected meat to school systems around the United States. Thereby insuring all American schoolchildren had a tasty, balanced meal at lunchtime.

Initially, Requests for Proposals (RFP's) were sent to a variety of unvetted meat vendors. Proposals were reviewed and evaluated by the SMA selection committee. Approved vendors were assigned to specific school districts. The program was known as the National School Lunch Act.

Fonso knew Metz Meats required a major makeover, but he didn't want to tear the place apart. His initial thought was evolution, not revolution.

The consultant's report was clear. Squeeze cash from a stack of aging account receivables. Grow the company's stagnant customer base. Modernize the antiquated distribution center. And, most important undertake a judicious pruning of senior management.

Five men sat around a slab of well-worn butcher-block, converted into a greasy conference table that could stain the elbows of your shirt on contact. The windowless room sat directly above the meat-processing group who were noisily hacking, chopping and trimming. The smell of fat drippings permeated the air.

CEO Fonso, now 24, looked more like a portly, old curmudgeon than a dynamic leader. He wasted no time at his first staff meeting.

"Fellas, I'm looking forward to working with some familiar faces to turn this thing around. I want the old man — founder Adolph Metz — smiling Up There."

Before the meeting, Fonso informed Sam Magro, his assistant manager for the past three years that he had been promoted to replace him. He was certain that move would insure the efficient production of Metz brand meats for years to come.

At 5-feet 6-inches, Sam bore a striking physical resemblance to Fonso. He also wore black-rimmed glasses and carried a potbelly stomach. Magro, like Fonso, was not a great student, and he'd dropped out of high school. Unlike Fonso, he played life straight. He joined Metz after responding to an ad seeking a "young man interested in having a career in the meat industry." His first job was refuse collection — he was the guy who collected the butcher's waste trim and packed it in drums for twice-weekly Sanitation pick up.

The soft-spoken, respectful Magro taught himself how to slaughter, trim and pack meat. Eight years later he was promoted to head butcher, then assistant manager. Everybody liked Sam's can-do attitude. He started from the premise there wasn't an operations problem that couldn't be solved with knowledge, patience and a little ingenuity.

The only thing that didn't add up about Sam was his choice of spouse, Barbara. She was bold and brassy, and spent whatever Sam made — sometimes even before he made it. Despite their differences, the relationship worked. They had been married 15 years and had two teenage kids.

$

Fonso's natty, single, dark-haired comptroller was Gino Metz, the old man's young silver-spoon grandson. Gino's reputation around the building? A gift to women — and mankind, who had pretty much had knocked up every Metz employee — male or female — he thought worth the effort.

Fonso took an immediate dislike to the wise ass

"Gino, let's talk receivables. My father always said in business cash is king."

"What did he do?"

"He was a butcher."

"Like in a butcher shop?"

"Yeah like in a butcher shop. Why?"

"There is a hell of a big difference between running a butcher shop and running a business," said Gino condescendingly.

Fonso chose to ignore the comment. "What I want…no what I need for next week is simple — a goddamn good explanation why it takes 120 days to collect 30-day old receivables."

"Where did you get that number?" asked a surprised Gino.

Fonso tossed a report across the table. "The consultants did an analysis during the reorg proceedings. Says our cash flow sucks and our collectibles system sucks."

"I'd have to look at the data."

"With all due respect you've gotta find money… Now."

"Next week may be tough," responded Gino. We've got quarterly reconciliations and…

"Gino, do our retail customers like Metz's premium products?"

Gino nodded.

"Do we ever foul up an order?"

"No."

"Do we deliver on time?"

"Always," said Gino nodding or the third time.

"So, why don't our customers to pay their bills on time?"

$

Next up was John Friedmeister.

"John," said Fonso, to founder Metz's oldest grandson, "how long have you been running business development?"

The tall man with black wavy hair and a bubble nose topped with a brown wart the size of a golf ball, responded in a thick, staccato German accent, barely comprehensible, "Zen, maybe twelff years."

"During your time with us, how many new accounts have we developed?"

"Many. But I dooo not valk around with record books."

"Okay." said Fonso, trying to be patient. "How many have we lost?"

"Ahhh few. But like I said..."

Fonso interrupted, "I know — you don't walk around with record books."

A scowl appeared on Fonso's face. His tone changed. "John, question. If we've got so many new customers and lost so few, why the fuck are revenues down 35 percent over the last three years?"

Dead silence. You could hear a pin drop.

"Here's your first assignment. Next week I want to hear your new growth ideas, see new timetables, etc. We clear?"

"Ya," mumbled Friedmeister.

$

Distribution Center Manager Rupert Hitzig was the staff's longest-tenured employee, a likable sort with gentle eyes and a warm smile. He was the proud son of a Jewish immigrant. He believed a fair day's work deserved a fair day's pay, nothing more, nothing less.

Rupert and wife Gisela, the daughter of a Romanian immigrant, met as teenagers on Grand Street. She was with her mama buying fabric. He was selling pickles from the barrel at Hymie's Deli next store. His opening line was, "Would you like a free pickle?"

Hitzig's department, unlike Magro's, had lots of moving parts — egomaniacal drivers, quirky mechanics, and a lazy, passive support staff who needed to be taught a new accountability. There was also the matter of an outdated truck fleet held together with chewing gum and rubber bands because of a lack of cash flow. Finally, there were always cantankerous AFL-CIO contract negotiations.

"Rupert, I understand the mess you're dealing with. I'd like you to think do-over. Take a few weeks. Build a plan that assumes we are going to add some big new customers," said Fonso with a reassuring smile.

"Check, Boss," he said nervously.

"Let's also talk about the unions off-line. We don't need everybody in that one just yet."

"Check, Boss."

$

Ricco Cicolo raised his hand.

"Boss, I have a good idea." The room braced itself.

"In case any you guys are wondering," announced Fonso, "the handsome hulk with the square shoulders and the pair of brass ones is my old friend, Ricco Cicolo. He's our new head of security...and anything else that needs investigating."

Fonso continued. "Ricco's good people. I expect all of you to help him get up to speed on the meatpacking business."

"Boss," said Ricco, "Have you see the latest Tom Mix movie?"

"No," chuckled Fonso.

"That means you haven't seen the latest Movietone News."

"Guess not."

"That announcer Lowell Thomas talked about people going hungry while hog-processors overproduced stock, and prices plummeted. They even showed farmers burying dead livestock."

"Ricco," snapped Fonso, "Tell me something I don't know."

"Heard of the SMA?"

Fonso knew Ricco never blew smoke. "Actually no," said Fonso, suddenly showing interest.

"My sources tell me the Department of Agriculture has created this new agency called the Surplus Marketing Administration to run the expanded Federal School Lunch program.

$

"The word on the street," continued Ricco, "is that the USDA has allocated $100 million for starters to buy surplus meat from approved suppliers." Ricco unceremoniously paused to burp. "I think all WE gotta do is get ourselves appointed an official Federal program sponsor."

"You've got my attention," said Fonso.

"Boss, suppose I told you that Congressman Jake Rutherford has just been appointed the head mucky-muck for the Program."

"I'd say we need to share some Fra Diablo with Jake," smiled Fonso.

Part Two
The Free Lunch Act

Chapter 15

———

September, 1938
Jersey City, NJ

The Clam Broth House at 42-46 Newark
Street in Jersey City was more than just a local
seafood joint. Since opening in 1910, the place had
become a hub for political deals, power-brokers,
and Mafiosi.

Tourists knew it as a big place with signature
sawdust floors and a bustling dining room. The
regulars knew it as a small place of intimate rooms,
off the main dining room, where business could
be discussed discretely. The house specialty was a
fabulous Lobster Fra Diablo smothered in a spicy
marinara sauce made with San Marzano plum
tomatoes.

"Jake, as you get to know me better, you'll find,
I like to get right to the point," said Fonso,

cracking a sauce-covered lobster claw. Red stains quickly splattered the apron around his neck. "Fuck, these things are delicious, but what a goddamn mess."

Rutherford laughed. "Get yourself a wife. She'll crack it for you."

"From what I gather," said Fonso, ignoring the wife comment, "This Fed Lunch Program could be a winner for Metz and your campaign kitty. How do we get to the top of the list?"

"Fonso, the SMA is a little different than my other committees. It's loaded with a bunch of small-minded, cover-your-ass administrators, who love long, complicated forms and the security of paper pushing."

"I'll hire somebody to fill them out. I'll hire two. Three, whatever it takes."

"There's one other wrinkle. I've been asked to appoint companies that not only deliver product on time, and on budget, but also give back to their community."

"Not a problem."

"Fonso, with all due respect, your reputation proceeds you. When was the last time you did anything for anybody?"

"You mean," glared Fonso, "besides your campaign?"

Rutherford paused. "My staff will get you a set of application forms. I'll assign one of them to give you a hand. Just remember, the apps need to be back at my office two weeks from tomorrow."

As the men prepared to leave, Rutherford paused. "Fonso, you know I'm always in your corner."

"By the way, Jake…fuck you about the wife. That's never gonna happen. They're like extra baggage."

$

The next day, Fonso cleared his calendar for an impromptu lunch with his old friend, Father Don from St. Patrick's. Father Don had been promoted to assistant to the Archbishop of New York, Cardinal Coogan.

"Always delighted to see an old friend. Particularly when he is buying lunch at the Rainbow Room," smiled the long, lanky Father Don. "I assume your urgency comes with a request?"

"Think of lunch as a belated thank you."

"So, how can I help?" said the priest.

"As you know, I've put my savings at risk trying to turn around the Metz Meat Company. I'm happy to report we are doing very well, and we've saved some 500 local jobs."

"God bless you my son."

"But I'd like do more. I read somewhere that the Catholic Charity Boys Club reports to you."

"I don't know if 'report' is the right word," replied the Father modestly. "As you know, my father was a big local supporter. I know he'd like me to maintain that tradition," said Fonso, morphing into an empathetic snake-oil salesman.

Father Don stared skeptically. He was well aware of Fonso's growing reputation as a master manipulator. "Did you have something in mind?"

"The Department of Agriculture has created a wonderful program to provide free lunches for underprivileged kids everywhere."

"What's that got to do with the Boys Club?"

"Father, let me put it this way. The appointment of Metz as an official Free Lunch supplier could help local kids from struggling families get a good hot meal, and provide the Boys Club with consistent donations every quarter."

"I applaud your goal, but I don't understand what you want from me."

"Father, if you could get the Cardinal to write a letter of recommendation based on the Gravenese family's past contributions to the Boys Club, I'm sure it would go a long way towards the appointment of Metz as an official Federal supplier. As a thank you, you have my word that 5 percent of all Metz program profits will go the Catholic Charities Boys Club."

"What a wonderful gesture," smiled Father Don. "I believe that can be arranged." He paused. "However, perhaps we could consider 10 percent. The cost of raising our boys continues to increase."

Fonso chuckled. Suckered by a priest. "Do they teach how to negotiate deals in heaven?"

Fonso stuck out his hand to consummate the agreement. But Father Don wasn't finished. "Remember those wonderful bikes you gave the Little Italy Boys Club?"

"I certainly do," replied Fonso proudly.

"It just so happens, the other day I was talking to Father O'Malley, our New York City Boys Club administrator, about those very same bikes. He said wouldn't it be wonderful if God somehow provided another 100 of them for the good boys of our city."

Two weeks later, Franklin Donato — yes, the same Franklin Donato — delivered 100 deluxe, new Schwinn bikes to the New York Boys Club warehouse at Brooks Avenue and 138th Street in the South Bronx.

Chapter 16

———

October, 1938
Washington, D.C.

Donna Joan Magro — even sitting at her cluttered desk with her hair in a tight bun — was the cutest government clerk Fonso had ever tried to make smile. She appeared to be intelligent, helpful, and a good listener — atypical government employee traits.

Donna took one look at the Humpty-Dumpty proportioned man smiling through his thick glasses, and returned to the business at hand.

"Mr. Gravenese, I've been asked to assist you with the SMA paperwork. That's a first for me, so you must be somebody really important."

"Not really," said Fonso modestly, "I'm just a guy with a little meat company who wants to help kids."

Donna thought his modesty seemed genuine. "Well, Mr. Gravenese, let's get started. These appointment forms feel like we're going to rewrite the Constitution of the United States."

Fonso smiled. "Call me Fonso."

Donna picked up her pen and began at the top of the form. "So, Mr. Gravenese what is the name of your company, its place of business, and when it was incorporated?"

"It's called Metz Meat Packing. We're at 22 Ridge Street in Englewood. We've been in business since 1891.

Donna stopped. "You're that Alfonso Gravenese?"

"I'm not sure. What did I do wrong?"

"My uncle is Sam Magro. He is one of your butchers. He's always talking about how you stepped up to keep the company running when those lazy Metz kids almost ran the company into the ground. Thank you so much for allowing him to maintain his dignity."

Two hours later, the form was completed.

"It's ready to submit. But I'd like to make a suggestion, if you don't mind," said Donna sweetly. "The SMA Commissioner really likes proactive community referrals. I would think about that, and bring the application back for formal filing when you have a little something more. Is that possible?"

Fonso smiled. "Almost forgot," reaching into his bag. "Here's a letter from Cardinal Cook thanking the Gravenese Family for their many contributions to the New York City's Boys Club. Will that do?"

"Perfect," she said, attaching it to the form with a paper clip.

Fonso decided to have a little fun at Donna's expense. "Oh, I almost forgot, I have a letter of endorsement from the Englewood Mayor. Maybe we should also attach that?" Fonso poured it on. He searched his bag. "Golly, Ms. Magro, I almost forgot. Here's a community proclamation signed by U.S. Congressman Jake Rutherford for bringing jobs to our community."

Fonso had a Cheshire-cat grin on his face. "Fonso, those are great," deadpanned Donna, "but a letter from President Roosevelt would be a little better.'

"Why don't you and Fonso discuss how to get one over dinner?" responded Fonso.

Donna cracked up. "I do come up from Washington every other weekend to spend time with my parents."

$

Fonso was really, really nervous. When had picked a girl up at her house to go out on a date, after meeting her father and mother?

The 24-year-old Donna was the first person in her family to go to college. Academically, she could have picked anywhere, but she chose to go local, and graduated from Columbia with a degree in business communications. Her father, Victor Magro, was a first generation Italian-American who took over his father's funeral parlor when he passed at age 87. Donna's mother was the former Mary Regan, the daughter of a decorated Irish-American police sergeant.

Donna's parents lived in a neat three-story brick house near Main and 22nd Street in Bayonne, New Jersey, an industrial blue-collar enclave populated mostly by Roman-Catholic Italians and Irish. The town had no distinguishing landmarks other than tiny Taylor Park, which sat directly across the water from lower Manhattan and had a picture-postcard view of the Manhattan skyline, the Statute of Liberty, and Wall Street.

Another plus: Bayonne was so close to the bustling New Jersey Turnpike that you could hear the drone of trucks and automobiles 24 hours a day. Fortunately, thanks to rows of giant circular storage tanks in an industrial wasteland at the edge of Turnpike, you could not see what you could hear.

$

"So Fonso," said her dad awkwardly trying to make small talk while waiting for Donna to come downstairs, "Donna tells me you own a company?"

"Yes, sir."

"A pretty big one I hear?"

"Guess so, sir."

"Understand you've done a lot of community work with Catholic Charities."

"Some."

"And, you've got the ear of a Mayor and Congressman."

"I'm sorry sir. I'm not sure what you want me to say."

"Where do you go to college?" asked Victor Magro.

"Never went. In fact, I never graduated from high school. But everything I have, I earned. Nobody ever gave me anything."

Mary came to the rescue. "Fonso, pardon Victor, he's only got one daughter."

"No offense taken. I'm an only child."

Mary was as curious as her husband, but, as the daughter of a detective, she took a different approach. "Fonso, I think Victor is just awed by the fact that such a young man can be in such a position of influence. Being responsible for the livelihood of six or seven hundred employees at 25, gosh almighty."

Donna sauntered down the stairs in a black skirt and a gray silk blouse with heels. She has also let her hair out of the bun she wore at work.

"Wow," smiled Fonso.

"Let's get out of here before they really ramp up the interrogation," smiled Donna. "My last date had to show his driver's license and passport before Daddy let me travel over the Bayonne border."

"Where are you kids off to?" asked Victor.

"Daddy, please. It's not like we are going to elope."

"It's okay," said Fonso. "I thought I'd take your daughter for dinner and dancing at the Rainbow Room in the City. It's a great night, and you can see forever."

Victor smiled. "Now, I'm impressed. Her last date was an up and coming actor. The big spender took her to dinner at the Empire Diner on 48th Street and 12th Avenue, next to the Yellow Cab parking lot."

Fonso was getting used to Victor's nosey sense of humor. "Mr. Magro, I guess that's why this time your daughter chose a mensch with money rather than a handsome hunk with change in his pockets."

Chapter 17

November, 1938
Rainbow Room, NYC

After Fonso and Donna left, Victor bitched, "We spend all that money on a college education, and she picks a little mutt that drops out of high school.

"Sure, 'nobody gave him anything.' I bet he just took what he wants. I can smell his kind"

"When she gets home, you've got to talk some sense into that girl."

$

Cocktails were fun, dinner was delicious, the conversation honest, and the Rainbow Room view of Manhattan breathtakingly romantic.

They walked around the open-air observation deck. They stopped to look at the Empire State Building twinkling in the sky. Fonso placed his hands behind Donna's neck, and gently pulled her body close. They could feel each other's breath. They kissed. Again and again.

The gender-shy Fonso surprised the hell out of himself…half-joking, half-serious. "Let's skip the engagement, and go right to marriage."

Donna responded in kind, "I'll make you a deal: marriage now, but a longer honeymoon to make up for no engagement."

Fonso went for the home run. "Okay, I'll get a driver to take us to Boston. I've always thought eloping would be a romantic way to marry your soulmate."

"When are we planning this elopement?" smiled Donna.

"I'm guessing I can have a limousine here in an hour. I figure it's a five-hour drive, maybe less to downtown. In the morning, we can find a priest, and get married on the steps of Faneuil Hall."

"You're not kidding, are you?" realized Donna, startled. She looked silently at the twinkling skyline, her back to Fonso. She turned with a big smile. "I say Yes! — if you can solve one little problem."

"Shoot."

"I want to be a virgin for my husband."

"You've never."

"No, never."

"Well that's easy. We'll get adjoining single rooms before the ceremony, and then a nice suite with a view and a double bed after we're married."

"You got a deal, butcher man."

They were married at 9:30 a.m. the next morning by a justice of the peace, stayed a day and night, then returned home to pack for their honeymoon. Somewhere in the middle of all this, Donna and Fonso called their respective parents.

Victor flipped, Mary laughed, and Philomena wept with joy.

Fonso also called Ricco to tell him he was in charge for the next few weeks. "Tell Friedmeister, he better be ready when I return, or I'll have his ass."

Donna called her boss at the SMA. "Donna, no worries. The government understands family takes precedence over work. The Lunch Program applications can wait. In the broad scheme of things, what's a few more weeks?"

$

After two glorious weeks at the tawny Cambridge Cottages on the secluded north end of Bermuda, the couple returned home. Fonso was madly in love. He wanted a happy wife, so he immediately cut a deal with the Victor and Mary Magro. The newlyweds would live in the four-room apartment on the third floor, until the first child arrived.

Fonso also sold his mother's house on Haight Avenue. She happily moved into a similar home on 22nd Street in Bayonne, a few blocks from where Victor, Mary, Fonso and Donna lived.

Chapter 18

June, 1940
SMA, Washington D.C.

"Mr. Gravenese, congratulations on your appointment," said Jim Thompson, new director of the recently created Surplus Marketing Administration.

Jim looked like something out of a Brooks Brothers catalog — blue pinstriped suit, starched white pocket-handkerchief, buttoned-down white shirt, and a traditional Brooks red club tie embossed with little white whales. He also reeked of Brooks classic 1940ish cologne — a crisp scent of citrus and jasmine mixed with a hint of patchouli and sandalwood.

$

"I'm honored," said Fonso, modestly. "We've worked hard to restore Metz to its prior position of prominence."

"I know. Our operations report suggests Metz has completed a hell of a turnaround."

Jim didn't know that Fonso had fudged the numbers a bit. On the SMA application, he had doubled the company's annual sales and tripled its projected production capacity. He figured, as a private company, which didn't have to support financials with anyone except lenders. So who was to know?

Fonso responded respectfully. "Sir, when you put your life savings into something, you've got a little extra motivation. Particularly with a new wife to support."

"Yeah, I heard. Donna is one determined young lady. He paused and smiled. I can't tell you how many times during the process your app magically reappeared at the top of the stack."

"Speaking of process, I think we should spend a little time reviewing our expectations. You and a few other vendors will be the first out of the box with the reconfigured SMA. My goal is to make sure we are all very, very successful.

"Our analysis suggests Metz's forte is processed meat products. Consequently, we'd like you to concentrate on manufacturing and delivering mainstream kid entrees, specifically hamburgers, hot dogs, bologna, and a little sausage. That okay with you, Mr. Gravenese?"

Fonso didn't know how to respond. He had never dealt directly with the U.S. Government. Was

Thompson merely being a cheerleader, or asking for something?

He decided to inject some charm. "Call me Fonso. Mom said it meant an endearing little fellow." He smiled, "Talk about giving somebody an inferiority complex."

Jim laughed. "I can relate. I prefer Jim. It's my translation of that stuffy moniker Mom stuck on my birth certificate — whatever was she thinking?

"Fonso," said Jim, returning to business. "Let's spend a few minutes on the process. Feel free to ask away. We've prepared an information packet for your internal briefings.

"Our process always begins with the purchase order (PO). It will define how many pounds of processed meat we are buying by product type, how much we are prepared to pay per pound, the point of delivery, and the expected delivery date."

Fonso thought for a moment. "Suppose your purchase price is lower than my cost of goods and delivery?"

"Very unlikely scenario. The SMA appreciates our vendors' care about doing the right thing, but we also recognize this is a business transaction between buyer and seller. Consequently, every month our pricing committee takes the average price per pound for USDA inspected meat, then adds 60 percent for processing, delivery and overheads. That should always leave you a reasonable profit, and the SMA a below-wholesale cost. Obviously, the more Metz meets or exceeds expectations in a given quarter, the more purchase orders it will receive in the next quarter, and so on."

"So orders can increase?"

"Absolutely. The SMA believes in rewarding those who do right by us."

Fonso was now sure Thompson expected something. The only question was how much.

"Obviously, Jim, the grade of meat has a lot to do with the price point."

"Let me answer this way, the kids are not expecting prime-aged anything.

"If you have no more questions, you just need to sign our vendor agreement. I've got your first PO right here."

Fonso signed the form, and quickly scanned the order. It was for 100,000 pounds of meat a month at 45 cents a pound, a significant premium to the prevailing wholesale rates. The PO also contained 30-day payment terms, and stated the government had the right to increase quantities with 15 days' notice. Fonso heard his heart pounding — this first SMA order equaled six months of Metz's current production. He paused to catch his breath.

"I know what you're thinking," said Jim. "Is the government going to drag out payment terms, and foul up my receivables? I promise there is nothing to worry about. The government remits payment in 20 days, I just wanted a hedge to 30 in case of some bureaucratic mix-up. Sometimes, the Federal Government has trouble putting stamps on its outgoing mail."

Chapter 19

———

July, 1940
Demarest, NJ

"Gino, the boss is back," quipped Fonso in an openly sarcastic tone.

It was days after Washington, and Fonso's first staff meeting after Bermuda. "What progress have we made on cleaning up the old receivables?"

"I've been working on the analysis. Should be ready in a few more days."

Fonso was not about to waste another minute.

"Ricco, I've got a little job." He reached into a folder and passed a paper to Ricco. "This is our top ten delinquent accounts arranged by cash owed Metz. Go pay them a personal visit."

Gino protested. "Fonso, I'm not really sure that's the way my grandfather would handle it."

"Ricco, maybe take Gino with you. You know like a team?"

"Boss, I don't think so."

$

Next was new business.

"I've got a pretty goddamn exciting announcement to make. We've been appointed a government vendor for the entire metro New York area under that Free School Lunch program that Ricco mentioned before Donna and I went on our honeymoon."

"Government business is a pain in the ass," responded John Friedmeister.

"How much business are we talking about? asked Hitzig.

"A hundred thousand pounds a quarter, maybe more.'

"Holy shit," responded Rupert.

"Yeah, but at what price?" wondered Friedmeister.

"Best I can figure, about 20 percent *more* than what you negotiated with our other customers. And they pay by certified check, 20 days after product delivery."

"Hard to believe," said Friedmeister.

"I don't really care what you believe. In fact, I've just decided I don't want to review your new account marketing ideas. "You're fucking fired."

"You can't do that."

"In case you missed it John I own the company. I can do anything I damn well please."

Fonso turned to Ricco. "Ricco, would you please walk John to his office to pick up his personal shit. Then walk him out to his car, and get him the fuck off my property. Make sure you tell the guards he is no longer welcome under any circumstances."

$

Rupert sat quivering.

"Relax Rupert. We have a lot of work to do, plans to make. You and Sam are going to be working closely, thanks to the government deal. This is our moment.

Ricco decided the first Metz customer who needed a visit was tough-as-nails Irishman Frank Hagen. About eight years before, Hagen had opened a bar and restaurant on West Farms Road in the Bronx called Rusty's. It was across from a bustling subway station where people changed trains to go as far North as 241st Street or took buses that traveled east to Morris Park Avenue.

Rusty's signature menu item was the Rustyburger. It was enormous. A ten-ounce patty of choice Metz hamburger meat plus French fries for only 40 cents. Hagen's idea was to use the hamburger as a loss leader to drive traffic to his mostly premium brand, premium price bar. He believed that if people drank on a full stomach, they wouldn't mind paying a bit more for their drinks.

Hagen's strategy worked. Rusty's boomed from the moment it opened at noon until it closed around 10 p.m.

Before long, Hagen had two Rusty's, then three, and by 1940, he had five dotting busy transportation hubs in the Bronx and on Upper West Side of Manhattan. During that time, he became Metz's largest customer— with the worst account receivables record — despite the fact that he was raking in a fortune.

His attitude was "I buy a ton, so fuck you." At six-foot-five with a head of scruffy red hair, and a mouth the size of roulette table, he put the fear of god in anyone who dared to mess with him.

Ricco had done his homework. At 11 p.m., He knocked on the front door of Hagen's neat single family home on Crosby Avenue in the Pelham Bay section of the Bronx.

There was no answer. Ricco knocked again, louder. There was some shuffling, and then door creaked open. Hagen stood in the doorway with a 36-ounce autographed Lou Gehrig baseball bat in his hand.

"Who the fuck are you?" roared Hagen.

"My name is Ricco Cicolo. I'm here to collect the receivables owed to Metz Meat Company."

"You gotta be fucking kidding."

Hagen swung the bat, Ricco ducked, twisted Hagen's arm, and ripped the bat out of his hand. He cracked Hagen across the mouth. Teeth and blood splattered across the porch.

Hagen's wife, Jean, and her 12-year old daughter, Margie, heard the commotion and came screaming.

Hagen struggled to his feet. Ricco bashed him again — this time in the stomach. Then dragged Hagan to a chair and tied him up.
Hagen's wife screamed, "You animal. I'm calling the cops." Ricco ripped the wire out of the wall.

"How?"

Ricco turned to Hagen. "Like I said, you owe Metz $12,378. Want to write a check now to avoid late fee penalties?"

"Fuck you," responded Hagen, blood spurting out of his mouth.

Ricco remained calm. He shook his head. "Wrong answer." He grabbed Margie, dragged her to the kitchen table, and smashed the bat across her hands. She fell to the floor racked in pain.

A few minutes later, a shell-shocked Hagen wrote a check for the full amount.

Word of Hagan's accounts-receivable negotiation quickly spread to Metz's other past-due customers. The checks came rolling in. Ricco never made another house call. Gino never appeared at another weekly staff meeting.

Chapter 20

October, 1940
Meatpacking District, NYC

Bright yellow sunshine played peek-a-boo with the railcars parked on upper Gansevoort Street.

A few minutes after seven in the morning, a shiny new black Cadillac convertible came to a halt in front of the Cisco Wholesale Meat Company at the corner of Washington Avenue and 11th Street. Fonso stepped out and looked around. He had not been there in eight years, but everything looked and smelled pretty much the same.

The place was as quiet as a ghost town. The refrigerated trucks and slabs of beef and pork had long since been dispatched to Manhattan, the Bronx, Brooklyn and Queens. (Sparsely populated Staten Island was not worth the time and costs of direct delivery.)

Owner Matty Cisco's shoebox-size office sat in the rear of the building, directly across from the entrance to the main refrigerator.

Cisco heard footsteps. Instinctively, he slipped his hand in the drawer and wrapped his big oversized paw around a 38-caliber Smith & Wesson. Fonso approached.

"What the hell do you want?" said Cisco abruptly.

"Don't you remember me?" smiled Fonso. "Think, eight years ago."

Cisco rubbed his chin with his free hand. "You're not that kid butcher from the Bronx?"

"That's me, Fonso Gravenese."

"I assumed when the orders stopped, Locatelli made you disappear."

"No. Dad died rather suddenly. I sold the shop, and moved on."

"So what the hell brings you here?"

"Take your hand off the gun, and I'll tell you. Promise, it's not a stick-up."

Fonso covered the last eight years in about five minutes — up to and including the Metz takeover, and the SMA appointment.

$

"Come a long way from the son of a butcher shop owner. How the hell old are you?" smiled Cisco.

"Twenty-five."

"Christ, you've already lived a lifetime," said 60- something Cisco. "Like I said, what the hell brings you here in that fancy Cadillac this early in the morning?"

"I got my first Federal Food Lunch purchase order yesterday," said Fonso, waving the purchase order. "They want me to start delivering 100,000 pounds of hot dogs, hamburgers and baloney a month. Maybe more, if all goes smoothly. I plan to do whatever it takes to make them a very satisfied customer."

"That's one slaughterhouse full of steers and hogs." joked Cisco, ignoring 'the whatever it takes.' "I know a few other guys that have been selected, but their initial orders are nothing like you're talking."

"Let's talk meat," smiled Fonso.

"I'm listening."

"I need a supplier who I can trust. Someone who has capacity, and who isn't going to play games trying to cheat me. When I was wet-behind-the-ears, you treated me with respect. Fonso never forgets."

$

Cisco was intrigued. "Let me see the paperwork." He looked at the pricing on the first order.

"No problem. I can provide all the USDA inspected livestock you need, but I'm not in the receivables business. It's cash on delivery. Nothing personal."

Fonso's credit was already maxed. Tens of thousands more was not in the cards.

Cisco sensed the hesitation, and gave Fonso a gracious escape route. "You're in a great situation. U.S. government receivables are good as gold. You've got options up the wazoo," he said. "Who's your bank?"

"Manufacturers Hanover."

"Daily double. They've been our lender for years. Those guys just love secured revolvers."

A revolver is a line of credit established by a lender for a maximum amount. The line of credit is usually secured by the company's account receivables and inventory. The lender protects his loan by also taking a security interest in said receivables and inventory.

Chapter 21

October, 1940
Demarest, NJ

Fonso was O'Brien's first appointment the following morning.

"How can I help my favorite customer?" asked O'Brien. Fonso explained the SMA appointment. O'Brien was delighted. "That really should jumpstart your reorganization." He was also amenable to an increased line of credit, with conditions. "Fonso, based on your financials, we do have to ask for a personal family guarantee."

"What do you mean, personal family?"

"We've got to get Mom's signature as the Haight Avenue owner of record in addition to significant assets are attached to your name…like that gold Rolex you're wearing, and the Caddy in the lot."

Fonso was displeased. "You mean… everything?"

O'Brien shrugged. "There is a factoring alternative, but I wouldn't advise you to go there, at least not with U.S. government receivables. These guys would scoop up your receivables in a heartbeat at 60 cents on the dollar. Traditional lenders call it desperate money, Fonso had a Manufacturers Hanover, or "Manny Hanny" secured line of credit for $250,000, and placed his first order with Cisco.

The next week, a line of refrigerated trucks were emptied by Metz employees under the watchful eyes of Hitzig and Magro. Halfway through the unloading process, Hitzig's burly lieutenant Charlie Gilardi approached. "Rup, there ain't no more hooks to hang them hogs and steers." Rupert double-checked all the refrigerated rooms. "Charlie, give the boys a break. I'll go find Fonso."

Fonso didn't want to know. "You and Charlie just do what you have to do. We can't have any problems with this first order."

Hitzig, not one to take chances, felt he had no alternative. "Charlie, have the floors wiped clean as best you can, and start stacking the stuff in rows."

Gilardi's bushy eyebrows went up. "You sure?" Both men knew the suggested process was a clear violation of Health Department standards. Hitzig gambled that the beef could be cut, ground, and boxed, and the hogs converted to frankfurter slurry and baloney — before the next unscheduled Health Department inspection.

They finished about 2 a.m. They were surprised to see Fonso walk in. "I want to thank all *my boys* for busting their butts." He gave everybody three crisp $100 bills and said, "buy your wives a bouquet of roses and take ém out for a nice dinner."

Everybody was pleased — except Gilardi. He saw the health violation as his opportunity to solve a bigger personal problem.

For years Gilardi had fantasized about being a singing star, cranking out gold and platinum albums. He was good, but not good enough. To pay for all singing lessons and demo records, he started to gamble. Before long, he was addicted to the thrill of betting on everything from the ponies to baseball games. Unfortunately, Gilardi rarely won. Eventually, his gambling losses exceeded his ability to pay his debts, and loan sharks became his primary source of funding.

The more money he lost, the more he bet to recoup his losses. The morning after the overtime gig, loan shark Johnnie Tripodi, showed up unannounced and took Gilardi aside. "Charlie, you owe me almost $8,000. There are no more tomorrows. If I don't see half of that money in 24 hours, you're not going to be able to lift a knife to cut a fucking pig. Do we understand each other?"

Charlie was desperate to raise cash fast. He concluded his best option was to turn informant. He called his local United Packinghouse Workers of America (UPWA) representative, Tomaso Hurley. Tomaso was rumored to take from employers and share with employees.

"Tomaso," said Gilardi from his home phone, "I have a situation that might interest you."

"I'm listening," said Hurley.

"There are some significant health and overtime violations at Metz."

"Talk to me about the health violations. I can't stand that little prick Gravenese. He's been trying to push the union out ever since he walked in the door."

"I heard," said Gilardi.

"Details," said Hurley.

"Not till we have an understanding."

"What are you thinking?"

"Eight big ones."

"Sounds high."

"Tomaso, let's cut the shit. We both know, eight grand is a fraction of what you're gonna rob from the Bank of Genovese."

Hurley knew Gilardi was right. "Deal. Start talking."

"Tomaso, I wasn't born yesterday. Money first, information second."

The following morning the two men sat on a park bench, a safe distance from the Metz plant. Hurley handed Gilardi an envelope. Gilardi quickly scanned its contents. "That's only four. Where is the rest?"

"The other four come after I verify the information. Trust me, Tripodi will wait for the rest."

Gilardi provided the where, when, and how of the health violations. He also told Hurley if the UPWA hustled, they would find a few sides sitting on the floor, since the butchers were still cutting. Hurley hustled over to announce a surprise inspection. He made a bee-line to the Metz fridge rooms, and was horrified by the appalling sanitary conditions.

"Rupert, you leave me no choice," Hurley announced. "I've got to issue Metz a Code-395 violation for unsanitary food-processing practices." Everyone knew such a citation would probably terminate their SMA contract.

"I appreciate your concern about the consumer," said Hitzig calmly. "But there are some extenuating circumstances to consider."

"Like what?" said Hurley.

"Why don't we talk to Fonso? He can explain it better than me." The two men found Fonso, who listened quietly to Hurley's litany of violations. Fonso reached into the drawer for his checkbook. "Tomaso, how much do the fines total?" Hurley pulled out an official-looking little black book, filled with notations. "Eight thousand dollars."

Fonso stared angrily.

"What can I say," said Hurley. "Increased Government overheads. Rising Inflation."

"I assume I make the check out to cash?" asked Fonso.

"Yes. I usually aggregate the fines, and provide a summary report to union leadership."

$

Despite the Hurley hiccup, Fonso kept his word with those that mattered. Ricco hand delivered a check to Cisco within 48 hours after the first SMA order was filled. Two weeks after that, Metz delivered 100,000 pounds of processed meats to the SMA distribution warehouse in Clinton, Maryland, an hour north of Washington, D.C.

$

As for Gilardi, he agreed to collect his second installment at Hurley's favorite restaurant in the North Bronx — a popular mob seafood haunt called Joe & Joe's, on Castle Hill Avenue. As the men devoured a mountain of lasagna at a corner table, Hurley passed The envelope to Gilardi.

"How much?"

"Three thousand, nine hundred and eighty. I took 20 out for the linguini and wine."

$

The more Hitzig traced the leak, the more all roads led to Gilardi.

"Can't be," bristled Fonso. "I asked the guy to sing *Mama, a popular Italian song,* at Father Don's birthday party." The lyrics pledged that a mama would always be respected and loved.

$

Ricco had a familiar suggestion. "Why don't I take Charlie aside, and get to the bottom of the matter?"

Gilardi reluctantly agreed to have dinner with Ricco. He knew Ricco didn't *just* invite people to dinner. As Ricco drove up Bruckner Boulevard in the Bronx, a nervous Gilardi wondered, "So, where are we going?"

"There's a great new restaurant on Castle Hill Avenue called Joe & Joes. I hear they serve the best lasagna in town."

The two men walked into the restaurant, and were seated at the same corner table shared by Gilardi and Hurley a few nights earlier. Ricco ordered the exact same meal Gilardi and Hurley had. Ricco excused himself to go to the men's room. As Ricco passed the bar, Gilardi noticed the bartender nod. Gilardi ordered another glass of wine. Ricco never returned. Gilardi checked the men's room. No Ricco. When he returned, the waiter asked if there was anything else. He assumed, for whatever reason, Ricco had stiffed him.

"Just the bill, I guess," said Gilardi.

"It's all taken care of," replied the bartender. "And, your cab is waiting out front."

Gilardi cautiously walked outside. Yellow Cab #2367 was idling at the curb. He looked inside, and saw only the driver. He looked around, the streets were deserted. He got in, and gave the cabbie his address.

$

When he didn't come home that night, Gilardi's wife called the police and filed a missing person's report. One week passed, then two. She called the precinct each day for some bit of information, anything. Nothing was forthcoming. Two months passed, then three. Without a body or any remains, the police officially declared him deceased.

Gilardi's funeral service was strange and strained. There was an empty, closed casket. No priest, no ceremony. Just a grieving wife and two grown children. Fonso, Ricco and Hitzig paid their respects.

Gilardi's wife, Marsha, reacted brutally to Fonso's hollow condolences. "You heartless bastard. I know you had something to do with this. I hope you rot in hell...alone."

Chapter 22

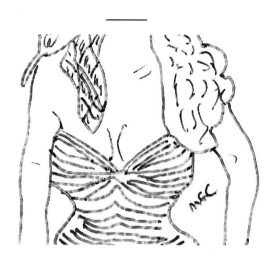

November, 1940
Demarest, NJ

A gorgeous blonde named Gloria with boobs large enough to sink the Titanic, leaned into Fonso's office. "There's a Mr. McGee here to see you. He says it's important."

Max McGee was the local rep for the International Brotherhood of Teamsters, and Tomaso Hurley's brother-in-law. The Teamsters were about two things — making sure their members got high hourly wages, including time-and-a-half for overtime. And making sure Union reps got their fair share of everything.

Based on his discussion with Hurley, McGee figured Fonso's unofficial overtime contract violations had two possible outcomes. Fonso could fess up publicly, and pay all his boys their due. Or he could confess privately, and pay McGee 20 percent of that total.

One twenty-minute contract discussion later, McGee left Fonso's office with a wad of cash in his pocket. Fonso summoned Ricco Cicolo. "I don't care what you do, but this shit has got to stop."

"This is the Teamsters," replied Ricco. "I may need a few more guys..."

Fonso interrupted. "Call in the Green Berets if you have to."

Instead of the Green Berets, Ricco called Max McGee, who didn't know him, or his relationship to Fonso. "Somebody told me you might be interested in overtime violations at Metz," said Ricco.

"Who the fuck are you?" McGee responded.

"One of those Metz employees who always gets shortchanged because I'm not one of Fonso's Boys." He paused. "But, if you're the wrong guy, let's forget this call."

McGee backtracked. "I didn't say that." Ricco suggested an exchange meeting over dinner at Carmine's Restaurant in Seaport Village on the Lower East Side. Ricco was particularly fond of the area because the cobblestone streets were deserted at night. And the pedestrian walkway under the FDR Drive leading to the East River was unlit.

McGee and his envelope left Carmine's first. He spotted Yellow Cab #2367 trolling for passengers. He got in and gave the driver his destination.

$

McGee's wife, Maureen, angrily paced the floor of their neat Bayside, Queens, duplex. It was now 2 a.m., and still no Max. She was certain he had shacked up with his sometime squeeze, Gloria-Big-Boobs, at her apartment in nearby Douglaston. After getting caught red-handed by a private eye, Max had promised his indiscretions were a thing of the past. Maureen had no clue Gloria was Fonso's secretary. Maureen figured the best way to send Max and Gloria both a message was to call the police, and tell them somebody was trying to break into her apartment. She gave them Gloria's name and address as the caller, and then went to sleep.

Max never came home. Gloria, Maureen, and Fonso never heard from Max again. Only Ricco and the cabdriver knew Max was at the bottom of the East River bolted to a concrete anchor.

$

The phone rang on Fonso's desk. "Damn good job," said Jim. "This is the first time the SMA has ever received an order two weeks ahead of schedule."

During the next year, Magro continued to improve trimming efficiencies, Hitzig ramped up delivery speeds, the SMA received every order on time or earlier. Consequently, Metz cash flow and profits exploded.

At the company Christmas party, Fonso announced every employee would receive a 5-percent cash bonus, based on their total earnings for the year. The place roared. Hitzig and Magro were ecstatic! Their hard work and loyalty had paid off. The following morning Fonso gave Ricco an extra bonus of 20 percent for, as he described it, "Ricco's extra work."

He also had Gloria arrange a holiday dinner to thank Jim for the SMA business. Fonso also invited Congressman Jake Rutherman. He knew Jim loved to feel important.

$

A few glasses of Sangiovese and a signature Clam Broth House seafood antipasto platter — then the parties got down to business. Jim was first. He raised his wineglass, "Fonso. Congratulations. The SMA has named Metz and Company the Free Lunch Program Supplier of the Year." The men clinked their glasses.

"But, there's something else. The Government believes outstanding service should be rewarded. So, as of January first, the Metz and Company Free Lunch monthly order has been increased to 300,000 pounds."

Rutherman was about to declare for a third term. He realized this was his moment. "Gentlemen, your partnership is really a great story about Government and industry working hand-in-hand. People should know."

"Fonso, how many new jobs will the increased order volume create?"

Fonso paused. "Fifty, maybe a hundred people, depends."

"Do you guys mind if my office contacts the press?"

It was showtime — Fonso style.

"Congressman, count me in. Maybe the good news can give your re-election bid a little boost against that anti-union Republican bag-of-wind, Jason Strach."

"Congressman," said Jim, "I hear nothing but nice things about you from Fonso. You can count on the SMA for our endorsement."

"Congressman," said Fonso, "I don't understand how the race is even that close. Strach wants to make the wealthy wealthier, while you just want all Americans to live the life they deserve."

"The reality is simple," said Rutherman. "The man's got lots of money."

"That reminds me," interrupted Fonso. "The Metz family all donated a few bucks to help your campaign. I know it's not a lot. But it's from the heart."

Rutherman turned modest. "Fonso, I didn't bring up the subject to…"

Rutherman glanced in the envelope. There were 20 thousand- dollar bills. "Fonso, thank the boys. Every little bit helps."

Rutherman looked at his watch. "Oops. I hope you fellas don't mind. I've got a little rally I need to attend."

$

After Rutherman left, it was now Jim's turn.

"Your support staff has been a dream to work with," said Fonso. "So we thought they might like a little extra Christmas cheer." Fonso handed an envelope of 20 thousand dollar bills to Thompson. Unlike Rutherman, Thompson stayed for dinner.

The three men were now officially brothers of a kind. Just to make sure they remained so, Ricco's hidden camera documented the gift-giving.

Chapter 23

December, 1940
Demarest, NJ

High-strung Hitzig almost had a heart attack when Fonso broke the news.

"Holy crap, 300,000 pounds! We'll need more butchers, more trimmers, more packers, more trucks, more production lines…"

Fonso knew he had three order fulfillment assets. Hitzig was a fastidious operations manager. Production supervisor Sam Magro had the confidence and loyalty of floor staff. Mean-mannered Ricco handled thorny company issues with efficiency and discretion.

Still, there were shortcomings that needed to be addressed. Fonso knew he had to raise his own game. He was no longer a two-bit, small-time entrepreneur. He was a respected community business force, destined for the big time.

As Hitzig said, the first order of business was to hire more qualified personnel.

Hitzig put the word out thorough the Union, trade ads, and colleagues that good-paying jobs with all sorts of benefits were available at Metz, right now. Meat trimmers and packers interviewed day and night. Fonso also sought staff referrals by paying handsome employee bonuses every time a referral was hired. The recruiting surprise was Gloria, who led the company in quality referrals at all levels, in all departments.

Fonso also approached Vinny and Richie Scaramuzzo about completing a needed plant expansion. After reviewing the product specs, Vinny candidly suggested Fonso consider a more experienced firm. "Don't get me wrong, my brother and I would love a multi-million-dollar construction project. But this is much bigger than anything we've ever done.

Fonso would not take no for an answer. "Vinny, do you want the best for you and your family? You know, the best costs money. I'm giving you the chance most people would kill for."

"Why?"

"Because I trust you. And, in the end, that's all the matters."

During the next six months, the Scaramuzzos transformed the pedestrian Metz building into a state- of-the-art production facility. They completed the task under budget and on time, including an office large enough to fit Fonso and his growing ego — far away from the chaotic production floor and the endless smell of fat renderings.

Pleased, Fonso awarded the brothers all his future projects. In time, Vinny and Richie parlayed those experiences into the highly-respected Scaramuzzo International Construction Company, which designed and constructed office towers around the world.

$

As Metz production exploded thanks to the SMA contract, there was one important area that still needed to be staffed and managed — the finance department.

Since Gino Metz had been dismissed as comptroller the year, the company's finances had been handled by a loose consortium of loosely-supervised bookkeepers, Fonso, and a highly sophisticated, part-time CPA, Fred Auslander.

"Fonso," said the tall, elegant, squeaky-clean son of a Swiss immigrant, "I believe the time has arrived. You need a Chief Financial Officer."

"That's one of my jobs," replied Fonso.

"It shouldn't be. Your job is to grow top line revenues and be the face of the Company. You are a woefully under-qualified CFO. You need more inclusive fact-based reports to increase production capacities; more cost-benefit analyses to make capital investment decisions; and, tight day-to-day controls — currently nonexistent — to better manage cash flows. Income taxes have to shrink and undeclared incentives better aggregated, among other matters."

Fonso got the point.

Auslander recommended a few search firms that specialized in financial executives. Fonso interviewed three or four candidates, but concluded they were all uptown snobs. He needed someone more street-savvy, more cunning.

$

By about 6 p.m. Friday night, everybody had left for the weekend. Ricco walked by Fonso's office on the way to his car. The blinds were closed, but the lights were on. He knocked. "Ever go home?" he asked.

"Home is a little chaotic right now. Donna is expecting, and her mother and father have taken over decorating the baby's room."

"I thought the deal was that when kids came along, you were moving out?"

"The deal changed."

"Shit…around here anybody tries to change the deal, and you cut their balls off."

"Can't do that with family," replied Fonso.

"You've been emasculated." said Ricco.

Fonso laughed. "Where the hell did a grammar-school dropout learn such a big word?"

"I've got this cousin, Robert Moccio, he went to one of those fancy business schools…Warttim University or something like that, in Philadelphia.

"You mean Wharton School of Business?"

"Yeah, that's the one," said Ricco. "He keeps telling me, Ricco, big money comes from knowing big words."

Fonso's ears perked up. "What does Robert do exactly?"

"Mostly look for a big financial job. He was the CFO at some Wall Street firm that got shut down over trading violations. His boss claimed the scam was all his idea."

"Bobbie created a system to buy and sell securities big customer accounts held in the street name. That way he could use the stock as collateral, and buy and sell shares and commodity positions without clients ever noticing. The formula was simple: pick winners, and repay the loans quickly. If a trader noticed, he gave him a spiff to turn the other way. His won-loss record was extraordinary: in three weeks, he had amassed $100,000 in gains. Unfortunately, an anonymous trader felt he was not getting his fair share, and exposed the scheme. An hour later, Bobbie was gainfully unemployed."

"What happened?"

"Far as I know nothing really, except he's having a hard time finding his next big gig."

Ricco didn't know that the IRS and Moccio had negotiated an undisclosed settlement. Moccio agreed to taxes plus penalties and interest on the undeclared gains, and the IRS agreed to waive their rights to press charges for income-tax evasion.

But the longer Moccio remained unemployed, the larger his tax bill grew. By the time he was introduced to Fonso, he was just weeks away from a lien being placed on his future earnings and the public embarrassment that comes from such a declaration.

Chapter 24

December, 1940
Demarest, NJ

Three days later, a handsome six-foot-two-inch well-groomed man faced Fonso sitting at his desk. He looked like something out of *Gentlemen's Quarterly* and sounded like something out of South Joisey.

Fonso wasted no time. "So Bobbie, what are you looking for?"

"Mr. Gravenese, don't you want some background?"

"Naaah, what's there to know? Ricco said you graduated from Wharton and got your hand caught in the cookie jar."

"Mr. Gravenese, I'm not sure that's the way I'd phrase it."

"Did you or didn't you?" asked Fonso. "By the way, I'm Fonso around here."

"I did."

Fonso chuckled. "Okay, no crime, there's a little larceny in all of us"

"What are you looking for in a CFO?" asked Moccio.

"I need a financially-polished Robin Hood. Take from a bloated government that <u>has</u>, and give it to a hard-working entrepreneur that <u>wants</u> — as in *me*."

"Make it as in *us*, and you've just hired your new CFO."

$

Moccio's first assignment was to find a creative solution to the impending Metz delivery dilemma.

Fulfilling the dramatic increase in SMA orders required more trucks than Metz actually owned. Hitzig wanted to do what he had always done — invest more money to buy more trucks.

"Rupert," said Moccio, in a three-way meeting with Fonso, "the need for 25 more trucks, and servicing the 17 we already have, will require a full-time maintenance department. By the time we add salaries, benefits, tools, garage space, and a bunch of other things, we could be placing an albatross around our neck that will be hard to get rid of should the orders slow, or should some of our core business shrink."

Hitzig and Fonso stared blankly at each other. "If you can fix the fucking albatross, you should be able to fix the fucken trucking problem," said Fonso. "I recommend we get out of the trucking business. Sell the fleet, and close the mechanic shed. Then we negotiate a flexible lease for brand new trucks from Pioneer Trucking in Avalon, New Jersey. They're willing to provide all the trucks we need, precisely when we need them. They'll take care of all the maintenance, trucker crew salaries, benefits and union dues."

Moccio passed a few sheets of paper to both men. "As you can see from the numbers, we can operate 42 trucks for same annual cost of owning and maintaining 17. And while it's true we don't own the asset, whenever one breaks down, it gets replaced by another."

"Rupert," said Fonso. "What do you think?"

"Seems like a no-brainer the way Bobbie explained it."

"Two last questions," said Fonso. "Suppose they don't deliver."

"Got us covered. The contract is written that if Pioneer defaults on their obligations — for any reason — we seize their assets."

A week later, Moccio had a signed Pioneer contract, and the trucks started to be scheduled and dispatched.

Fonso decided not to ask the second question. What percent of every truck lease did Moccio get? He guessed it was 25 percent, which was okay by him. Fonso never realized Moccio also owned 25 percent of Pioneer.

$

Surprising nerdy, but crafty, Rudy Gigante, the Teamsters rep who replaced Max McGee, took one look at the truck-leasing deal. He smelled more than animal fat renderings. He smelled a private deal.

"Fonso," said Gigante over coffee in Fonso's office, "that Wharton punk you hired, is cutting out the Teamsters."

Fonso played dumb. "How so?"

"This Pioneer lease shit. My Teamsters collect less dues because your drivers are gone. Is that fair?"

Fonso decided not to die on that battlefield. A dispute with the Teamsters could spread like wildfire to the other unions, which could lead to a widespread strike that could shut down the whole plant. And put the entire SMA relationship in jeopardy.

"Rudy, how about we keep a side book? You get a monthly incentive on truck deliveries?" He figured the thousands of dollars the trucks earned each day would more than make up for the "monthly taste."

Fonso asked Moccio to handle the Gigante deal personally. He was confident the matter would be handled discretely, since Moccio already had his own hand in the Metz cookie jar.

$

Soon Moccio had both good news and bad news.

"Fonso, the orders are cranking, Sam's got production humming, and our latest quality assurance report says we've got nothing but satisfied customers. But..."

"But what?" asked Fonso.

"Cash flow is starting to lag," said Moccio.

"How can that be?"

"Side agreements," responded Moccio. "They keep getting bigger."

"Cost of doing business," said Fonso. "Why didn't you alert me sooner?"

"It's not all that easy to hide the stuff, and still look professional to the banks."

"What are you suggesting?"

Moccio recommended keeping a second set of books with the real numbers. Moccio called them "the home copy." They would operate like an early alert system. Both sets would contain Metz revenues, cost of goods, and profit estimates. But the second set would also include line items detailing the when and where of special payments to the Metz Company's growing cadre of blatant liars, subtle obstructionists and unethical expeditors.

Only three people in the whole world knew of their existence: Fonso, Moccio, who prepared them, and Fonso's trusted lieutenant Ricco.

The three men agreed the books would only be removed and updated once a month after hours. They would be stored in a small safe behind a picture that hung on the wall in Fonso's office. Fonso also decided he would be the only one who knew the combination.

What went unsaid was that Fonso felt Moccio was the kind of person who would do anything to save his own skin. So he issued himself a little insurance. Once the second set of books was updated each month, Fonso would take them home and place them in a tuxedo bag in rear of his clothes closet.

The bag contained the only tuxedo Fonso ever owned. The one time he wore it, Donna laughed and said he looked like a penguin. Fonso didn't like being called a penguin. He also knew it was unlikely Donna would ever bother with the bag.

$

A few days later, Moccio reviewed the newly instituted second set with Fonso in his office. Fonso was shocked at the cost of his generosity.

The two men agreed cuts needed to be made. Fonso told Moccio he needed some time to think about who and how much.

That evening Fonso laid quietly in bed with a small notepad. He was making lists and estimating cost reductions.

Donna, in the mood for some serious lovemaking, entered the room in Fonso's favorite sexy red negligee. She snuggled next to him, and tried to turn out the light. "My, my," purred Donna, "we seem quite preoccupied."

Fonso decided not to respond. He went back to identifying potential job cuts in his notebook.

"Why are you so preoccupied with that dam pad?" asked Donna, frustrated.

"I got some bad news about cash flow from Bobbie Moccio."

"How can that be? Jim told me the Metz trucks are delivering 24 hours a day."

"It's a little more complicated than that."

Donna smiled. "Well, you are the world's undisputed, reigning heavyweight king of bullshit. You'll figure out something."

Chapter 25

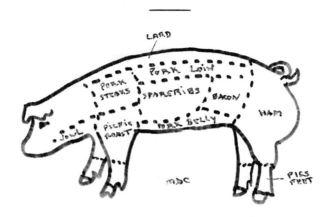

Hogs are the primary source of numerous cuts of meat, including hot dogs and baloney. Commercial-grade versions of these hot dogs and bologna are made by placing seasoned meat trimmings into giant steel vats. Seasonings are added and the meat is mechanically ground until it has the consistency of a thick slurry. The slurry is then pumped into long clear edible casings, moved to a smoke house, where the product is fully cooked, and cut into the appropriate shapes and lengths.

November, 1941
Demarest, NJ

Fonso invented two new strategies to resolve the cash flow issue, neither of which was technically legal.

First, he returned to his roots. He and Sam Magro spent hours on the production floor, experimenting with new trimming techniques to increase per-hog yield. They figured out a way to get a lot more yield per hog by using a narrower trimming knife around hard-to-reach places like the carcass. Sam thought the increased yield might be tough, fatty, and not particularly tasty. He suggested to Fonso that they experiment with different hog cuts and amounts after the day staff left.

Fonso had one mission: lower his cost of goods. The two men experimented for four nights. Fonso kept pushing Magro to replace Grade-A product with more and more of the cheap yield. Eventually, Magro said no more. "This stuff tastes like flavored liquid plastic. It's an insult to the Metz name."

Fonso ignored Magro's observation. "Are the hotdogs and frankfurters edible?'

"Technically yes."

"If the kids eat them are they going to get sick?"

"No."

"Do you think the kids will actually complain to somebody?"

"Highly unlikely. They're just elementary school kids."

"Precisely," said Fonso. "Nobody will ever know the difference."

Sam hesitated. "That still doesn't make it right."

"Would a 10 percent raise make it easier to fill our orders?'"

Magro wanted to maintain his integrity and say no. But his wife Barbara was racking up bills at an ugly pace. Both he and Fonso knew he could use the money.

Magro paused. "Tell you what. Add a $10,000 signing bonus up front and we'll start making the new formulation tomorrow."

Fonso was surprised the Magro incentive was so low. He was prepared to pay Magro three times that amount.

$

The second cost-reduction strategy required the cooperation of Matty Cisco.

Fonso got right to the point. "Matty, for a lot of reasons, I need to lower my cost of goods on Free Lunch shipments."

Cisco assumed he knew what was coming. "I told you right from the beginning, I'm not in the receivables business."

"No, a deal is a deal. But I think I've come up with an idea that would work for both of us. Suppose you change my balance of shipment contents."

"What the hell does that mean?"

"USDA inspected meat is more expensive than uninspected meat. Right? If you shipped me a blend of 70 percent inspected and 30 percent uninspected meat, I'd save a bundle. Right?"

Cisco balked. "Fonso, I've spent too much time building my business the right way. I don't want to send crap to the SMA.".

Fonso's tone changed. "Suppose there was no SMA business. Suppose Fonso went elsewhere."

"You wouldn't."

"Try me," glared Fonso.

Cisco thought about his options. Was the comprise worth the risk to his reputation? If he agreed, could he cover his tracks?

Fonso's tone changed again. "Matty, do you have kids? Are they in the business?

"No way. They're in college."

"So what happens to the business?"

"I'm not planning on going anyplace anytime soon."

"Me either, but suppose it happened. Do you think the kids will get the true value of the business?"

Fonso paused for a moment.

"Suppose we get a little creative here. You provide the mixed meat, and I'll give you a 10-percent interest in Metz."

"Something to think about, I guess," said Cisco. "When did you need that first mixed order?"

Chapter 26

Christmas Eve, 1942
Demarest, NJ

At 3 p.m. on Christmas Eve, the plant closed down for the holidays.

Fonso was about to leave his office. He looked around and smiled at his good fortune. The restructured Metz Company and its Surplus Marketing Administration contracts had been a cash machine for almost three years. He had paid off all the bank notes, and managed to sock a few million away for a rainy day. The future appeared to be nothing but sunny days. Santa had brought Fonso a Merry Christmas!

Suddenly, the door snapped open. Three FBI agents showed their badges, introduced themselves, and handed Fonso a search warrant.

"What the hell is this about?" screeched Fonso.

"We have reason to believe you've violated a number of federal laws," said the lead agent, barrel-chested, curly-haired Logan Bray, gun jutting out of his side holster.

"You guys are crazy. I run a legitimate meatpacking company. I'm not some common criminal you can just push around."

"Mr. Gravenese, you are not under arrest…yet. We are here to gather evidence. However, any representations you make can and will be held against you in a court of law," continued Bray.

Bray directed his associates, "Start checking the refrigerators. Mark and segregate the uninspected stock for pick up."

"Metz Meatpacking is a premium supplier. We don't own or ever sell products using uninspected meat," said Fonso with conviction.

"That's not what our sources have testified," retorted Bray

Fortunately, Fonso knew the end-of-year Surplus Marketing Administration orders had been filled and shipped, leaving the refrigerators with only a small amount of premium aged beef.

"Please, Mr. Bray," sneered Fonso sarcastically, "let me help you. In addition to the main fridges, we have a few smaller ones in the rear. Wouldn't want you to miss anything."

Bray wasn't finished. "Where do you keep your books?"

Fonso was surprised but prepared. "They're in the top drawer of the cabinet behind my desk."

Bray skimmed the office copy, which included detailed revenues and expenses entries using industry-standard General Accepted Accounting Principles known simply as GAAP. He appeared to be looking for something specific. "Where's the other set?"

Fonso played dumb. "The books are the books."

"Where's the wall safe?" asked the lead agent.

Fonso smelled a rat. "What makes you think I have a wall safe?"

"A little bird told me."

Bray tapped on a picture hanging over Fonso's desk. "What's behind here?"

Fonso smiled cynically. "A wall."

"Listen you little shit," said Bray approaching Fonso.

Fonso stood his ground. "Do you guys have a search warrant?"

"Not at the moment," replied Bray.

"Tell you what," said Fonso, "despite your rude behavior, it's Christmas. Behind the picture is the petty-cash safe. Please, let me open it for you."

Bray's sidekick searched the safe. "Only thing in there is about five grand in small bills. Maybe *he* was wrong," said the agent.

Fonso now knew who tipped the IRS.

The FBI left frustrated, tails between their legs. Fonso stood by the door and waved. "Thanks for stopping by. Have a Merry Christmas and a Happy New Year."

Despite the surprise FBI visit, Fonso made it home in plenty of time for Christmas dinner followed by Midnight Mass. The joyous sounds of Christmas hymns filled their Church as the Gravenese and Magro families sang traditional carols. Fonso looked around. The building was awash in red poinsettia plants, bright colored Christmas ornaments and a spectacular manger with the three wise men under a big Christmas tree. He smiled at the coincidence.

$

On the other side of the north Bronx, the Robert Moccio family Christmas turned into a long wait for their father. He never came.

The family filed a missing persons' report. Days passed. All the police were able to determine was that Moccio had gone to Macy's on Herald Square to pick up some last-minute Christmas presents. One unsubstantiated report stated a man of Moccio's approximate height and build entered Yellow Cab #2367 with two shopping bags brimming with gifts.

The police contacted every Yellow Cab company in New York City. None had a registered cab #2367.

Chapter 27

January, 1943
Los Angeles, CA

Fonso knew he had not seen the last of the FBI. He told Donna about their visit. She wasn't surprised — she had overheard rumors during the SMA Metz vetting process.

She agreed with Fonso's conclusion. "I think we should consider hiring the best defense lawyer money could buy, just in case." The last thing Fonso wanted was a smudge on his record. His instincts told him there was even more money to be made in government programs.

Donna volunteered to do the research. Her rationale was simple. "Who else can we trust?" She identified a Los Angeles attorney, Dwain Clark.

"Los Angeles," asked Fonso. "That's 3,000 miles away. You couldn't find somebody closer?" Donna wasn't crazy about the distance either. But Clark, a retired FBI agent, had a reputation for knowing his way around an indictment. In ten years, Clark had never lost a case.

Donna didn't know that the handsome, silver-tongued Clark had quietly retired with a full pension at the age of 41. There were rumors, none of which was ever substantiated, that he had been on the take from a number of mob-related corporate enterprises. Technically he was squeaky clean. He passed the Los Angeles Bar and established his practice in Beverly Hills.

His ego was as big as his reputation. His practice sat in an elegant, expensive suite on Wilshire Boulevard down the block from the landmark Beverly Wilshire Hotel. He quickly became one of the busiest defense lawyers in L.A., representing organized crime figures. His unpublished client list read like a Who's Who of American mobsters: Dipolitto, Battaglia, Licata, DeSimone, Licavoli, Milan, Testa, among others.

Clark's specialty was white-collar crime, particularly Federal cases involving bribery, kickbacks and payoffs in high places. The word was, perhaps promoted by Clark himself, that he never had a dissatisfied client.

Donna arranged a first meeting at Clark's favorite watering hole, the celebrity-studded

Brown Derby on Wilshire, within walking distance to Clark's offices.

Donna thought the Brown Derby was a local, good-value diner. So Fonso was stunned when the cab stopped in front of a pretentious building shaped like an English Bowler hat. As Fonso stood in the two- story lobby, he felt as if he was standing upside down. He stared up at the unusual interior supports.

A distinguished gray-haired man in a tuxedo approached. "Fun isn't it? Nowhere but L.A." Then, "Mr. Gravenese, Mr. Clark is waiting."

The men walked toward a rear table with an unobstructed view of the front entrance — a long-standing mob preference. Fonso noticed a tall beige wall decorated with caricatures of famous Hollywood stars. At the table directly below the caricatures of Cary Grant and Myrna Loy sat Cary Grant and Myrna Loy. Poker-faced Fonso was impressed.

Clark stood up to shake hands. The scene looked like a meeting of the popular cartoon characters Mutt and Jeff. "Fonso, let's eat and talk," smiled the personable Clark. "I never do business on an empty stomach."

Fonso stared at the mile-long menu. "Christ, I could spend the day just reading."

"Forget the menu," said Clark. "The specialty is the Cobb salad. Incredible combination of tastes and textures, like bacon bits, gorgonzola, chopped turkey, eggs and a bunch of other stuff."

Then he got right to the point. "Does the FBI have a case?"

"Absolutely not."

"Bullshit," said Clark. "I hear you've spread the wealth to everybody in New Jersey but the Governor."

Fonso took out a cigar and lit it. "How the hell do you…"

"That's why I charge the highest hourly rates in town. I know what I need to know. Never forget… it's all about information. He who controls the information, controls the game. I'm guessing the Government doesn't have any hard evidence. Just the testimony of one or two disgruntled bums who took bribes, and are now trying to save their skin."

"How do you know it's two?"

"Doesn't matter. Two, three, ten. Everybody has dirt. We'll discredit them all."

$

The men spoke for another hour. There were many things Fonso liked about Clark's brashness and confidence. But he wasn't sure how well his style would play in the more conservative New York courtrooms. Clark sensed Fonso's concern.

"Fonso, if you decide I'm a little too L.A. for your taste, don't worry about it. It's not like I'm desperate for clients. When are you going back?"

"Tomorrow."

"Where are you staying?"

"The Hilton in downtown."

"The Hilton downtown. The worst hotel, in the worst section of town. Tell you what I tell everybody that comes out for the first time. You've got to stay at the Beverly Hills Hotel on Sunset. It is an absolute kick. After lunch, we'll stop at my office. I'll have my secretary make all the arrangements. It's my gift to you, no strings attached."

$

The pink-stuccoed Beverly Hills Hotel sat majestically on a small rise off Sunset Boulevard, oddly garish and discreet. Jungle green banana tree wallpaper was everywhere. Celebrities walked the public rooms in virtual anonymity.

Clark didn't just make arrangements. He reserved a two-story rear cottage. It was *the* area to relax or play if you were named Humphrey Bogart or Gregory Peck.

The bell captain took Fonso on a tour of his oversized cottage. It was larger than his apartment in Bayonne. As Clark suggested, Fonso called room service to order the hotel's McCarthy chopped salad and a Sambuca with warm roasted coffee beans from the Polo Lounge. While he waited, he started to watch one of his favorite TV shows, *I Love Lucy*.

The doorbell rang. A stunning blonde starlet who was a dead ringer for the actress Jean Harlow stood in the doorway wearing a low-cut dress with a generous side slit.

"Mr. Clark wanted you to know that there will be a little delay in your dinner order." She sensuously rolled her tongue around her lips. "Perhaps you would like to start with dessert first?"

Fonso took his glasses off and smiled. "Thanks, but no thanks. Dinner will be quite enough." He closed the door, and went back to watching Lucy and Ethel Mertz making a mess of chocolate pieces on an assembly line.

After dinner, the phone rang.

"Hey Honey," said Donna. "When I heard they put you in a cottage at the Beverly Hills, I figured I better do a bed check." They both laughed. But Fonso wondered. How did Donna know where he was?

Chapter 28

January, 1943
Bayonne, NJ

The evening after Fonso returned from Los Angeles, the in-laws invited Donna and Fonso to dinner.

"So what were you doing in the Land of Fruits and Nuts?" asked the ever-nosey Victor Magro.

"Interviewing attorneys."

Magro became alarmed. "What's wrong? Isn't 3,000 miles a long way to go to find an attorney?"

Fonso felt his company was none of Magro's damn business. But to keep peace in the family, he decided to weave a little fantasy. "Mom and Dad, you know your daughter and I have worked long and hard to rebuild the Metz brand. In fact, we've invested all of our savings plus the money that my father passed on. In the process, I've been forced to deal with a host of unsavory characters from old man Metz's past. Apparently, he bribed meatpacking officials, teamsters, and, maybe even a government official or two. I'm not exactly sure."

Victor bristled at the accusations. "Odd, I thought the Metzes were a fine family. I remember Adolph's funeral about five years ago. All the family could talk about was how proud they were that a German immigrant had come to America and build a first-class company, using old world recipes."

"Were you aware this fine family had been draining the company dry for years?" glared Fonso. "Do you know what this fine family said when Donna and I announced the SMA appointment? Do you know what this fine family said when we showed them the potential impact our appointment might have on revenues, profits, and potential bonuses?"

"I get your point," said Magro.

"I want dedicated workers, not disgruntled complainers."

"I really can't comment on the business," said Mary. "But I will say, in all the years my father served on the police force, the name Metz and wrongdoing never appeared in the same sentence."

"Mary, with all due respect, I believe the FBI has been monitoring Metz family activities for quite some time."

"Aren't we being a little paranoid?" challenged Magro.

"Not when two agents show up at my office unannounced, and tell me anything I say can and will be used against me in a court of law."

"I think they're bluffing," said Magro.

"Suppose you're wrong? Are you going to be my attorney?"

"Fonso, I don't think you should rush to judgment. I mean, why hire an expensive attorney unless you're charged with something? In America, you're innocent until proven guilty," said Mary.

"Mary, with all due respect, you've got it backwards," said Fonso. "If you're Italian, you're guilty until proven innocent. It's been that way since I was a kid on the streets of Little Italy. Every cop thinks you're a Garafolo."

$

"Fonso, tell Daddy what the FBI man said?"

Donna weighed in. "Daddy, Fonso doesn't want to alarm you. But, they told him to find a damn good attorney who knows his way around white-collar crime."

Donna closed skillfully. "Daddy, neither of us want the Gravenese or the Magro family name dragged through the mud. Besides haven't you always taught me to stand up for what's right?"

Victor applauded his daughter. "Atta girl, Dee Dee, give 'em hell."

$

Donna explained about her research and how one of the names that came up consistently was Dwain Clark in Los Angeles.

"Dwain Clark," said Mary. "Isn't he that high-profile mob attorney?" Clark's relationships took Donna by surprise. She changed the subject by dropping a bombshell. "Do you realize everybody missed my clue," said Donna, beaming.

Fonso, Mary and Victor stared quizzically.

"I said Gravenese *family*, as in husband, wife *and child*."

"Congrats, Kids," said Victor uncharacteristically giddy. "Fonso, how far along is she?" Fonso looked confused.

"*We* are four months," said Donna.

Mary got her daughter's unspoken message. "Oh my goodness, Donna. You mean he really didn't know?"

Donna shook her head. "I've been trying to find the right moment. But Fonso's either working late or rubbing elbows with politicos. But Donna did the research."

"Fonso playfully tapped himself on the side of the head labeling himself "Stupido."

Donna laughed. "Stupido or no stupido, one healthy, loving baby will be on our doorsteps before Christmas."

Fonso's made an on-the-spot decision. "Dad and Mom, Donna and I haven't discussed this, but how would you like the Gravenese family to live here for the foreseeable future. Our apartment has plenty of room, and you can see the baby whenever you want. And if Donna decides to go back to work, you can be our official babysitter. I mean why waste a good college education?"

The solution delighted everyone.

Fonso had two reasons he wanted Donna to remain gainfully employed at the SMA. First, she'd have access impending opportunities long before they became public knowledge. Second, she could be their early warning system for impending investigations.

$

Donna shared her thoughts as soon as the couple returned to their apartment.

"Was my mother right about Clark?"

"Well, he does have a broad clientele."

"Let me be really clear," said Donna. "I'm willing to take some chances, and maybe once in a while walk up to the edge. But, there is absolutely, positively no way I want to get in bed with the mob or a mob lawyer. And, be forewarned. That was my last academy award performance in front of dad and mom."

$

Fonso reluctantly called Clark about a week later with his decision. "I think I better stay East. If and when…"

Clark interrupted. "As I said, no need to explain. But forget about 'if and when' the word is *when*." Clark paused. "By the way, if any of your government ventures need a little boost or just the right connection, give me a call. I know a lot of people who know a lot of people.

Chapter 29

February, 1943
Newark, NJ

Fonso called Congressmen Rutherman. "Jake, trust all is well with the family? I'm calling because I need some advice. Could we talk in person?"

"I'm not sure that's such a good idea at the moment. The FBI have already been here."

"What did they say?"

"They want the unvarnished truth. They said you're a terribly clever crook they plan to turn into a white-collar-crime poster child. I probed gingerly to find out what they really know. It's hard to say exactly. But you definitely should hire a lawyer, just in case."

"That's why I was calling. I need a referral."

"Fonso, I can certainly make a suggestion. But for Christ sakes, don't involve me."

"Involve you? Why the hell have I been paying you every month for the past three years?"

"Stop yelling. Somebody might hear you."

"Let's be real clear," Fonso said, "I keep records. Good records."

Rutherman continued. "My suggestion is Walter Riperton. He's a straight shooter and tough as nails. He plans to run for political office in New Jersey next year. If he decides to represent you, you'll get the benefit of his squeaky-clean image."

"*Decides* to represent me? Can't you do something more?"

"He's expecting your call."

$

Unlike Clark, Riperton insisted on meeting at his bland, uninspired office in crime-ridden Newark. There was no meal, no Cobb salad, just a cup of Sanka instant coffee, and some direct questions.

He had scary, threatening eyes, a big pointed nose, and a rock square chin.

"Mr. Gravenese, dealing with the FBI can be a tricky matter. Tell me more about how you conduct your business, and what you think the threats are all about?"

Fonso gave his rags-to-riches version of life, the jobs he had created through innovation and hard work.

Riperton wasn't buying. "Is it true that your key employees like Magro, Hitzig, and that thug Cicolo, all drive expensive black Cadillacs?"

"Fonso likes to reward loyalty and hard work."

Riperton leaned over and stared at Fonso. "I hear Fonso also apparently likes to reward a whole bunch of part-time and full-time employees."

Fonso became indignant. "Listen, Mr. Riperton, I've been supplying the Federal Government, helping kids, and donating to causes."

"Mr. Gravenese, you're quite an enigmatic figure."

Fonso stared blankly.

"What I mean, Mr. Gravenese, is that you are an unusually complex individual who sometimes gives and sometimes takes. And, I'm guessing you can't honestly tell the difference."

$

Ricco took Fonso by surprise, "Boss, my instinct tells me we should lay low and stay local. Hiring Riperton is like getting an endorsement from the Pope."

Two days later, Fonso again sat in front of Riperton, who passed Fonso a contract. "Here are my proposed terms," said Riperton. "In short, I'll be your eyes, ears and mouth, so long as you tell me the truth, and pay your bills on time. You are also protected by client privilege, something I have never violated in 21 years as a defense attorney. Given what I anticipate to be a potentially complex case, my fee is $25,000 a month plus expenses, with a four-month advance. I'm happy to look at adjustments every three months."

Fonso took out his checkbook and wrote a check for $100,000. The men shook hands. "I suggest we start early next week, so we stay one step ahead of the Feds," said Riperton.

Fonso took a document out of his pocket. "We may need to start sooner. I was served with a discovery request just before I left the office."

Discovery is a request for information to help the prosecution prepare its case before going to trial. Prosecutors are free to ask for documents they feel are relevant to the case, and, must disclose those witnesses, expert and otherwise, to be called during the actual trial. In many cases, after discovery, parties to the legal action agree to a plea bargain, where the prosecution offers a reduced sentence or fine in exchange for an acceptable admission of guilt.

"Let me see it," said an alarmed Riperton, who spent the few minutes reading the document in silence. Fonso was accused of numerous counts of fraud based on willful delivery of substandard meat products to the SMA, and the illegal use of bribes at various government levels to obtain and/or maintain SMA contracts.

"Are there any paper trails anywhere that suggest or imply that you knowingly purchased substandard livestock to use in the processed meats delivered to SMA distribution centers?"

"Absolutely not," responded Fonso trying for justified outrage.

"Good. Good…Who is Matty Cisco?"

"One of my primary wholesale distributors. Why?"

"The prosecution has already subpoenaed him to testify."

"And Max McGee?"

"A dirty Teamsters rep who always had his hand out. But don't worry about him."

"Why?"

"Let's just say, he understands," said Fonso.

"And Charles Gilardi."

"A gambling addict that used to work for me."

"Where is he now?"

"I really have no idea."

"Does the FBI?"

"Highly unlikely," smiled Fonso.

"I'm starting to understand," said Riperton.

"What about your books and records. Do they identify any of your supplemental disbursement activities?"

"Absolutely not," said Fonso who thought Riperton did not have a need to know about the second set of books stashed in his tuxedo bag at home. "I would never…"

It was now clear to Riperton that he had a client in a precarious position. "Fonso, let's cut the crap. I think you should admit to sloppy management oversight and loose controls. Swear complete ignorance about delivering substandard product and act completely shocked about any under-the-table inducements. Make up stuff about things you missed. I don't care what they are, just sound naïve. Be repentant and ready to accept any reasonable court-ordered fine for your mistakes."

"One humble man coming up," smiled Fonso.

"While you practice humility, I'll talk to Father Don and Congressman Rutherman about being character witnesses. Thank Christ you did some good things for the Boys Clubs and brought new jobs to Jersey."

$

Discovery took place in the spanking new Bergen County District Attorney's office on Main Street in Hackensack.

Lead prosecutor Benjamin Overlook was smart, young, and fiery but inexperienced. This was his first major case. Riperton decided to disarm the young attorney by sounding kind, gracious and extremely cooperative. He played the same theme over and over again — "Mr. Gravenese is happy to cooperate in any way. He has nothing to hide."

He knew the case rested on a weak foundation. The prosecution had no direct witnesses. No Moccio, no Gilardi, and no McGee. And every Metz employee was a Fonso loyalist.

Q. Mr. Gravenese, how were you appointed an SMA supplier?

A. I filled out the government packet.

Q. What role did your wife play in the process?

A. My wife's a secretary. She gave me the packet, and brought it back when my CFO and I completed the forms.

Q. Can your CFO confirm that?

A. I don't know where he is.

Q. And, what about Mr. Gilardi's complaint about health violations? Where is he?

A. You tell me.

Q. Did you falsify bookkeeping entries?

A. I wouldn't know how to do that. I never graduated from high school.

Q. Can we discuss the matter with your controller?

A. Absolutely. But I don't know where he is.

After more questions, more dead ends, Overlook tried a different tactic. He called Hitzig to testify.

Q. Mr. Hitzig. Your role at Metz?

A. I was production and distribution manager.

Q. Did you either direct or see SMA violations during the Company's participation in the Free Lunch Program?

A. No.

Q. Mr. Hitzig. You are under oath.

A. Is that a question?

Q. Were there any shortcuts taken in product specs during production?

A. Never happen on my watch.

Q. Let me rephrase. Were you witness to any health violations during the entire process?

A. No.

Now Riperton's turn to put the nail in the coffin. He called Father Don and Congressman Rutherman as character witnesses. Game over. Cleverly, Riperton asked for a short recess to throw Overton a bone.

"May I make a suggestion," said Riperton. "Clearly, somebody screwed up somewhere. My client neither knew about the alleged problems or willfully engaged in creating them. However, as the sole owner, he realizes he is ultimately responsible for shoddy management oversight. We are willing to pay a $50,000 fine for our negligent mismanagement, with no admission of guilt.

Overlook took the bait, and started to negotiate the amount. Fonso and Riperton wanted him to feel he won. They ultimately agreed to pay $100,000 — about one-half of 1 percent of the profits generated by the program. As part of the agreement Metz was removed as a Surplus Marketing Administration supplier. Fonso was ordered to sell Metz Company at a discount to a responsible consumer goods company to save 300 area jobs.

$

In Fonso's mind, he had done nothing wrong. A few bribes to a few people to insure a lot of well-paying jobs. He wasn't a boss, a consigliere or capo in some violence-ridden family named Colombo, Gambini or Lucchese.

His generosity to employees at Christmas was legend. He paid salaries 50 percent above market, holiday cash bonuses to all, and the occasional spanking new Cadillac to his inner circle.

There was also his continued support of metro New York's Catholic Charity Boys Clubs, and his frequent appearances as a good will ambassador and master of ceremonies.

On the day of his departure, Fonso was defiant and unrepentant, determined to affirm his legacy...His speech was a litany of accomplishments, spiked with the proper hint of humility. His eyes welled with tears. "I want to thank all of you for helping me bring Metz back from the dead. I hope you feel your long hours and loyalty were amply rewarded."

Every Metz employee cheered, convinced they had shared in the wealth.

"It wasn't so long ago, the business community laughed, and called me a fool for investing every dime my family had. But we had the last laugh, didn't we?"

The crowd stamped their feet.

"I know some of you will eventually go into business for yourself. Just remember the key to success: If you make something of value, there will always be a market."

Fonso put his glasses back on and raised his right hand, "Fonso promises one more thing — they can knock Fonso down, but he'll always get back off the canvas."

$

With no Metz responsibilities and three million in safe deposit boxes, Fonso developed a guide to future decision making.

1. Avoid government programs that contain performance standards.
2. Expect business associates to steal a little from you. But make it scary dangerous to steal a lot.
3. Never offer anyone a bribe. Give them performance bonuses.
4. Inside-the-box ventures generate fair profits. Outside-the-box ventures make you filthy rich.

Part Three
The Price Control Act

Chapter 30

With the onset of *World War II* every *American was asked to make sacrifices, so our troops would not go without in the heat of battle. In the largest citizen program ever organized, the Federal government passed the Emergency Price Control Act. The Act established the Office of Price Administration and Civilian Supply. The Agency was entrusted with the job of rationing items to the general public deemed necessary to maintain a well-motivated military — notably protein-rich meats, automotive gasoline and year-round clothing.*

To avoid public anger over the shortages, the Agency established a process. Families were issued weekly war ration books that contained a number of Red and Blue stamps based upon family size. When shopping they had to consider three factors — the actual cash price of the item, product availability, and the number of stamps required in addition to the cash price.

The well-intentioned, bureaucratic agency opened for business in the spring of 1942. It did not officially close its doors until May, 1947, long after the war ended.

This five-year window gave duplicitous visionaries like Fonso an extraordinary license to swindle. The price and control system was so complicated that it was relatively easy to circumvent the rationing process. Willing and financially able consumers just paid a premium price for what were called "black market" goods.

There was no shortage of willing retailers. The OPA estimated that a staggering 10 percent of all U.S. retail business were fined, and another 15 percent received some kind of documented OPA warning, short of criminal prosecution.

April, 1943
Meatpacking District, NYC

The Metz experience had taught Fonso the basics of corporate finance. He learned how to reestablish a struggling company, how to employ off-the-book techniques to make increased cash flows disappear, and how to suck up to banks, legislators and government agencies.

Now he would go on to the advanced course — despite his slightly tarnished image. He owned the right assets: 2-3 million in the bank and a select group of trusted lieutenants who would follow his lead. And always the Machiavellian mindset to take advantage of a gaping U.S. government loophole.

His goal was to build his new enterprise, Omaha Meatpacking Limited, into the unquestioned leader in the distribution and sale of black-market meats. His target audience — the thousands of retailers who wished to circumvent food-stamp rationing.

Fonso knew there were three keys to success.

1. A dependable source of quality meat.

2. An unlimited supply of ration stamps.

3. A marketing plan to acquire customers.

Fonso renewed acquaintances with his old friend, Matty Cisco on 124th Street, to discuss product supply.

Cisco had made a lot of money during Fonso's Free Lunch scam, in some ways he owed Fonso.

Fonso knew Cisco's priority — his grandchildren.

"Was in the neighborhood. Thought I'd just stop by to say hello. How are the grandkids?"

"Getting big. Thanks."

"As I recall, you had eight?"

"Good memory. Four boys and four girls. Now aged ten to sixteen," responded Cisco proudly.

"Any in the business?"

"The meat business? Hell no. I want them to get college degrees. Have careers. Maybe doctors, teachers. Doesn't matter."

"Eight grandkids in college. That's a lot of tuition. Guess your kids been building a college nest egg?" Fonso had done some research. They weren't.

"My kids. How could they?" said Cisco. "John works for the sanitation department. Billy is at the post office. They're good providers. But…"

Fonso interrupted. "So, I guess college is going to be grandpa's ticket…Matty, has the war affected business?"

"Let me put it this way, this stamp rationing fiasco has made it a lot more difficult to earn a fair profit."

"I may have a way to build the kids college nest egg, and increase your business," said Fonso. "We could have an encore. My research says there are a lot of little guys making a ton in the black market.'

"Fonso I don't think so. I never have…

"What do you mean, never have?' *You* did pretty damn well in *my* lunch program. My idea is simple. Institutionalize the sale of black market meat for as long as the government lets us. I've already named the company — Omaha Meatpacking Limited."

"Sounds important."

"That's the idea."

"My thought is your operation becomes the supply arm of Omaha. I'll be responsible for rounding up customer orders, and you fulfill them.

"The idea sucks. Rationing means there are only so many stamps, only so much meat for people to buy."

"Suppose I told you I could get all the stamps we need to sell all the meat we want to all the butchers who want all their customers to have more."

"I would say we could sell a ton of meat. Maybe even at a premium. But, where are you going to get the stamps?"

"You deal with the meat. I'll find the stamps," smiled Fonso. "You manage the inventories, and make your usual markup. Participating butchers will pay Omaha a monthly fee for the right to buy, and to receive all the stamps they need."

"In other words," said Cisco, "I absorb all the overheads, take all the inventory risk under your company name...and make my usual markup."

Fonso knew, if his scheme worked properly, there would be millions in fees. "That's a reasonable point," he said. "How about you get an *additional* 15 percent over your usual profit on all the meat you ship and deliver."

Cisco sensed more juice that could be squeezed from the lemon. "Since I'm doing all the heavy lifting, I think 25 percent is fair."

Fonso reacted as if he was getting robbed. "What's fair?" I take 100 percent of the risk, and get three-quarters of the profits on one tiny part of the business? As far as I'm concerned, you just crossed the line." He got up and headed toward the door. "Let's just forget the whole damn thing."

Cisco didn't want to lose the deal. "I never want to be known as a deal-breaker," he said. "How about I receive 20 percent but we also extend payment terms. No more cash on delivery. Rather cash within 45 days of delivery. That way if you collect promptly, you can make a few percentage points."

Fonso had already figured 15-day terms would make him a ton of short-term interest. A 45-day float will triple those projections. And if one day he could figure out how to avoid income taxes, all the better.

$

Fonso wasn't quite finished with Cisco.

After 30 years in the meatpacking industry, Cisco had dealt with virtually every wholesale distributor in America. He knew who was good, who was bad, who had a big mouth, and who could be discreet.

Night after night Cisco and Fonso sat in Fonso's living room developing their initial target list. The floor was flooded with bits of white paper, handwritten notes, index cars with contact information, and a little spiral bound pad that listed wholesaler and retailer idiosyncrasies that could be the difference in closing or not closing a sale.

As the men worked, Donna served the men espresso and cannoli, then sat down to listen. Cisco was uncomfortable with Donna being there. Fonso assured Cisco, "My wife is one of us. Besides, somebody's got to turn this mess into an organized data base, so I can start making calls?"

"You're going to make the calls?" questioned Cisco. "We've picked 400 names. That's a ton of details."

"Matty," said Fonso, "Leave that to me, along with the stamps. This rationing gig isn't going to last forever. So we've got slaughter the pigs, before the trough is empty."

Chapter 31

June, 1943
Lake George, NY

"Your new job will be to identify a reliable source of government ration stamps. Everything else will take care of itself," Fonso told Ricco. "And just make sure everybody pays on delivery. No receivables."

Ricco had identified which mob family controlled which stamps, geographically and operationally.

Chicago was an important Federal Price Control Agency distribution hub. Stamps were stored in a south side warehouse and dispatched to Price Control offices west of the Mississippi. The Lentini family paid Government dispatchers to reroute inventories to official sounding addresses that constantly changed.

In South Florida, the Lomiscolo family preferred to print their own stamps in the store basements on Flagler Street in downtown Miami. They found illegal immigrants were reliable counterfeiters who kept their mouths shuts. To insure loyalty, Lomiscolo paid well and provided fake passports.

The Palumbo organization in New York visited the U.S. Post Office headquarters on 33rd Street during the night shift. There they simply stuffed stamps in canvas bags while well-compensated Government security guards stood watch. The next morning official inventory adjustments were made by select members of the accounting staff who arrived early.

Together, the three families controlled 80 percent of the production, collection, and distribution of black-market ration stamps.

$

The group's unofficial spokesman was Joe Lomiscolo. He insisted the first meeting take place at the picturesque, low-key Sagamore Hotel on the north end of Lake George — far from the Feds, the FBI, the IRS, and the press.

Fonso walked into the conference room alone. He was surprised by the presence of three impeccably tailored and groomed men in conservative pin-striped suits, white handkerchiefs, white shirts, and red club ties. If he didn't know better, he could have been in the boardroom at the General Electric Company. There were two giveaways. The room reeked of cheap cologne and the men sounded like characters from a James Cagney movie.

"Gentlemen, thanks for your time," began Fonso cordially. "Let me start with a little background."

"Let's cut to the chase. Dwain suggested we meet, so here we are," said the greasy, wavy-haired Lomiscolo.

"You know Dwain?" asked Fonso.

"We all know Dwain," smiled Lomiscolo.

"What the fuck do you do exactly?" interrupted bald Anthony Palumbo. "The word is you manufacture money. Gotta respect that."

"Now Anthony," counseled Lomiscolo, "what did we agree about swearing. Please. It makes us seem like ordinary thugs."

"Go for it, little man," directed impatient, Mickey Lentini, with a bulldog face, a birthmark on his right cheek, and a single gold tooth in the front of his mouth.

Fonso's removed his black-horned rimmed glasses and put them on the table. "The Federal Government is in the business of giving away free money. Politicians invent fancy do-good agencies with fancy names, and appoint idiots to run them. Then they invite us to fill our trucks with as much as we can drive away.

"How many of you have actually sold two million pounds of uninspected meat to the U.S. Surplus Marketing Administration?" Fonso continued smoothly.

"Suppose I told you I fed thousands of kids with meat nobody wanted. And walked away with three million bucks after expenses, which included a measly $100,000 Government fine and a few bucks in legal fees to defend my good name."

Fonso now had everybody's undivided attention.

"Guess what? Yesterday's Surplus Marketing Administration is today's National Office of Pricing and Controls. The morons don't realize that printing food rationing stamps is like creating a license to steal.

"I'm not talking about selling a few stolen stamps. I'm talking about using millions to make millions. When butcher shops buy their meat from us, they get a bunch of extra ration stamps to use however they want." Fonso continued. "We're ready to sign up 400 large butcher shops and chains to participate in our program. And they've got retail customers lined up outside their shops ready to buy the meat. That's why I'm happy to buy all the stamps you can provide. All I ask is that you charge a price that makes sense for everybody in this room."

"Give us a few minutes to talk privately," said Lomiscolo.

$

The three men returned to the table with smiles on their faces.

"Fonso," said Lomiscolo, leaning back in his chair. "How many butcher shops are there across America?"

"I don't know for sure. Maybe 10,000 good-sized ones, give or take."

"We've decided we don't want to be nickel-dime stamp suppliers for 400 butchers. We want to be 50-50 partners with Omaha Meatpacking."

""How would that work?" asked Fonso.

"Simple," summarized Lomiscolo. "We'll compile an accurate list of at least 10,000 potential customers. We'll also sign up participating butchers in a manner that avoids delivering small orders all over the place."

"One more thing," added Lomiscolo. "Every week you give us a list of retailers who refuse to participate or pay late. We'll work that list until there is no list."

"From my end?" asked Fonso.

"You handle meat deliveries, customer service, fee calculations, banking activities, and partner disbursements. And make damn sure the butchers pay their bills before they get their stamps. "

Fonso put his hand out to consummate the deal. Lomiscolo had a final demand. "One final understanding. We don't want our names anywhere. Just deliver cash, and detailed reconciliations, once a month. We'll give you reasonable notice about where and when."

$

Palumbo also volunteered to handle the initial signups. He figured it made good business sense to fine-tune the sales pitch in the less populous mountain-west, and then roll out to metro centers like New York, Chicago and Dallas.

Things went well until he approached Eddie Jordon of Grand Junction, Colorado. Jordon was a patriotic American butcher who started with one butcher shop, and now proudly owned seven. He believed in free enterprise, free speech, religious freedom and the Second-Amendment right to own guns. His two sons were in the Army fighting Japs and Nazis. Eddie let everybody know by hanging two flags from his front porch in the center of Grand Junction.

The Palumbo family met Jordon on a Wednesday evening after his main shop had closed for the day. He went ballistic about the black market program. He thought the idea of ripping off the Government was downright un-American.

First Jordon told Palumbo's team to leave. They persisted. He pulled his Winchester 12 rifle from a hidden shelf near the cash register. He walked the boys to the front door. Once they were outside, he started shooting in the air until they were long gone.

When Palumbo's men told him about the Jordon's stubbornness, he got extremely agitated. Palumbo didn't want word to spread within the meat community that his family could be bullied. It would be bad for the Omaha Meatpacking business plan. And it would be terrible for his reputation with the other Families.

Friday evening Jordon drove his refrigerated truck on Route 70 from Denver with a truckload of steers for the following week. It was dark, and snowing lightly. As he began to descend through the mountain pass, he applied his brakes. They failed. He tried to get on the nearest runaway truck ramp. The steering wheel locked. The truck picked up speed, jumped the barrier, and plunged 200 feet down the mountainside. Then it burst into flames.

Denver area butchers got the message. Signup was 100 percent. Palumbo called the accident an example of how things "just sometimes happen for the better."

$

When Fonso heard about Jordon's accident, he was giddy with delight.

He had traded 100 percent of his black market participation fees from 400 butchers to 50 percent of the fees from 10,000 butchers. He would also keep 100 percent of the undisclosed short-term interest from receivables. And he now had a free police force to supplement Ricco's activities.

Chapter 32

August, 1943
El Morocco Club, NYC

The El Morocco, sometimes nicknamed "Elmo," on East 54ˢᵗ Street was Manhattan's nightclub for the power elite and New York-based celebrities from the mid-1930's to the late 1950's. It's signature, one-of-a-kind, blue-zebra striped motif was created by high-society designer, Vernon MacFarlane, and his gay photographer partner, Jerome Zerbe. Visually, the place was zebras run amuck: zebra chairs, zebra table cloths, zebra banquettes, and even menus printed on zebra striped paper. It some ways it was New York's answer to the Beverly Hills Hotel equally garish Banana Tree wallpaper.

$

After the Sagamore meeting, Fonso did a few projections. The numbers suggested millions would be flowing to Omaha Meatpacking for years to come. Now he to figure out how to ramp up net income by eliminating income taxes. He knew he needed an experienced CFO who could keep track of all the deals and discernments, gain the confidence of the banks, and offer some intelligent tax suggestions. The candidate had to be absolutely discreet and have a streak of larceny.

Fonso had someone specific in mind. He would just need a little persuasion.

$

"Mr. A," asked the El Morocco waiter, "The usual?"

"Make it two," said the ultra-conservative Fred Auslander. Fonso was surprised this seemingly ultra-conservative financial advisor had suggested lunch at such an over-the-top landmark. Soon the men were sipping tall glasses filled with a creamy liquid and topped with zebra-striped paper umbrellas.

"Yup, Piña Coladas," said Auslander. "I know that sounds ridiculous at the El Morocco. My wife Mae and I had them on a recent trip to Puerto Rico. Now she cannot get enough of them. I think her craving has rubbed off on me."

Lunch was a quiet affair with attentive, doting service at surprisingly reasonable prices. The beautiful people preferred the night scene and exotic dinner-only entrees like the Tagine á la Morocco, a saffron seasoned stew made with filet mignon.

For 20 minutes the two men caught up on the last three years. Auslander told Fonso how he was introduced to the in-your-face Catskills hotel magnate, Jenny Grossinger, at a Manhattan dinner party. Within months, Auslander became Jenny's personal financial advisor. His rigorous investment process and insider stock selections made Jenny more money in one year than she made in the last two years running her 320-room hotel. Jenny spread the word and before long every major Catskill hotel owner was an Auslander client.

As Auslander reminded his clients, "making money is one thing, keeping it from the tax man is a completely different matter." That's where his personal Swiss Bank connections made him stand out from every other advisor in metro New York. Auslander asked Fonso, "how many C.P.A.'s do you know that have a brother who runs a major Swiss Bank?"

During the 20th Century, U.S. citizens wishing to avoid significant taxes could, with the right connections, deposit unlimited sums of money in anonymous, interest-bearing Swiss numbered bank accounts. Under Swiss bank regulations, no bank was required to disclose the names or information regarding account owners.

"Your turn," said Auslander.

"Well its not as exciting as your last few years," said Fonso professing modesty.

"Fonso, this is Fred. From what I hear you made a ton, even after the government settlement. I've got to compliment you my friend. You have the vision to find money where nobody else even thinks to look. Let's order, then tell me more."

Fonso scanned the menu. Nothing looked even vaguely familiar. "Try the Tagine," said Auslander. "You won't regret it."

"The menu says that's only served at night."

"Not for Fred." Auslander waved someone over. Auslander whispered in the man's ear. He nodded. "John will take care of it," said Auslander. "That's owner John Perona.'

$

Fonso made his offer. "Not having the right chief financial guy, cost me millions."

"It wouldn't be forever. I figure the Government's rationing program has a five-year life, maybe six tops. The Metz fiasco taught me something valuable. Things were always moving. I was sort of a one-man gang — making sure production was efficient, sucking up to Government officials, listening to employees complain about their pay and benefits, and so on. Somewhere along the way, I made some administrative mistakes, and the establishment dinged me for it. Fortunately, Riperton's a good attorney, so I was able to get out of the mess for chicken feed. There was more to it. The controller, who was a relative of the original founder, was a disaster."

"What were your annual revenues?"

"About 40 million at our highpoint."

"And you didn't have a CFO?" said Auslander incredulously.

"What's past is past," said Fonso. "What I need is highly qualified financial professional I can trust."

"Obviously I'm flattered," said Auslander. "But I'm not really in the market for a corporate job."

"What would you say if I told you in five years — maybe less, you'll never have to worry about money again."

Fonso explained his Omaha Meatpacking business, leaving little to the imagination. He made Auslander a generous compensation package on the spot.

Auslander was intrigued by the projections but frightened about the mob relationships. "Let me think about it."

"What's there to think about?" pressed Fonso. "Oh, you want more. Okay, how about we create a side agreement."

"I'll you 30 percent of the estimated tax savings we deposit in my Swiss bank accounts."

$

A week later Auslander unveiled his new, improved business strategy in Fonso's office. It was based upon the two things he knew Fonso craved above all else. How to make Fonso filthy rich, and how to morph the tainted Fonso into a respected corporate leader. The main points were:

- "Remain a private corporation, so we don't have to waste time and energy meeting laborious public-disclosure reporting requirements.
- "Don't disclose anything to anybody, other than a few selected insiders.
- "Minimize Federal tax exposure by designing legal structures so you own

nothing but control everything. Take advantage of international tax havens.

- "Position yourself as a local business leader, a community contributor.
- "Be a serious political donor; one who supports pro-business initiatives.
- "Minimize prior associations with Metz by locating Omaha Meatpacking offices someplace other than Englewood."

Fonso realized he had recruited the right man to help this high-school dropout secure advanced standing in corporate finance. But convincing Auslander was not an easy sale. As the cash started to roll in at Omaha, Fonso was increasingly concerned he could quickly have another Metz financial fiasco. He made Auslander the ultimate offer: a signing bonus equal to the fees Auslander would receive from Jenny Grossinger over the next twelve months.

Auslander gave Fonso the number without hesitation or calculation. Fonso accepted on the spot. The two men decided to open offices in Teaneck, NJ.

Chapter 33

December, 1943
Teaneck, NJ

"How was Auslander's first day at the office?" asked Donna.

"My head's still spinning from all his suggestions."

"Anything make sense?"

"Unfortunately, every one of them made perfect goddamn sense."

"Did you agree on priorities?"

"Christ, you sound just like him."

"It cost my father $60,000 for me to learn to say what are your priorities. Only lesser intellects use phrases like 'so whatta ya gonna do?'"

Fonso laughed. Donna was the only person in the world who could make fun of him without fear of reprisal.

"Three things jumped out at me," responded Fonso. "Avoid taxes, own nothing, and get a trusted assistant."

"I don't know much about the first, agree with the second, and the answer to the third is Josephine Bernardi."

"Who the hell is Josephine Bernardi?"

"She was my classmate at Columbia. After graduation, she planned to attend law school. She even got accepted at Duke. But she met this handsome football player, Gino Marchetti of the New York Giants, on a cruise to the Bahamas. They fell madly in love and got married. The very next season Gino tore up his knee, and never played again.

"Out of frustration, he took up a new form of exercise — beating the shit out of Josephine for no good reason. She finally built up the courage to throw the bum out. Now she's looking to earn some money, because Gino claimed he had no assets in the divorce proceedings."

Fonso gulped. "Are you sure?"

"Look, she's smart as hell, perky, attractive, and terribly organized. I bet she could charm the hell out of your macho retailers."

"Done," agreed Fonso.

$

Josephine turned Ricco's head from the first day he saw her.

She had a Doris Day smile that could light up a room. She wore just the proper amount of makeup and carried herself with an elegant confidence. She had done her homework on who was who.

"Good morning, Mr. Cicolo," my name is Josephine Bernardi. I'm Mr. Gravense's new executive assistant," she said. "I assume you're here for the weekly operations meeting?"

Tongue-tied and totally surprised, Ricco nodded. "Fonso didn't say anything about..."

She quickly interrupted. "That's going to be one of my jobs. Mr. Gravenese has asked me to enhance the internal communications among the corporate staff."

"Ahhh, you're Fonso's new secretary?"

"No."

"But I thought you just said..."

"I said I was Mr. Gravense's new executive assistant."

"What's the difference?" Ricco shrugged. By now the entire staff was listening to the banter.

Josephine responded without hesitation. "With all due respect, a secretary does what she is told, and only what she is told. An executive assistant processes her bosses' request, and, tries to fill them by exceeding expectations."

Ricco head was spinning with foreign phrases like enhance communications, executive assistant, and exceed expectations.

$

Over the next few weeks, Ricco uncharacteristically began checking with Fonso on the smallest details.

"Boss," said Ricco, "one of our biggest customers is..."

Fonso interrupted. "Ricco, why don't you just ask her out? I don't think she bites."

"Boss, I'm here on business."

"Ricco," laughed Fonso. "This is me, Fonso. Could I be that brain dead?"

Ricco was horrified. "Boss, I wasn't... I would never..."

"Ricco, relax. All I'm saying is the nickel-dime questions you're suddenly bringing up, were never an issue before Josephine. You just took care of things and told me later."

"Do you really think she'd say yes?" asked Ricco embarrassed. "She's a lot smarter than me. I'm not sure I know how to treat a lady like that."

"Tell you what. Call Donna. Josephine is one of her best friends. She can help you. I've got two left feet with women myself, in case you haven't noticed."

$

A week later, Ricco knew what he needed to know about Josephine, both the good and the bad. He arrived at the office carrying a dozen red roses wrapped in newspaper, and walked over to Josephine's desk.

Are these for Mr. Gravenese?" she said teasing Ricco.

"No. They're for you. I thought I'd ask if maybe," fumbled Ricco, finding it difficult to look directly at Josephine. "If maybe you wanted to go out to dinner in twelve days? — on the Saturday after next."

Josephine melted at the unpolished man's attempt to be sweet and gentle. "Suppose I said no?"

"I'd jump off the George Washington Bridge."

"Now we wouldn't want that would we? Mr. Gravenese would be very disappointed." She smiled. "So I guess the answer has to be yes."

Ricco let out a sigh of relief. His face filled with a big grin. The girls in the office applauded.

"Ricco," wondered Josephine, "I do have one question. Why twelve days?"

"It will take me that long."

Josephine had no idea Ricco was planning to make their first date a memory that would last a lifetime.

$

During the next few weeks, Matty Cisco appeared to become Ricco's best friend. There were calls back and forth. Fonso noticed. Josephine noticed. The assumption was that the men had some new business idea he would eventually propose to Fonso.

Chapter 34

January, 1944
Hackensack, NJ

While Ricco focused on his date with Josephine, Donna focused on Auslander's business advice. "Explain the own nothing in a little more detail," said Donna one evening at dinner.

"You want the real answer?"

"No I want you to lie to me. Remember… we're supposed to partners for better or worse, till death do us part?"

"Fred suggests the less I own, the easier it will to avoid unnecessary income taxes. Paying taxes is for chumps."

"How much income are we talking about?"

"Some number of millions, depends on what the new company earns."

"Is this all necessary? Don't we already have enough in the bank thanks to the Surplus Marketing Administration?"

Fonso leaned back on the wooden chair. "Think bigger. That three million is after-tax earnings from our stupid years."

$

"What about our private life?" asked Donna.

"You mean like buying a house?" Fonso blamed Auslander. "Fred suggests not now. He thinks it's best if we stay away from the IRS."

"What's owning a house got to do with the IRS?"

Fonso really didn't want to be bothered with a house, so he switched gears. "Besides, there's a lot of space, your parents love having their daughter around all the time, and…"

"Let me see if I've got this right," said Donna indignantly. "You're the president of a major wholesale distributor that specializes in black-market meat and stolen rationing stamps, generates millions in profits, pays no taxes and has no discernable assets. Right?"

Fonso nodded.

"And we plan to live in a four-room apartment until you decide enough is enough money."

Fonso sat silently for a few moments, then stared into Donna's eyes. "Baby, here's the deal. I love you and all that, but only you can decide if you are in or you are out."

Donna wasn't about to bail out. She was in too deep.

$

Date night finally arrived.

Ricco pulled up to Josephine's first-floor apartment at 234 Main Street in Hackensack, a tough but inexpensive neighborhood.

He knocked on the door. Neither recognized the other. Ricco was tastefully dressed in a gray-checkered cashmere sport jacket, starched white shirt and red Brooks Brothers tie. He was also reeked of a pine-scented, masculine cologne.

Josephine's flawless complexion was accentuated by just the right amount of mascara, lipstick, and rouge. Her skintight black dress revealed her generous proportions and shapely legs.

Ricco was tongue-tied. "You look like... wow, what a dish."

Josephine laughed. "And you, my handsome gorgeous man, smell like a forest."

Ricco apologized. "Stop stop," said Josephine. "I like you because you're a man's man. I want to laugh, have a good time, and just see where things go. And, as Fonso said, I don't bite."

"Fonso told you?"

"He's your best friend. He just wants you to be happy."

Ricco led Josephine to his new Cadillac convertible. It was a crystal clear New York summer night. "What a beautiful car," she remarked.

"I'm starting to get the picture. Fonso gave it to me to impress you. He called it an operations bonus. I'm guessing he didn't want me to tell you that."

They laughed as Ricco pulled away. "Where are we going to dinner?"

"I found this quiet little Italian place uptown. I hope you like it." He drove to 124th Street and Twelfth Avenue. He came to a stop in front of

Cisco's wholesale market. "Here we are." He opened her door and put his hand out.

"Where is here?" wondered Josephine

They walked into Cisco's place and were immediately greeted by a tuxedoed waiter. "Good evening, Miss Bernardi. We hope you enjoy Chef Rao's selections."

The man led Josephine and Ricco through a magical maze of blinking candles and fresh flowers to a giant freezer door which opened door to reveal a romantic red banquette for two. Lenox china, Waterford crystal goblets, and rare wines from Tuscany and Umbria that matched each course. The couple started with freshly pounded tuna Carpaccio, moved through pasta to an il secondo, and ended with an arugula salad in a lemon balsamic dressing.

It was almost midnight. "Ricco, I will never forget this evening. Thank you so much." She then reached across and tenderly kissed him.

"We ain't done yet," said Ricco. "Dessert."

"Let me guess," said Josephine. She outlined the most outrageous thing that came to mind. "We're going to have cannoli, latte and a vintage grappa tasting at a corner table on the Staten Island Ferry looking at the New York skyline."

Ricco was stunned. "How did you know?"

$

Dessert finished, Josephine fell asleep in Ricco's arms as they readied to dock. She was secure in the thought that all was finally right with the world.

In a strange twist of fate, Alfred Gilardi, the son of Metz employee Charlie Gilardi who mysteriously disappeared, was a passenger on the same Ferry. He spotted Ricco. He angrily paced across the beige linoleum deck toward the couple. Ricco recognized Alfred from the memorial service. He gently placed Josephine's head on the bench and met the man halfway.

"You son of a bitch," shouted Gilardi. "Killing my father and then having the balls to show up at the funeral."

Gilardi pushed Ricco. A ferry guard came running. The commotion woke Josephine. Ricco pulled out his gun.

"Okay big man," shouted Alfred. "You gonna make me disappear too."

Josephine screamed. "Ricco, what are you doing?"

He looked at her then he turned to Gilardi. He put his gun away.

So this was the first date Josephine would remember the rest of her life!

$

No matter how much he begged and pleaded, Josephine refused to go out with Ricco again.

Two weeks turned into two months. The uncomfortable stalemate affected office morale. But, Fonso and Donna had a plan. Each would invite their friend to dinner at the house without the other's knowledge.

Ricco arrived first in casual attire. The men shared a glass of Barolo, Fonso's favorite red wine. Donna answered the doorbell. She walked into the living room with an equally casual Josephine.

"If one of you makes for the door before we get this straightened out, you're both fired." said Fonso.

$

The couple sat and talked. "Look, you gotta understand the Gilardi thing. He did some bad stuff.

"How does that you justify your violent behavior?" asked Josephine.

"Look, I'm not perfect. But I'm sorta like the head of company's police force."

"Sorta like in a police force that lives by its own bizarre code of conduct," said Josephine.

"It's the code of the street. I don't know anything else," apologized Ricco. "To me, it's just business. And in business sometimes you just gotta do things."

She shook her head. Ricco was the first man she ever met who seemed to have no frame of reference about right and wrong.

Ricco pleaded. "What I do know is I love you like no man has ever loved a woman. And I will love, honor and respect you all my life."

Josephine was torn. Was the gentle guy in front of her an illusion? How deep did Ricco's flaws run? Was there such a thing as *the* perfect man?

Ricco was desperate, but the words came difficult. "I swear on my mother's grave you're it. Forever."

$

Two months later the couple was married at St. Patrick's Church on Mulberry Street by Father Don. Afterward, Ricco had an old-fashioned sandwich wedding on the street of Little Italy. He invited friend and foe to celebrate. The party ended about 5 a.m. as the empty zeppole truck headed into the sunrise on the Manhattan Bridge.

Chapter 35

———

February, 1944
Teaneck, NJ

While the boys worked at growing Omaha Meatpacking revenues and profits, Auslander focused on tax avoidance.

Auslander had Aemon O'Brien's confidence from past dealings. Their first step was to understand more about Manufacturers' international banking relationships, including transfer caps, non-disclosure protections, intra-bank communications and documented case studies.

"Fred," joked Fonso meaning it, "I have no idea what you're talking about."

Patiently, Auslander explained his plan, using Fonso's third-person kingly reference. "Fonso's undeclared cash profits need to be wire-transferred to an interest-bearing offshore bank where the money can grow without IRS interference. I'm guessing the numbers are going to be huge, given projected profits from thousands of retail accounts and a significant short-term interest float.

Fonso got Auslander's general drift.

"We also need to know what Manufacturers will or won't do regarding income disclosures. My instinct tells me they will make nice but won't play.

"Why?"

"They don't know the game and probably don't have any interest in learning. Banking in America is not like Europe."

$

Auslander had a backup plan.

"Remember my brother, Wilfred, in Zurich? He'll be happy to open a series of numbered bank accounts in the names of you and Donna, and whomever. Swiss Bank privacy laws allow us to open as many accounts as we want and to park unlimited sums of money without any IRS disclosures.

"Wilfred's also got a network of correspondent bank contacts around the world, if we need them. Typically, they operate under guidelines that circumvent international banking conventions."

"How much does it cost for Omaha Meatpacking to go international?" wondered Fonso.

"The banks charge reasonable transfer fees and ask the saving accounts to remain in their banks at least one year from date of deposit, so they can generate some short-term interest."

"Sounds fair. How do we get things rolling?"

"First, we need to sign a few holding documents, transfer authorizations and nondisclosures. Then we'll make first deposits in person.

"$250,000 per account will get their attention."

"How the hell do we get that much money through Swiss customs?

"We just pack a suitcase and fly to Zurich. My brother Wilfred provides the customs staff with our arrival particulars. Switzerland is very pro-capitalism.

"I think I'm going to like Switzerland."

"It is a charming, beautiful country. I predict you and Donna will quite enjoy vacationing there. Leave it to me. I will make arrangements for all of us," said Auslander.

"Who is us?"

"You and Donna. Ricco and Josephine. And me."

"Let me think about Ricco and Josephine," hesitated Fonso hesitated. "May be too early."

Auslander called Wilfred at the Swiss Bank Corporation, the country's most prestigious bank. The home office was a stone-and-granite monolith that towered over the competition in the heart of the financial district.

"Wilfred, you have an important new American client. We need to make the usual arrangements."

"How many accounts?"

"I think we should start with three or four, with initial deposits of about a quarter of a million each."

"Do you anticipate other deposits?"

"Based on my projections, about the same amount quarterly for the foreseeable future."

Wilfred paused. "I see…I think we may need a few more accounts, and perhaps some correspondent facilities. We can handle all those details after you arrive."

"Dear brother, I know we are in your good hands," said Fred Auslander.

"By the way, Frederick, did you hear? I believe congratulations are in order. Your younger brother has just been appointed President of the Swiss Bank Corporation."

Chapter 36

March, 1944
Jersey City, NJ

The Clam Broth House in Jersey City was a study in contrasts — noisy and crowed in the sawdust- covered main dining area, and peaceful and private in the back room. Auslander, Fonso, and O'Brien chose the back room.

"Let's order some fried clams," laughed Fonso, "while we talk clams."

Auslander ignored Fonso's corny joke. "Aemon, as you know, Fonso has an instinct for business opportunities. Our research suggests that thousands of hard-working American butcher shops are sorely underserviced. Consequently, Omaha Meatpacking has decided to act as a sales and marketing agent between livestock producers, butcher shops and the end consumers dealing with the complexities of rationing stamps."

"That sounds promising for Omaha and the Bank."

"Agree. That's why we need a line of credit for short-term lending."

"I'm not sure I understand," said O'Brien.

"Aemon," said Auslander, trying to clarify, "Occasionally, there may be a 30-to-60-day lag between customer deliveries and final payment."

"O.K. But Fonso already has a significant revolving line of credit. Are you looking for an increase in the loan facility?

"We're looking to restructure and expand. The current revolver is personally guaranteed, contains a high interest rate, and has significant late pay penalties," reeled off Auslander.

"I don't mean any disrespect, but Manufacturers is treating Fonso no differently than any other higher-risk customer."

"Higher risk? Has Fonso ever been delinquent on paying the line down?" asked Auslander. "Has he ever balked about collateralizing his line of credit?"

"No."

"What we are proposing is nothing more than business as usual. Fonso remains timely, and we give the Bank risk comfort by allowing it to collateralize his line with retailer receivables."

O'Brien hesitated. "Unfortunately from the Bank's perspective, Fonso's little SMA problem, subsequent admission of guilt, and payment of a fine for wrongdoing…"

Fonso rose in righteous indignation. "Aemon, I didn't do a damn thing wrong, other than let that Adolph Metz's moron grandson keep the books, out of respect to the old man. That's why I got Fred is involved in Omaha. He's been a trusted advisor to some of America's most successful business owners."

"Such as?"

"Frankly, I'm insulted that I've even got to answer that question. I fucking assume you've heard of Jenny Grossinger and Thomas Jenke, the multi-millionaire owners of a couple of five-star resorts in the Catskills called Grossinger's and Brown's?"

Fonso's convictions, and the fact that he was the branch's largest single customer, caused O'Brien to hedge. "Let me see if I can get corporate to buy off on asset collateralization of your line."

Auslander wanted more than lip service. "Well at least we're making some progress. But, at what rate?"

"I'm thinking prime plus four."

"You must be joking," retorted Auslander. "You and I know a good customer rate is prime plus one-half."

"Tell you what," said the crafty Auslander, "prime plus one will get you an introduction to Jenny Grossinger."

O'Brien knew he was in competition for a corporate promotion. Acquiring even part of the business of a super-rich high-net-worth customer like Jenny Grossinger, might move him to the top of the list.

"O.K.," said O'Brien. "How do we approach the Grossinger referral?"

"After we sign the revised credit agreements."

Neither Fonso nor O'Brien knew that Auslander was aware of O'Brien's promotional aspirations. They also didn't know Manufacturers had rejected a Jenny Grossinger expansion loan three years before, prompting her to take all her business to the Chase Bank. So there was zero-to-no chance that Auslander would reintroduce Grossinger to Manufacturers. He had two simple goals. Get the credit line drawn to his specs. Then drive the two-faced O'Brien crazy by stringing out the Grossinger introduction... indefinitely.

Part Four
Swiss Anonymity

Chapter 37

April, 1944
Lucerne, Switzerland

Auslander knew from experience evading U.S. federal income taxes required more than a trip to Zurich.

First, there needed to be safe deposit boxes in unknown names at Manufacturers Bank, so unrecognized cash profits could be securely tucked away. Even though they knew O'Brien would give the couple unfettered access, Donna used her maiden name. Twice. Auslander suggested having a box in Josephine's maiden name for later. Fonso again declined.

"They are almost family, but let's make sure everything works smoothly before we involve too many others...What about you?" asked Fonso.

Auslander saw his moment to test his worth. "Christ, even I'm a hired gun." Fonso knew what Auslander wanted, but he wasn't in a giving mood yet. No answer was not the answer Auslander was expecting.

Once Fonso and Donna stuffed the drop boxes with cash, offshore entities had to be created. And, controlling interests in each entity had to be carefully structured so that each succeeding company had the controlling interest in the previous one.

Fredric and Wilfred Auslander also had to agree which willing countries had banks willing to follow precise transfer instructions and which countries had the best track record in the nondisclosure of US assets.

In the end, Auslander and a friendly corporate attorney — Auslander's stepbrother Manheim, who owned multiple addresses in a variety of international tax havens — created four complex corporate entities. Cross Roads International, PCCB Inc. (the PCCB stood for absolutely nothing.), East Asian Industries, and New World Connections, that were registered in Turks & Caicos, the Cayman Islands, the Isle of Wright and Lichtenstein.

Fonso soaked in every note, every sharp, every flat, every chord. The little man from the Bronx was well on his way to acquiring, a pedigree he would eventually need for his ultimate foray on mainstream Wall Street.

$

Auslander's financial labyrinth was almost complete. One step remained: opening the appropriate numbered Swiss bank accounts. Under Swiss banking that had to be done in front of a registered bank person.

"Fonso, I would suggest you and Donna fill a few suitcases with thousand-dollar bills for our Swiss vacation. We can take in some of the tourist sights, before and after we finish our business."

Auslander's plan was designed to confuse authorities. They would fly to Zurich with five pieces of luggage, check three at the airport storage center — the ones with $250,000 in cash — and take the other two on a tour of some popular tourist destinations.

When they returned to Zurich, they would visit Auslander's immediate family, and make a stop at the Swiss Bank Corporation to personally congratulate Wilfred on his promotion.

$

First stop was Lucerne. The 1,000-year old, picturesque city sat on the Reuss River. They stayed at the 17th Century Hotel des Alpes, a two-minute walk from the main tourist attraction — the city's 14th Century Kapellbrücke wooden footbridge. Their hotel was also just a five-minute walk to some of Europe's most sophisticated shopping on Schwanenplatz in the city's Old Town district.

Fonso decided to surprise Donna by buying her an heirloom Patek Philippe watch for $53,000 U.S. He had the payment wired transferred from Manufacturers Hanover (without letting Auslander know).

Later that evening, he took the watch from his pocket and placed it next to a hand-written card and dozen long-stem red roses sitting on the living room coffee table. Donna emerged from the bedroom in her robe.

Fonso smiled and pointed. "Happy Monday evening."

She was blown away. Everything was so un-Fonso. She read the card. "I love you. I wish I knew how to be more romantic."

Rare moments like this helped Donna accept Fonso's chosen profession as a skilled con-man with an insatiable appetite for more. She was also increasingly comfortable with the benefits wealth provided.

To her, their whole crazy existence was okay, so long as Fonso remained faithful. As a Catholic, committing adultery was the ultimate mortal sin. She promised if she ever found out Fonso cheated, she would cut his heart out.

$

After a pleasing night of physical revelry, Donna woke first. She opened the thick brocade bedroom curtains. The floor-to-ceiling windows flooded the room with light and offered gorgeous views of Mount Pilatus in the nearby Alps.

As Fonso, Donna and Auslander ate breakfast admiring the views, Donna made a rare request. "My mother has always wanted one of those colorful painted Swiss clocks to put on her fireplace mantel."

"I know just the place," said Auslander. Max Zuffenloffer's shop is just a few blocks from here on Schwanenplatz. The family designs and makes all the clocks, down to the hand-painted cases."

Donna entered the store with clocks ticking and wooden birds cooing. She thought she had entered a Grimm Brothers fairy tale. A friendly gentleman in a starched shirt and bowtie, white hair and mustache, walked over. "Frederick, so nice to see you. Long time." The men hugged.

"Donna, this is the proprietor Max Zuffenloffer. "Max, Donna is looking for one of your delightful hand painted musical clocks for her mother's fireplace."

From his rear room Max fetched a shiny burgundy clock decorated with hand-painted humming birds and red-breasted robins. The clock case rested on four curved brass legs. "This box plays a song I particularly like," Max told Donna.

"Max, it is so beautiful."

He showed her how to turn the little arm in the back of the piece. The clock began to play *To Each His Own*. Donna began to hum the lyrics.

> *If a flame is to grow*
> *There must be a glow*
> *To open each door there's a key*
> *I need you I know*
> *I can't let you go*
> *Your touch means too much to me*

To everyone's amazement, Donna reached for Fonso's hand. She prodded him to dance...right there, right then. Fonso laughed, shook his head and began to dance. When the music finished, Fonso took a bow and joked. "I can't wait to see your father when your mother asks."

Max suggested he ship the keepsake. "We Swiss are masters at moving items with care."

Auslander smiled at the unintended double entendre.

$

Auslander announced, "Next stop Mount Titlis in Engleberg, home of the longest natural ski jump in the world. I've made reservations at the Central Hotel at the edge of town near most imposing peaks."

Fonso remembered the slopes of Morris Plains. He shuddered. "No chance I'm going to do that."

Auslander failed to mention that the only way to reach Engleberg was via a tiny narrow-gauge train line owned by a private railway, Zentralbahn. The Z-Line ran straight up the side of the mountain, providing breathtaking panoramic views, a close-up of high-performance skiers zooming by at breakneck speeds, and a change in atmospheric pressure that made you momentarily lightheaded.

That evening the portly Fonso rolled over and over, unable to sleep comfortably. When he finally dozed, he roared louder than a coal-fired locomotive. Donna decided to sleep on the living room couch with the bedroom door closed.

In the morning, she slipped back into bed next to Fonso, who had noticed nothing. The couple had breakfast of muesli and sausages on the open-air patio so close to the mountain she could touch the snow granules.

"I know this trip is about business," laughed Donna, "but I'm having a hell of a good time."

Chapter 38

April, 1944
Zurich, Switzerland

Bahnhofstrasse, Zurich's main downtown street, was home to three of Switzerland's commercial banks — The Swiss Bank Corporation, Union Bank of Switzerland, and UBS.

Fonso, Donna and Auslander walked down the street in a damp mist with raincoats and umbrellas. Each clutched a small suitcase stuffed with thousand-dollar bills. Auslander stopped in front an imposing white marble building with four columns. The building appeared to be a replica of the New York's main public library at 42nd Street and Fifth Avenue, only it was about 50 percent larger.

Auslander waved his arms. "Welcome to the new home for the Gravenese family fortune."

Fonso's appetite for more had brought them to the doors of one of the world's most powerful institutions. "I hope they have no issues with money suitcases," Donna said.

Fonso put his hand over her mouth. "Not so loud."

They walked through the front door into a gigantic, austere room. An impeccably dressed guard approached. "Mr. Auslander, I presume? Follow me."

The threesome was led to two large polished wooden doors at the end of the hall. When the doors opened, Donna felt as if she had entered St. Peter's Basilica in Rome. There were 23-karat gold-leaf ceilings with black walnut moldings and flying buttress alcoves furnished with desks. Fonso shook his head. He thought to himself, saving clients a few bucks on taxes must be a *very* profitable business.

A svelte, regal man rose from an oversized mahogany desk about a football field away. He walked over to greet the group. "Frederick." The brothers hugged warmly. They'd been close as children, growing up in the pre-Hitler years.

"My dear older brother, it appears that crass America lifestyle has suited you. Yes?" smiled Wilfred.

"American democracy is the same and yet different than our Swiss democracy," responded Auslander. "Both respect the same common values

—

the accumulation of wealth and the power it provides."

Fonso interrupted the lovefest. Listening to a discussion of comparative financial systems held little interest. "My name is Fonso Gravenese. I believe your brother has spoken about my needs."

"So sorry, Mr. Gravenese. Frederick and I have not seen each other in almost three years. He started to offer refreshments, but hesitated. The difference in age, grooming, and sophistication between Fonso and Donna was striking.

"Some coffee and a taste of our wonderful Swiss strudel?"

"Absolutely," Donna piped up. "By the way, please call me Donna. The rude man who interrupted your brother is my husband, Alfonso Gravenese."

The brothers smiled politely. Wilfred, a devout chauvinist, was privately appalled that Fonso let his wife speak that way about him in public.

"Based on your instructions, Frederick, I have prepared all the paperwork. Let me explain what I have done. I have established three separate accounts. One in Mrs. Gravenese's married name and one in her maiden name. And one for Mr. Gravenese. For convenience, either party can act as a sole signatory on all of the accounts. Frederick, I assumed you would act as executor should something happen to either party."

"Excellent," said Frederic Auslander.

"The only thing remaining is the amount of the initial deposits."

"Mr. and Mrs. Gravenese are there any questions?"

Fonso looked at Auslander. "Why you as executor?"

"Who else do you suggest we discuss these accounts with?"

Fonso opened the suitcase. "The suitcases contain about $750,000. Just split it equally between the accounts. That ok with you Donna?"

Fonso casually began to remove the bills.

"The bank will take care of that," said Wilfred.

Fonso laughed. "Just make sure we get the empty suitcases back before we leave. We've gotta do some shopping. I notice leather here is pretty expensive."

Donna wasn't sure if his comment was supposed to be a joke. But Donna was certain of one thing — in the eyes of the law she was now a full-fledged felon.

Wilfred pressed a button on the side of his desk. A woman came in, took the suitcases, and returned minutes later with some typewritten papers and deposit slips. She handed them to Wilfred and left. Not a word was spoken. Wilfred explained the secrecy ground rules.

"Mr. Gravenese, these papers confirm your new accounts. As you can see, the only identification is the account numbers. We maintain your personal contact information in separate, fully-secured files. In other words, no government anywhere can put a call on that information."

"How do we keep track?"

"Your balances, interest and such, can always be accessed by Telex. Although we would prefer you contact your Swiss Bank Corporation personal banker for obvious reasons."

"Does he also handle deposits?"

"That's an entirely different matter. You as the account holder have to initiate the transaction. You make deposits by visiting a correspondent bank. They will wire transfer the funds to us. You and Donna can also visit Zurich and deposit the funds directly with us."

Fonso had one final question. "How do we meet our personal banker?"

"Mr. Gravenese, you have already done so. Frederick's projections suggest you should have the best our bank has to offer."

Fonso was surprised and pleased that he now had an international bank president in his pocket.

Chapter 39

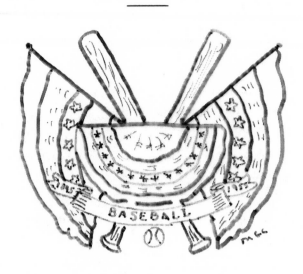

July, 1947
Teaneck, NJ

The next three years at Omaha Meatpacking International passed in the blink of an eye for Fonso, Auslander, his mob partners and company employees.

Auslander fined-tuned his tax-avoidance strategy. Like clockwork, first revenues every quarter found their way to Wilfred in Zurich.

Annual taxable revenues always seemed to mirror operating expenses such as salaries and benefits and rent and utilities. Despite millions in cash flow no taxes were ever due or paid by Omaha.

The mob delivered on its promises. They built a detailed three-ring binder that included 11,000 of

America's largest retailers and provided an uninterrupted flow of real and counterfeit ration stamps.

Fonso rehired the affable Sam Metz, his former production manager at Metz Meats. In a matter of months Sam exceeded all expectations by building a discreet account-service department.

Sam turned out to be a better sales person than Fonso ever imagined. His pitch contained the perfect reverse psychology. "The Omaha Meatpacking bonus program is limited to those retailers who always pay cash on delivery and are always discreet." His warning was intentionally concise and threatening. "One strike and you're out."

Sam hired loyal, sales people and gave them an experienced support staff. Tens of millions in sales revenues and program participation fees rolled in every month — without much need of Ricco. During this growth period, Fonso quadrupled his cash compensation and gave Sam a black Cadillac convertible. The latter signified Sam was now part of Fonso's intimate inner circle.

$

Fonso acted on another Auslander suggestion: Develop an image of a business leader who generously gave back. He became a visible supporter of numerous local causes — refurbishing the citizen park overlooking the George Washington Bridge, buying bicycles for the Boys Clubs, and building a state-of-the-art baseball field for Bayonne little leaguers.

He also had Ricco and his team actively solicit donations from his three-ring binder. Ricco's pitch was simple. "Make a donation for the kids, or you're out of the stamp program."

$

Construction of the baseball field was Fonso's absolute favorite project. Baseball was Fonso's only passion (after money and Donna). He still owned the Rogers Hornsby baseball glove he negotiated with his father over 25 years ago in Little Italy. He commissioned the Scaramuzzo Brothers to build the field to actual minor-league specs. In turn, the brothers donated a bench area that held 1,000 seats and two dugouts. Fonso named the park Chadwick Field in honor of Henry Chadwick, the father of baseball. He even commissioned a full-size replica of the famous Chadwick bronze that sits near the entry to the Baseball Hall of Fame in Cooperstown, New York. Father Don agreed to dedicate the field in exchange for a five-figure donation to New York Catholic Charities.

Fonso, who had a sixth sense for publicity, also hired a public relations firm. They advised Fonso to turn the dedication into a major newspaper and radio event, and to place Omaha Meatpacking signage and hotdog trucks everywhere.

After the event, the firm produced an impressive media kit that was sent it every local area politician and every retailer donor with a personal thank-you note.

No disclosure was ever forthcoming that Fonso also held a media-incentive drawing. Any reporter that got a story published, was eligible to win a $5,000 cash prize. Each story got one raffle ticket. Not surprisingly, metro New York coverage exceed all norms for similar past events. Fonso held the drawing in private to identify the winner. He decided everyone should be a winner. It would help the next time he needed a publicity boost.

As Fonso remarked later, "we got a few million dollars in publicity for a dirt field and a $50,000 statue."

$

Fonso was also proud of his growing reputation as a local center of influence. He typically backed political candidates that saw business as he did. Most important, he hitched his star to Jake Rutherman's wagon by becoming the largest single donor in the Congressman's successful bid to become a United States Senator. He also paid to speak at Union membership meetings. He strongly supported the re-election of Englewood's pro-labor Mayor Johnathan Dinkins (who was also Rutherman's cousin).

In exchange for Fonso's ongoing support, Rutherman provided Fonso advance notice of new Government funded business opportunities, and impending FBI investigations into Omaha Meatpacking business activities.

Fonso loved being invited to walk alongside the Senator and the Mayor at the annual St. Patrick and Columbus Day parades. It made the diminutive titan of industry feel like an industry mover and shaker.

$

Fonso learned some important lessons about the Swiss Bank process during the ration-stamp scheme years — lessons that would serve him well in future ventures.

Accumulating tax-free wealth in Switzerland was surprising easy if you followed a very specific process.

Periodically, Fonso and Donna would remove cash from their safety deposit boxes, pack it in plain boxes, and mail it directly to Wilfred via the U.S. Post Office. To eliminate any suspicion about frequent mailings, they sent the boxes to several different post office locations, never visiting the same one more than once every six weeks. As the cash rolled in, their appetite to accumulate metastasized. One million became two. Two became four.

Eventually, Fonso felt compelled to reveal the process to Josephine and Ricco, who were given their own safe-deposit boxes at different banks. Periodically they stuffed boxes with cash and mailed them to Switzerland. Wilfred's hand-written notes would subsequently confirm receipt of contents. Donna kept an accurate tally of how much belonged to Fonso and Donna, and how much they planned to share with Josephine and Ricco's.

The process went without a hitch for the next year and a half. As a token of their loyalty and discretion, Fonso bought each of them a Cadillac. Josephine chose a tan Eldorado convertible, while the more conservative Ricco chose a dark Coupe de Ville sedan to replace his two-year-old Caddy.

Josephine quickly realized enormous sums of cash were being accumulated and redirected. The more they moved, the more she became convinced that she and hubby Ricco should have their own Swiss bank account. "Fonso owes us more than a few Cadillacs," she said privately to Ricco…"I want an account which we control."

"You want me and you to go to Switzerland?" asked Ricco.

"You bet I do. I know you guys are close friends. But suppose he needs money and disappears with all of it?"

"Fonso would never do that. We're brothers," boasted Ricco.

Chapter 40

April, 1951
Hackensack, NJ

Ricco and Josephine had often discussed the advantages of starting a family. Ricco claimed he liked the idea, but wasn't in any rush. Besides, their use of the rhythm method of birth control seemed to be working. Josephine spent a bit of time each month identifying her fertile days, and then the couple would avoid having sex during those times.

While the couple danced around the issue, Josephine's mother alternated between fear and guilt. She wanted a grandchild. Josephine was her only daughter. "Josephine, do you realize your biological clock is ticking? You're going to be 30 in a few months? Josephine, do you know the risk of abnormal childbirth increases over 30? Josephine, daddy and I can't wait to hold our first grandchild."

Josephine listened, but said nothing.

$

A few days after Christmas. Josephine backed their shiny Caddy down the driveway of their new home in Hackensack. As she reached over to turn the radio on, Ricco noticed the buttons on her wool pea coat pop, revealing a tiny bump.

Josephine had always been fastidious about maintaining her svelte, perfectly proportioned figure. She frequently mocked the perennial pouch around Ricco's belt, even suggesting as they aged he might be taken for her older uncle, the kind that paid to have their niece accompany them to social events.

Ricco reasoned Josephine's obvious weight gain was now his chance to turn the tables. "Ho, ho, ho, look who's getting a little of that middle-age spread."

Josephine smiled. "Maybe there's a reason."

"I know," responded Ricco, clueless. "It's called too many dinner reservations."

Josephine looked into his eyes. "Dr. Bernardi thinks there may be another reason."

Ricco became concerned, thinking Josephine had contracted some illness. "Why didn't you call? I should have been there. I'm so sorry. What did the doctor say?"

"About five months."

"For what?"

"Men! Think about it."

"Oh, my goodness," blurted Ricco, "You're having a baby."

"No, *we're* having a baby."

Ricco didn't know whether to laugh or cry. "I don't understand…what happened. We were doing so well with your charts."

"What happened to my charts...That's all you've got to say?"

Ricco answered with another question. "What was that five months thing?"

"I'm already four months pregnant. Nine minus four is five."

Ricco was in shock. He didn't talk to his wife for two days. He was angry at her for getting pregnant!

$

A few months later, Ricco ensconced, on the couch watched the New York Knicks play their hated rival, the Boston Celtics, on their spanking new Dumont television. The tightly contested game went into overtime.

Josephine asked calmly, "Is the game over?"

"What a hell of a game. Harry Gallatin made a last-minute shot to get the Knicks into overtime."

"How long is overtime?"

"Five minutes."

Twenty minutes later, Josephine asked, "Is the game over?"

"This is incredible. The Knicks made another last minute shot. This time Sweetwater Clifton. The game is going to double overtime."

"Speaking of water, mine just broke," said Josephine. "We really need to go."

"Go where?"

"To the hospital. The baby's ready."

"Be a good mommy? Tell our kid this is the first Knick-Celtic double overtime game in history. Just a few more minutes."

Josephine was alarmed. "Goddamn it, Ricco, get off that chair, and get the car. We've got to get to the hospital right NOW. Dr. Bernardi is waiting."

The couple pulled up to the emergency room entrance. Dr. Bernardi met them, completed a quick exam, and sent Josephine directly into the delivery room.

He stared at Ricco. "Where the hell have you been? That baby's partially out."

$

In an hour, Ricco and Josephine Cicolo were the proud parents of a baby boy they would name Alfonso, in honor of his Godfather, Alfonso Gravenese.

Chapter 41

———

January, 1952
Little Italy, NYC

The baptism of Alfonso Ricco Cicolo at old Saint Patrick's Church in Little Italy did not lack irony.

Ricco had happy childhood memories as he stood proudly next to his son's Godparents in the chilled, dimly lit church.

Father Don slowly immersed the child in the holy water, praying that little Alfonso would not emulate his dad. Father was fully aware of Ricco's violent behavior from parishioners who prayed to God that he would rot in hell.

The baby's reaction to the immersion seemed almost prophetic. He silently stiffened and firmly waved his hand as if to protest his entrance to Catholicism.

Father Don participated — despite the Cardinal's better judgment — because he knew his former parish was hanging on by a thread. The children of many of first generation Italian-Americans in Little Italy had migrated to the other boroughs, Westchester County, and Long Island. Some 15,000 parishioners had shrunk to less than 1,000, and more and more Chinese immigrants flooded the Canal Street area.

Fonso's pledge to replace the aged pews and pulpit, and restore the crumbling statues of St. Peter, St. Joseph, and the Blessed Virgin Mary to their former glory, was an offer Father Don couldn't refuse.

After the Baptism ceremony, the 50 or so family and friends in attendance went to lunch — compliments of Gravenese Foods — at Paolucci's, the popular family-style establishment off Mulberry Street across from Ferrara's Pastry shop, where Fonso and Ricco first met.

Bringing up the rear, Fonso took a nostalgic stroll down his own memory lane. He sat on the stoop of 80 Spring Street where he learned to beat the bigger boys in yo-yo contests by applying olive oil to his string. He paused at the corner of Hester and Mulberry where he first observed his father swindle his own neighbors. Finally, he poked his head in the door of the Ravenite Social Club at 247 Mulberry, where Ricco's father first introduced him to members of the Garafolo family. Nothing much had changed. Simple tables with white tablecloths, pictures of the Blessed Virgin Mary, St. Joseph, and the Holy Trinity on the far wall.

$

The baptism heightened Donna's concern about her own biological clock. She longed for a child or two of her own. So did her father, Victor, who seemed to raise the topic at every dinner. "So when are you kids going to make us grandparents? Time's awasting."

It was not as if the couple hadn't tried. Out of frustration, Donna suggested they visit their doctor, complete some tests, and identify some solutions to her fertility dilemma. Fonso went along reluctantly. "It's not my damn problem," he stated arrogantly.

Dr. Cafora walked in the room holding the specialist's report. "Donna, unfortunately your intuition was correct. There's no way you can become pregnant."

"Told you," said Fonso.

Cafora looked Fonso in the eye. "Fonso, it's not Donna. It's you. You're sterile."

"How the hell can that be?"

"I looked back at your medical history, such as it is. Your condition may be hereditary, or it may be a side-effect of experimental eyes drops administered when you were a child, or some combination of both. Fact is, that medication was removed from the market years ago because of complaints about unnatural side effects."

$

Fonso said little during dinner. Donna knew he was upset, but she had a practical solution.

"Honey, I was thinking the sterility thing is not the end of the world. You're a perfectly healthy male otherwise, and you'd make a great father. Maybe we should consider adoption?"

Fonso recalled a conversation with his father long ago, about why he did not have a brother or sister. "My father told my mother he would not have a child that was not his own blood. I guess I feel the same way."

Donna decided this was not the moment to debate the topic.

$

The subject reared its head a few days later as Fonso and Donna had dinner in her parents' apartment. "What a beautiful Baptismal ceremony in your old parish," said Victor. "I think it was quite generous of you and my daughter to throw the party at Paolucci's." Donna's mother nodded.

"They're very good friends," said Fonso. "Like family."

"Speaking of family, it's none of my business, but you know me...are you planning on keeping up with the Cicolos?" said nosey Victor.

"You're right," said Fonso indignantly, "it's none of your business."

Victor didn't like Fonso's tone or answer. "It *is* my goddamn business. Donna is my only daughter, and we can't wait to be grandparents."

"It's not going to happen," responded Fonso curtly.

Donna tried to lighten the atmosphere but choose an unfortunate set of words. "Dad, what Fonso is trying to say is that Dr. Cafora told us Fonso shoots blanks."

Fonso glared at Donna with fire in his eyes. He got up and left, slamming the door on the way out.

When Donna returned home, Fonso let it fly...in the majestic third person. "Fonso has made you a rich woman, and there is more to come. He has asked nothing in return. He is honored in his community, loved by his employees, and treated with respect by all his friends. Do you understand?"

$

A few weeks later a letter arrived from the IRS asking him and/or his tax advisor to attend a hearing at the IRS regional office in Manhattan. The topic —

underpayment of corporate income taxes for the three past years. The letter included the IRS's adjusted statement of expenses, which translated into taxes due of $1,237,586 plus interest and penalties.

"What the fuck is this," screamed Fonso.

"Stay calm," said Auslander. "You never challenge the IRS using intimidation. And, by the way, I don't respond well to the tactic either."

Auslander was fairly confident the returns were generally bulletproof. Fonso had only taken a salary of $30,000 per annum, the same as his other senior managers, and every business deduction could be justified. That left only two possible challenges: personal expenses like cars, dinners and donations, that virtually every CEO in America buried on their expenses, and the net profits exported to Switzerland.

If it were about personal expenses, reversing the deductions would never add up to a million dollars in taxes due. If it were about Switzerland, Fonso wouldn't have received a letter from the IRS, but rather a hand-delivered legal complaint from the FBI accusing him of Federal income tax evasion.

He concluded the entire audit was a poorly conceived witch-hunt.

$

The IRS examination room was stereotypically austere, and the expressions on the reviewers' faces dour.

Quickly, Auslander realized these guys were amateurs. They tried to raise Fonso's ire by focusing on reversing a few minor business deductions. Auslander's response was to overwhelm with documented receipts, so when they got to the judgmental expenses, he could negotiate a nominal settlement that made the IRS feel they had won.

The strategy worked. At 4 p.m., just six hours after they arrived, an amicable settlement was reached.

"Based on our calculation," said the agent, "over the past three years, Mr. Gravenese has attempted to deduct a total of $20,700 in personal expenses as business expenses. With penalties and interest, he owes the IRS $8,322, Mr. Auslander, do we agree?"

Auslander fumbled with his calculator, as if to double check. That was the prearranged signal for Fonso to do his thing. "I must say gentlemen, I'm disappointed that you've picked a legitimate Italian-American businessman to hassle while the Bell Companies and the Generals Electrics bury millions. If I had the resources, I would sue for discrimination."

Aulander then played the "good cop." "Fonso, we could argue with these gentlemen for weeks. You'll wind up paying me more in fees to me." He looked at the auditors. I have a suggestion for a fair settlement. Since Mr. Gravenese did nothing wrong intentionally, I suggest we eliminate the penalties. According to my calculations that will also reduce interest due a bit. The totaled owed is $5,218. If we agree, Mr. Gravenese will write a check out now and we'll consider the audit closed."

The examiners smiled and nodded like they had just killed a wild boar in the forest.

$

To Auslander's surprise, the auditors had a few more questions — for him. "If you don't mind Mr. Auslander, we just have a few additional questions for our records. "Be my guest," said Auslander.

Q. Mr. Auslander, what nationality are you?

A. How is that relevant to your claim against Mr. Gravenese?

Q. Is it true you hold a Swiss passport?

A. If you're asking if I was born in Switzerland, the answer is yes. But I proudly am a dual citizen. America is my home.

Q. Is your brother Wilfred a dual citizen also?

A. What has he got to do with any of this?

Q. Are you close?

A. He's my brother.

Q. Do you talk frequently?

A. We keep in touch. Mother is almost 81 now.

Q. She must be very proud of his recent promotion?

A. Is that a question?

Auslander and Fonso got up and left. The IRS had made their point. Auslander better watch his ass because they were watching him.

Part Five

Food for Peace

Chapter 42

August, 1953
Paramus, New Jersey

In late 1954, President Dwight D. Eisenhower signed the Agricultural Trade Development and Assistance Act which simultaneously created the Office of Food for Peace.

By signing this legislation, the President laid the basis for a permanent expansion of U.S. exports of surplus agricultural products, with lasting benefits to ourselves and peoples of other lands. The bill, a solution for food deficient, cash-poor countries, created a secondary foreign market by allowing food-deficient countries to pay for American food imports in their own currencies instead of in U.S. dollars.

The law's purpose was to expand international trade, to promote the economic stability of American agriculture, to make maximum use of surplus agricultural commodities in the furtherance of foreign policy, and to stimulate the expansion of foreign trade in agricultural commodities produced in the United States.

Senator Rutherman invited Fonso to dinner at the popular Steak Pit Restaurant on Route 4 in Paramus.

Ostensibly, he wanted to thank Fonso for his unwavering support during the Senate — but also to provide him with a bit of valuable insider information.

"Fonso, keep your wallet in your pocket tonight. You're a guest of the United States Government," smiled Senator Rutherman

As a surprise, Rutherman had the Pit's owner book the popular Louie Prima and Keeley Smith and their band, Sam Butera and the Witnesses. Rutherman knew Fonso loved the Steak Pit and Prima. Louie walked over to the table before his second set. "Good evening Senator. Is this Mr. Gravenese?"

Fonso smiled like a little kid who had just been given a lollipop. "The Senator tells me you like my *Angelina*?" (Prima's best-selling song.)

"Love it," said Fonso.

Prima went back to the tiny stage, "Louie wants to tell you about his first girlfriend, Angelina. Is everybody ready?"

> *I eat antipasto twice*
> *Just because she is so nice*
> *Angelina*
> *Angelina…*

A boys' night out was just what Fonso needed. The war had long since been over, and the stamp rationing discontinued. Fonso had tested a few new hog-butchering ideas, but had not identified anything big enough or challenging enough. Consequently, he maintained a skeleton staff (Josephine, Sam and Ricco) while he monitored his Swiss millions and traveled with Donna to exotic international destinations. As Fonso boasted to friends and family, "We can visit the Grand Canyon and paddleboat down the Mississippi River when we're too old to wander the streets of Karachi and Cairo."

As dinner wound down, the two men sat with candied cannoli and coffee. "We're discussing something in the Senate that might be of interest," said Rutherman. He gave Fonso a detailed sneak preview. "The Senate is about a month away from establishing a Food for Peace program at the Department of Agriculture to solve a major world problem. The economies of our World War Two allies are recovering at a much slower pace than here in the states. One of their most pressing needs is food at fair prices. Ironically, our farmers are growing soybeans and cottonseeds, and crushing them into vegetable oil at a record pace. So some of the very foods our allies could use are piling up in storage tanks in the South and Midwest — and creating a lot of unhappy farmers."

"I'm not sure I get it."

'The main stumbling block is these countries have currencies nobody wants right now. So they can't pay for these surpluses."

"So let's just give it to them."

"Can't do that. The President feels that would set a terrible long-term precedent. Imagine a world where every country in financial trouble asks the United States to deliver truckloads of money."

"Never happen." said Fonso.

"The Senate has already debated that issue. Food for Peace solves the problem. Companies can deliver surplus oil to countries that are strategically important to United States interests. The purchasing country pays in their currency, however unsteady, then the Federal government pays participating exporters in U.S. dollars," replied Rutherman.

"That way the countries get all the refined food oil they need to make all kinds of products, and exporters know they will not be exposed to currency fluctuations in the Japanese yen, German mark etc."

Fonso was starting to smell opportunity.

"Suppose the actual price these countries are willing to pay is less than the producers' cost?"

"We've got that covered with generous government subsidies. The producer is guaranteed minimum profit of 15 percent, and the exporter, who has no inventory risk, earns an additional 5 percent commission, after all expenses."

"I get the drift, the exporter is a middle man with sales and marketing skills and accounting controls," said Fonso.

"Bingo," said Rutherman.

"How does the exporter know which countries and officials to focus on?"

"Good question. Again, got you covered. The Department of Agriculture has a list of precisely which countries can make best use of the surpluses, and which government officials are the decision makers."

Fonso smiled. "Unlike most Government programs, Food for Peace seems well thought out."

"Is it something you would be interested in?"

"Yes. But why me? I'm a butcher by trade."

"Fonso, please. Humility doesn't become you. You're a terribly clever businessman and salesman who can figure out how to benefit you *and* your country. Imagine, traveling the world, rubbing elbows with decision makers, and coming home with suitcases of cash."

Now Rutherman was talking Fonso's language. But Fonso knew the suitcases of money wouldn't be coming home.

"As a sponsor of legislation, I can nominate you as a participating exporter. That will give you a head start on competitors."

"Export away," smiled Fonso. The men shook hands.

Chapter 43

October, 1953
Washington, D.C.

Some months after the Rutherman dinner, the *New York Times* reported the introduction of the Food for Peace program. The Department of Agriculture publicly issued the program's first Request for Proposal. The RFP sought qualified suppliers to act as exporters.

As per Fonso's agreement with the Senator, he and Auslander had received and completed their RFP weeks earlier. As promised, Senator put Fonso's application at the top of the stack.

But the Department of Agriculture, (DOA), was well aware of Fonso's unsubstantiated transgressions during the Free Lunch Program. The DOA selection committee seriously questioned whether a man of his moral integrity should be one of the first representatives of America's post-World War II largess.

"Gentlemen, I think we may be overreacting to some questionable media coverage at best.," said Rutherman to the committee as they vetted International Grain's application. "For the record, Mr. Gravenese is guilty of only one thing: tirelessly supplying our nation's children millions of pounds of nutritious meat during a most difficult time in our history. He paid a fine for an accounting error made by his incompetent controller."

"Doesn't that call into question his firm's ability to monitor and control potentially complex Food for Peace transactions?" asked the squeaky-clean, Evangelical DOA Chairman Standard Williamson.

"With all due respect, Mr. Chairman, I know the situation fairly intimately. The controller in question, Gino Metz, was the grandson of the firm's deceased founder. Mr. Gravenese employed him out of family loyalty. He was trying to do the right thing, and wound up being castigated for his good deed.

"It's also worth noting, Mr. Gravenese has brought jobs to the New Jersey business community, and had been praised for his many philanthropic activities."

Williamson wasn't quite convinced. The tall man stroked his long black hair. "And what about his alleged connections to organized crime?"

Rutherman responded with just the proper hint of righteous indignation. "Mr. Chairman, as far as I know, nobody has ever documented one of these alleged connections. Let's not forget this is America, and in America, you are innocent until proven guilty."

Rutherman had one final comment. "Gentlemen, I would like to direct you to Page 3 of International Grain' RFP. Mr. Gravenese states his CFO is Frederick Auslander, CPA. Mr. Auslander's bio suggests he has held a number of senior financial roles in a number of fine companies."

It was time for the group to vote. Minutes later, the appointment of International Grain as the program's first exporter was approved by a 6 to 0 vote.

$

"We're in," said an excited Fonso, waving the formal DOA appointment letter.

"Congratulations," said Auslander in the firm's modest new digs in blue-collar Bayonne, New Jersey, directly across the river from Manhattan. Fonso figured the town was close to the financial action on Wall Street, had plenty of room for industrial expansion, and was cheap. It was also a convenient commute — a ten block walk to his in-laws on 22nd Street.

The next step was a meeting in Washington to discuss program operating ground rules, reporting requirements, initial participating countries, etc.

While in Washington Fonso and Auslander were immersed in vegetable oil specifics. He knew from Rutherman about the record surpluses of plant-based cottonseed and soybean. He learned that America's production was a virtual monopoly. The country controlled more than 70 percent of the entire world's entire grain inventory.

Fonso learned the grains yielded two types of oils. A cheap, commercial grade, produced by an unsanitary and nauseating process of chemical extraction with unstable solvents. This created high-yields of oils used in soaps, perfumes, lubricants, paints, wood preservatives, and other industrial products.

A smaller portion of the seeds was crushed or pressed, then naturally refined. This produced lower yields of higher-quality, full-flavored, edible oils such as olive, coconut, and peanut that could be used wholly, or blended into mayonnaise, salad dressings, cooking lards and table margarine.

Auslander analyzed U.S. production costs. He found that the chemical process yielded four times as many gallons per hundred bushels of raw material. But technically the stuff was inedible because of the solvents.

Auslander's analysis also indicated that as seed surpluses grew, vegetable oil refiners changed the laws of supply and demand. They no longer bought from farmers directly. They started buying their raw materials through specialized commodity traders who operated under the provisions of the U.S. Commodity Exchange Act, first instituted in the 1930's.

With his new found education, Fonso realized he eventually would need to produce and refine both types of oil. He hoped his first sales trips would help him determine the balance of the two, because the production economics were so different.

The second thing he needed to master was how to buy commodities through this network of commodity traders few people seemed to know much about.

His first DOA-directed sales call was Spain.

Chapter 44

$

Spain, under the dictator Generalissimo Francisco Franco, had enormous post-World War II economic problems — widespread deprivation, soaring inflation, and black-market rationing. By the early 1950's, per capita gross domestic product (GDP) was 40 percent of the average for West European countries.

In 1953, the United States and Spain signed a mutual defense agreement. In return for permitting the establishment of United States military bases on Spanish soil, the Eisenhower Administration provided substantial economic aid to the Franco regime. More than one billion dollars in economic assistance flowed into Spain.

While the economy began to respond, a large obstacle to lasting reform was the corrupt, inefficient, and bloated bureaucracy. London's Financial Times *described the Franco era as "the triumph of primitive market skills operating in a jungle of bureaucratic regulations, protectionism, and peddled influence."*

November, 1953
Madrid, Spain

Fonso left for the airport with Auslander and Ricco and a detailed Food for Peace operating manual. Auslander believed that Spain, an economically unstable country, was custom-tailor made for Fonso's style of wheeling and dealing. Ricco was selected over Donna, who was furious that Fonso had chosen his brawn over her brains.

$

There were substantial delays in their Pan Am Airway flight at Idlewild Airport (since renamed JFK) adjacent to blustery Jamaica Bay. The men thought about turning back. It was Ricco's first flight, and he was already nervous.

"Suck it up, you big baby," chided Fonso, handing Ricco a double Scotch. Travelers in the first class lounge chuckled at the sight of a 5-foot-5 bowl of Jell-O telling a 6-foot 3-inch block of granite to suck it up.

Four hours later they were over the mid-Atlantic. The pilot's velvety calm voice asked passengers to buckle up because they were about to enter a patch of turbulent air. Fonso complained, "Why can't the fucker go around the problem?"

The plane bounced and gyrated for the next hour. By the time things calmed down, Ricco was a mass of perspiration. As they left the plane, a stewardess said, "Thanks for flying Pan Am. Hope to see you the next time."

$

They were met by a courteous driver holding a misspelled sign "Gravnee" at the rundown Madrid airport.

The men sped through a variety of dark, windy streets on the way to the landmark 50-year old Hotel Ritz, a 167-room former palace in the heart of Madrid's Golden Triangle of culture across from the renowned Museo del Prado. Fonso looked outside to get a feel of the city. There were no street lights, no pedestrians. He looked at his watch. It was only 7 p.m.

The reception desk manager was professional, informative, and spoke perfect English. "I have been instructed to let you know that Minster Adolfito Aiza, will meet you for breakfast at 8 am at his table in the main dining room."

From their Washington briefings, Fonso vaguely recalled Aiza was the ranking decision maker, personally appointed by Generalissimo Franco, to insure the success of the initial surplus food negotiations and deliveries. Gentlemen, I know you've had a long day, but our bar is open for another hour. If you wish, we can even keep it open longer. Also, our staff is available 24 hours a day. They occupy two attractive suites at the end of the hall on the top floor of the hotel. They are the only rooms with a door bell."

$

Fonso had a restless first night because of a displeasing dream that recycled over and over. He was outside shivering in the cold in some foreign city, hopelessly lost. Suddenly, he saw a row of small cottages with smoke coming from their chimneys. He knocked on door after door. There was no response. He reached the end of the row. The last two cottages were different than the rest — they each had a doorbell. He paused a moment to decide which bell to press first. He chose the one with a tiny light in the window. The door opened. There stood a furious Donna, screaming about cheating on her. She picked up a red wood-and-leather fireplace bellow and began to pummel the hell out of him.

Chapter 45

November, 1953
Casa Lugio Restaurant, Madrid, Spain

A distinguished, well-groomed gentleman with a glowing Mediterranean complexion waved to Fonso, Ricco and Auslander from a corner table in the rear of the dining room.

"Welcome to España," said the smiling man. "I am Minister of the Interior, Adolfito Aiza."

The men exchanged a few pleasantries, ordered breakfast, and then got down to business. Fonso provided his background as an American businessman known for his abilities to deploy government social programs for the benefit of the general public. "I'm proud to say we've helped millions of school kids obtain free lunches, and ordinary Americans have balanced meals during the period of war rationing."

"Good. Now you have volunteered to help your allies around the world," said Aiza, (not revealing he was educated at Harvard, and had a master's degree from Wharton School of Business).

"Unlike yourselves, I am a career politician in the service of my people. As you probably know, my country struggled through a terrible three-year Civil War. Fortunately, our great leader, General Francisco Franco, came to power in 1939, and has ruled intelligently since. When World War II broke out, we declared our neutrality. Our European neighbors accused us of siding with the Germans and Italians. So, we have been political outcasts and economically deprived for many years. Our citizens have endured much.

"On the bright side, General Franco, and myself, share the same views as America with regard to world peace, and the containment of communism. That is why we signed the Pact of Madrid, last year. We are happy to welcome American military bases to Spanish soil."

"With all due respect," interrupted Auslander, "we appreciate the background, but we are business appointees. We have nothing to do with government policy."

"Understood," smiled Aiza. "But to do international business you need to understand the customer...no?"

Fonso stepped in. "I agree completely."

"Yup," nodded Ricco.

"Mr. Gravenese, who exactly are these men? In España we believe the less people know the better."

"That is the same in America. But Frederick and Ricco are my family. Frederick handles all money matters, and Ricco handles all operations."

"My family is smaller," smiled Aiza, "Only me and the General." Aiza mentioned nothing about the fortune he had earned in the black market during the war, nor about the thousands of dissidents he made disappear, at the behest of the Generalissimo during the past decade.

The Minister looked at his watch. "I do have another appointment waiting. May I suggest you see some of our city today, and we finalize our first transaction tomorrow morning at my office, say 10 am?"

"Done," said Fonso.

"I assume this is your first trip to España?"

Fonso nodded.

"Good. I have arranged for my driver and bodyguard Juan Carlos to take you to important places in our city. There is nothing better than firsthand experience."

$

Juan Carlos stopped the unmarked government limousine in front of a modest-looking restaurant called Casa Lucio in the La Latina area, one of Madrid's oldest neighborhoods. Casa Lucio, was established in 1952 quickly became the place in all of Madrid to eat fried eggs and chips, a place for famous people to dine out of the limelight.

Fonso stared skeptically. "Trust me, you will like," said Juan. "Lots of famous people stop in. My favorite dish not on the menu called Callos."

"What is it?" asked Ricco.

"How you say in English? Stewed cow stomach in spicy sauce. Tell Cristina to make extra spicy, the Juan Carlos way."

Fonso insisted. "Ricco, you only live once. Maybe the cow will bring you good luck."

Reluctantly, Ricco ordered the dish. It turned out to be delicious. As the men ordered espresso at the meal's end, three men and a woman sat down at the next table. Ricco and the woman where almost shoulder to shoulder. He went to move his chair. Suddenly, he was staring in the face of perhaps the best-known Italian actress and screen sex symbol, **Gina Lollobrigida**.

$

Juan Carlos suggested they take in a few museums. Fonso had brought a Kodak Brownie camera, instead wanted to visit the local, working-class neighborhoods. He explained his modest beginnings, and how to this day he lived in Bayonne. Despite his success, he would never forget where he came from. Juan got the gist.

"Want to see my birth home?" said Juan.

"Yes," said an excited Fonso.

"We go to Carabanchel, if you promise not to tell the Minister? It is not a place on the approved tourist list. But, it is the real Spain."

Carabanchel was a rough, working-class district in the southwestern suburbs of Madrid, the scene of fierce fighting during the Spanish Civil War, and home to Carabanchel prison which housed the most political prisoners during the Franco era. The narrow, winding cobblestone streets were dark and depressing. There were no streetlights. The walls covered with graffiti.

"See this," said Juan, as he stopped the car in front of a hand-painted, scuffed mural. It depicted a woman and child on a donkey with a man leading it though a battlefield littered with bloody bodies. "You feel the pain," said Juan. "This is what happened not far from here, during the people's civil war. Terrible time." Tears streamed from Juan's eyes. "I remember."

"May I take a few pictures?" asked Fonso respectfully, thinking he might never pass this way again. Juan nodded. Fonso opened the door. "You guys coming?"

Ricco got out. Auslander looked around and decided to remain in the car, "You guys are crazy."

Fonso walked into a local church. Once inside he saw a few familiar statues of the Blessed Virgin, and Christ on the cross. He blessed himself with holy water, and left.

They walked down the street toward another mural. Fonso, acting like a true tourist, handed the camera to Ricco. "Take a shot of me in front of the mural." The flashbulb lit up the street for an instant. Three young, mean looking men came around the corner dressed in jeans and worn leather jackets.

The tallest of the three looked at Ricco. He said something in Spanish that neither Fonso nor Ricco understood. Ricco saw fire in the man's eye. He spoke in a heavily accented English, "You tourist from where?"

Ricco responded, "America."

"Why you take picture? You want to make fun of poor people?"

The two men were soon surrounded by four men. One stood in Fonso's face, towering over him. "Give me money, little man." demanded the man.

Ricco pushed him back. "I wouldn't do that if I were you."

"Ugly, don't tell me. This my neighborhood."

The four men pulled knives out of their pockets. Ricco reached for his shoulder holster and just started shooting. One fell, then another. The mural was now stained with blood. The two other men took off like the wind down the street.

As Ricco got back in the car, Juan Carlos smiled. "You know how to handle difficult moments. Minister would be proud."

Chapter 46

November, 1953
President's Palace, Madrid, Spain

Fonso had expected Minister Aiza's office to be opulent. Aiza saw the disappointment.

"You expecting something else," smiled Aiza. "We work for the people. It is inappropriate to appear wealthy and powerful, while our citizens struggle daily."

Fonso smiled knowingly.

"Why is that funny?"

"No," said Fonso. "I quite agree. As a businessman, I spend the money to build my companies, reward employees. We keep our overheads modest like you."

Aiza stared blankly. "Overheads, what are overheads?"

Auslander took over. "Minister, what Fonso is trying to say is that we are social capitalists. Our business goal is to do good for the common man, while at the same time figuring out how to make a reasonable profit for our efforts." Fonso laughed to himself at Auslander's line.

Aiza paused. "Frederick, if I may call you that, where are you from? You do not sound like Mr. Gravenese."

"I was born in Switzerland, and educated at Oxford."

"No wonder, you do not sound American."

"What sounds American?" asked Fonso.

Aiza smiled. "Fonso sounds American. So may I call our American partner Fonso?"

$

Aiza assumed too much.

"As you know, we have done our part in the agreement with your President Eisenhower to build a communist-containment strategy. Franco was staunchly anti-communist.

"As we speak, the Naval Station at Rota in the Atlantic corridor, and the Morón Air Base in the south, are opened and operating. And the weapons facility at Torrejon is under construction.

"After discussion amongst the Ministers, we would like the first order of vegetable oil to be one million gallons; 80 percent industrial grade and 20 percent commercial. Our desire is to rebuild certain industries, open new ones, and provide people jobs."

Auslander did a quick calculation. "Under the terms of our agreement, the United States will ship the quantity requested at 50 percent of the market price in pesetas. Based on current currency rates of seventy pesetas to the dollar, that amounts to 70 million pesetas."

"Agreed," said Aiza, knowing full well the value of the peseta had plummeted due to skyrocketing inflation and the country's economic woes.

America was subsidizing about 75 percent of the actual costs paid to American farmers and refiners. Separately, the Federal government also owed the transaction's middle man (Fonso's new International Grain Company) a 15 percent commission in U.S. dollars.

On the way home, Auslander summarized the complex transaction for Fonso and Ricco. "America gets military bases on their soil; Spain receives the vegetable oil at 17 pesetas per gallon instead of the market price of 70 pesetas or a dollar a gallon; and we get paid $10,500.000."

Ricco's eyes popped. "I'd say that is a fucking win, win, win, win, win. Ahhhh Fonso."

$

In two weeks, the oil was delivered to Spain's busy southernmost port, Cádiz. The next day Aiza called Fonso personally.

He explained there was a problem with the first shipment. When the drums were removed from the ship, they were found to have small dents from the trip across the Atlantic. "We estimate about 50 percent of the oil was lost," said Aiza. "So we are transferring 35 million pesetas to the bank selected by your government. "

Fonso had no idea how to respond, but he knew he had just been out-conned by a fellow conman.

$

Fonso's discussion with the Department of Agriculture showed how important the Spanish bases were.

After explaining the Aiza call, Fonso suggested Chairman Williamson's department call Aiza's bluff by sending inspectors to examine the so-called leaking drums.

"Do you actually think the drums will be intact when our men arrive?" said Williamson.

"With all due respect, Chairman, that's really not the point. Dropping a few inspectors in the mix sends a message to Aiza not to screw around with the United States," said Fonso, displaying his street savvy.

Williamson leaned back in his chair and laughed.

"With all due respect, Mr. Gravenese, it's you who doesn't get it. Do you really think we care if one of those guys steals a little from us? President Eisenhower wants military bases in Spain. The long game is to contain the fucking communists."

Fonso suddenly realized he was a pawn in a bigger chess game.

"I suggest you take a cram course on partnering with these bastards. They're all the same. Their country is in the toilet because some guy is robbing the house blind. A second guy creates a coup to overthrow the bastard. He tells everybody the first guy is stealing from them, and that he will stamp out corruption, so everybody has a better life. Then he creates his own army. They are bigger thieves, and even more violent. People are conditioned to keep their mouth shut or they disappear.

"The second guy's objective is to stay in power as long as he possibly can, making sure he lines the pockets of his friends and family by depositing U.S. dollars in banks around the world."

Williamson's assessment was music to Fonso's ears. He saw opportunity everywhere. But, first things first.

"Chairman, does all this political gamesmanship mean we wasted time? That there are no commissions…"

Williamson interrupted. "Hell no, Mr. Gravenese. You and your group are providing an important service to your government. You keep giving the oil away, however it's structured, and we strengthen our military presence." Williamson paused. "Can you be discreet?"

Fonso nodded.

"I'll tell you something. But if you ever repeat, I'll deny the whole thing and kick you out on your ass. The military has given DOA an almost unlimited budget for these unexpected vegetable oil claims. We're not stupid, you know."

In two weeks International Grain's first commission check arrived. Auslander deposited eight million at Manny Hanny, and while Fonso and Donna put the other two million in safety deposit boxes at a variety of non-Manny Hanny bank branches around Bergen County.

"Keep in mind," said Auslander. "The real commission, after taxes, is about half what we deposited."

At that moment Fonso didn't care about tax bites. He gave his lieutenants, Auslander and Ricco a spot bonus of $100,000 and Magro $50,000.

Fonso, who had recently discovered his overnight security manager worked two jobs to make ends meet, bought him a new house not far from the park in Bayonne with a little yard, and more than enough room for his three growing kids. Fonso's generosity toward loyal employees was legendary.

Donna and her mother went on jewelry shopping sprees. Later, she proudly showed her purchases to Fonso in their apartment. "You know that stuff isn't free," smiled Fonso. "You've got to work for your pay."

"The older you get," she teased, "the more you talk in riddles."

"I need you to mail some boxes to Switzerland tomorrow."

Fonso's generosity did not extend to himself. He continued to wear the same crumpled suits, drive the same car, and live in the same apartment with the same furniture.

$

Fonso officially returned to Aiza's office to procure Spain's new order. Unofficially, he was there to build relationships. He figured somewhere, somehow they would be useful.

"Thank you for processing our damages claim so promptly," said Aiza. "Generalissimo and I are pleased America keeps its word."

Fonso decided to blow smoke on a level he had never imagined growing up on the streets of Little Italy.

"Off the record, based on my discussions in Washington, I can assure you our government believes our relationship with Spain will be long and mutually beneficial."

"Good, good," said Aiza. His attractive blonde secretary entered. She walked over and whispered in his ear. Aiza nodded.

"Fonso, I told the Generalissimo you were coming. He would like to meet you. He is waiting for us in his office."

$

Generalissimo Franco, in full, finely-tailored military regalia, and Fonso in his crumpled black suit, shook hands. "Welcome, welcome," he said with a serious scowl and a high-pitched voice. Fonso noticed they were about the same height.

"Come sit down," said the Generalissimo with a brusqueness that seemed inconsistent with the warmth of his words.

"As Adolfito has told you, these are difficult times in our country. But we are here to serve the people."

"Understand. My goal as a business representative of the United States, is to help you."

Generalissimo Franco's switch clicked on. "Maintaining authority in a country such as ours, requires the Generalissimo to always keep dissidents in check. One day you take this position, the next a different one. Truth, by its nature, must remain flexible."

To Fonso, it was as if he was listening to his clone in military garb. "Remember as your friendship with the Generalissimo develops you may hear terrible things from his enemies. He understands when someone is in a position of power, everybody wants a share. He asks you to believe only what he says. Agreed?"

Fonso smiled. "Agreed."

The two men shook hands. Aiza and Fonso returned to Aiza's office. "So as I mentioned earlier, Spain would like to purchase another one million gallons of oil, under the same terms as the first."

Chapter 47

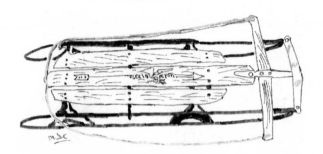

Christmas, 1953
Morris Plains, NJ

To celebrate his sales success in Spain, Fonso decided Christmas 1953 should be one to remember for himself and Donna and Ricco and Josephine.

The Christmas tree in the Gravenese living room was surrounded by two six-foot-long boxes wrapped in shiny foil paper and a big red bow.

Fonso played Santa Claus. He told the women to open the boxes. "Santa, how do you expect two little girls to move these monsters?" asked Donna.

"That's why we invited Ricco."

Unwrapping the packages revealed two double-seat Flexible Flier sleds.

"Okaaay, now what?" asked Donna slowly.

"Look outside," said an excited Fonso. "Twelve inches of pristine white powder."

"Soooo?"

"So I thought we'd take a ride to Morris Plains and do some sleigh-ridding. I did a little research. The Mountain Way School has a hill that is supposed to be great fun."

The women were less than enthusiastic. Fonso kept selling. "It's less than an hour from here. And after we run some hills we can have some hot toddies and steak at Arthur's Tavern. It's a landmark. People come from miles around."

"You're serious," said an astonished Donna. "Aren't we a little old for that kind of thing?"

"Old," said Fonso. "I'm 31. They'll be lots of people our age. When was the last time you just let yourself go? Acted like a kid?"

Fonso continued to rationalize. It was one of the things bizarre things Donna loved about him. He had the capacity to believe his own bullshit... when the need arose.

"Think of Morris Plains as an alternative to Madrid."

It was Josephine's turn to protest. "I don't own the right clothes for messing around in the snow."

"Figured that might be an issue. Open the other boxes."

The packages contained properly fitted parkas, gloves and waterproof boots.

"I'm impressed," said Donna. "How did you manage to get all the sizes right?"

"Gloria," said Fonso referring to his assistant.

"So there are some brains behind those boobs," said Donna, who wasn't joking.

$

The next morning was perfect sledding weather — sunny, crisp, and not a hint of wind.

As the foursome stood at the top of the first hill, the women chuckled at the appearance of the men. The tall, broad-shouldered Ricco resembled a giant snow monster. The rotund, bespeckled Fonso looked like a snowball with eyeglasses.

The two sleds zoomed down the hill, snow blowing in all directions. They were as giddy as a bunch of teenagers.

Despite the near perfect conditions, they noticed the hill was virtually empty. Fonso approached one of the park rangers. He explained they were on the kiddy slope, that most everybody else was sledding down the more advanced hills on the other side of a patch of pine trees.

"Kiddy slope," laughed Ricco.

"Shut up, you big oaf," teased Fonso playfully. "Follow me." Climbing the hill with the sleds left the two men a bit breathless. When they got to the top, Fonso discovered the other side was more like a ski slope. The angle of decent was almost 70 degrees, the hill itself about 1,500 feet long.

Donna looked at Fonso. "You sure?"

Fonso noticed parents, teenagers and kids traversing to and fro. "Christ, if they can do it so can we." Fonso then raised his fist to the sky. "We are Jerseyites."

Josephine smiled. "What the hell are Jerseyites?"

Fonso weaved a most imaginative fable. "Jerseyites are the direct descendants of the Norsemen who braved ocean storms to cross the Atlantic from Scandinavia. They reached Bergen County in the 12 Century. Jerseyites have inherited the Norse traits of courage, bravery and endurance. Some Jersians eventually immigrated to places like the Bronx and Manhattan. But values are values."

The girls doubled over in laughter. An uninhibited Fonso was indeed a rare sight. So rare in fact that Ricco was confused and convinced. Until that moment, he had no idea he could be of Jerseyite descent.

$

Ricco and Josephine went first. Ricco's muscular arms and strong upper torso allowed him to maintain full control over the sled's direction. On his descent he skillfully traversed between the pine trees. Before long the couple was out of sight, although you could hear Josephine's yelps of delight.

It was Fonso and Donna's turn. They headed straight down. Fonso was unable to maintain the same control. The sled picked up speed. Dead ahead sat an unavoidable bolder blanketed in snow. "Hang on," said Fonso, sounding like a wartime pilot. The sled hit the bump, bounced two feet off the ground, then continued its downward flight.

"Oh my god," yelled Donna as they were headed straight for a clump of trees. She closed her eyes and held her breath. Fonso braced himself.

SMASH. A direct hit. Fonso's head bounced off the tree. His glasses shattered. He was out cold. Donna was more fortunate. Fonso's body cushioned her blow.

Ricco was concerned the unconscious Fonso had broken something. Donna started sobbing uncontrollably. She kissed him gently. He woke up with a big smile on his face. "Is it time for cocktail yet?" It was Fonso's way of saying he was okay.

$

Fonso insisted he was fine, just a little sore. Donna made them visit a local hospital emergency room just to be certain. The X-rays indicated Fonso's diagnosis was correct. The doctor gave Fonso a few pills for the pain. And suggested he think long and heard about sledding again that winter.

The foursome headed to Arthur's Tavern. The place exceeded expectations — aged corn-fed rib-eye steaks, giant salads topped with bacon bits and gorgonzola, and one crusty waitress.

The waitress looked at Fonso's shattered lenses and bruised face. "He yours?" Donna nodded

"Couldn't do any better?'

"He's rich."

"That's different. A hell of a lot better than marrying for love."

Fonso didn't find the repartee particularly humorous. Fonso addressed the waitress. "Make yourself useful. Get me a goddamn double Johnnie Walker on the rocks."

As they ate and laughed, Fonso had another double, and another. By the time dessert arrived Fonso was feeling no pain thanks to the liquor and the pain pills. Donna decided to make a final toast before Fonso passed out. "To our group's next adventure…hiking through Alaska to the North Pole."

Fonso sat by Donna's side as she sped down Route 24. To no one's surprise, Fonso's eyelids closed. He tilted to his right and fell fast asleep, cheek resting against the window. Donna looked in the rear- view mirror. Ricco and Josephine were making out like two teenagers. He had his hand up her dress and she had her tongue in his mouth. They both were moaning and groaning.

When Donna reached the Cicolo home, the couple thanked her for driving. Fonso was still sound asleep when she pulled into their Bayonne driveway. Clearly he was too heavy for her to lift. Yet it was way too cold to leave him outside. She gently shook him. He didn't flinch. Donna shook him harder and harder. Fonso started to mumble in the middle of a dream. Suddenly he awoke, comically dreaming out loud.

"When I looked in the trunk, they weren't there. I told the bartender we gotta go back to the hill and find the sleds."

Somehow they managed to get upstairs.

As Fonso sobered up over a cup of coffee, he again asked where the sleds were. Donna explained. "When Ricco poured you in the car at the base of the hill, I made a management decision. I gave the sleds to a local family with two strapping teenage boys. Like the doctor said, you sledding days are over."

"What doctor?"

Chapter 48

———

February, 1954
Karachi, Pakistan

Fonso spent the rest of the holidays contemplating a future where International Grain was a Food for Peace sales agent, refiner and exporter.

He wondered. Could IG triple-dip? Would the Department of Agriculture notice or care?

An impressed Chairman Williamson called. "Fonso, great job. I understand the Madrid meetings went so well Generalissimo placed the order?"

"Where did you hear that?"

"My source tells me *she* witnessed the whole thing."

Fonso thought about the meetings. He recalled the attractive blonde who whispered. He laughed.

"Tell me you've got an operative right under the Generalissimo's nose."

"I'm not telling you anything," replied Williamson. I'm DOA, not CIA."

"Got it," said Fonso.

"Next stop is Karachi," said Williamson. "Just do what you did in Madrid."

"Karachi? Where the hell is Karachi?"

"Pakistan."

"And, where the hell is Pakistan?" said the boy from Little Italy.

"Fonso, if International Grain is going to do the international circuit," laughed Williamson, "management better take a geography class."

Just months prior, Fonso would have laughed at his own naiveté just months before. But doing business in Madrid changed his worldview. He now realized understanding international cultures and histories offered unlimited business opportunities, virtually unknown by what he perceived as an insular, smugly superior American business community.

"Standard," replied Fonso, "at least give me A for effort."

"That I will."

"And, how about some background on why we are spreading the wealth in Pakistan?"

"Why not? I've always got a few minutes for our best ambassadors." Williamson gave Fonso a quick briefing the U.S.-Pakistani relationship.

"After the war, we were unable to persuade India to join an anti-communist pact, so we turned to Pakistan, which was prepared to join a Middle Eastern alliance in return of military and economic aid. Our military command decided that Pakistan, and its neighbors Turkey and Iran, would be ideal countries to counter Soviet influence. So we cut a General Franco-type deal with their popular leader Muhammad Ali Jinnah."

"Do you mean popular, like in elected, or popular like in dictatorship?"

"A little of both. He was elected after independence, but can remain in power as long as he wishes, if the major parties agree. And he controls the major parties, partially by direct appointment."

Fonso just shook his head.

"There's also one other little cultural twist you need to beware of: Muslims are more skeptical of the Christian West, so they are not about to allow American troops and bases on the ground. But they are happy to take hundreds of millions in upgraded military equipment and weapons to strengthen their army, air force and navy, which is fine with us, because that provides a stronger regional anti-Soviet deterrent force."

"And," said Fonso, learning to connect the dots, "because Pakistan has a zillion people, they need U.S. farm surpluses, which we're happy to provide at a deep discount to the market."

"Bingo. Give the man a silver dollar."

"When is our first visit?"

"Fonso, I hate to ask you to hit the road at this time of year, but, for reasons I really can't disclose, it important to start shipping vegetable oil, and its derivatives, quickly."

"Hey, it's summer," said Fonso cheerily, thinking more millions, faster. "The height of tourist season."

Williamson did not have the heart to tell Fonso July and August were monsoon season. In fact, the year before almost eleven inches of rain fell on Karachi in a 24-hour period, causing major flooding, road washouts, and a loss of power and electricity for almost a million people.

$

Fonso, Auslander and Ricco were met personally by Ahmed Hussan, the Minister of Agriculture, at the recently renovated Karachi International Airport. Hussan, an attorney who graduated from the highly-regarded Aligarth Muslim University, was an influential figure in the new Pakistan government, having been appointed personally by Pakistani leader Ali Jinnah. Hussan was known as a devout Muslim with a strong sense of integrity, who always operated in the best interest of his newly independent homeland.

"We welcome our American friends," he said with a respectful bow. Fonso and company had no idea what to do, so they bowed back. Hussan was impressed. He assumed the men had taken the time to understand cultural nuances, since he had done the same.

"Mr. Gravenese, tomorrow we talk business. Today, our Leader prefers you rest, maybe see a few sites on the way to the hotel."

The car passed the Empress Market, and stopped in front of a large religious structure on Shahrah-e-Iraq, a busy street in transition. The wide street was a maze of commercial buses and men in ankle-length outerwear (Thawbs) and white turbans (Kiffiyehs) on camels trying to avoid collisions.

Hussan spoke as he led the group up a set of long winding steps, "This is my country's largest Catholic Church. It is called St. Patrick's, just like yours in New York City."

"I thought Pakistan was primarily a Muslim culture?" asked Auslander.

"Our leader preaches moderation. All religions are welcome in Pakistan."

Slowly as they continued on their way, the car had to slowly make its way through a throng of people at the densely populated Frere Hall Gardens, where snake charmers, musicians and fire-eating performers entertained. Fonso asked Hussan if they could stop.

"Why?" asked Hussan.

"I would like to take a picture of the musician trumpeter serenading the dancing snake. Nobody in America would believe me without proof. Besides what puts the whole scene over the top for me is a double for one of my favorite American jazz musicians. A fellow by the name Dizzy Gillespie."

Hussan laughed. "That *is* Mr. Gillespie. He visits frequently because Pakistanis love jazz. Sometimes he plays in the open-air markets, sometimes he plays at Le Gourmet club in your hotel."

The exhausted men headed for their rooms with a last bit of advice from Fonso, "Get a good night's sleep. Tomorrow should be another lesson in negotiation."

Chapter 49

February, 1954
Marketplace, Karachi, Pakistan

Hussan was a gracious host. Next morning, glasses of hot tea and a dish of small round shiny cookies sprinkled with pistachios sat at the modest table in his modest office.

"I thought we'd start our meeting with a cup of Chai and cookies we call Naan Khatai. The two have been part of the Pakistani breakfast tradition for centuries."

"Centuries?" wondered Ricco. "I thought Pakistan was a new country?"

"Our country may be new, but our land has customs that are many centuries old," said Hussan. "May we begin our business?"

Fonso nodded.

Hussan removed a manila folder from his desk drawer. "Leader Jinnah and I have discussed Pakistan's needs. We would like to begin with a shipment of 500 gallons of commercial-grade vegetable oil. Our people certainly have needs, but we believe improving the Pakistan economy takes priority. More jobs mean happy citizens. If all goes well, we can order more? Yes?"

He took an official purchase order out of the folder, and handed it to Fonso. "At the current exchange rate of 105 rupees to the dollar, we owe the United States 52,500,000 rupees. Would that be correct?"

Auslander took out his pad and pencil to confirm. "Correct."

"We can have a check drawn to International Grain for half the amount before you leave. Final payment will be provided on receipt of product. Is that acceptable?"

"Technically," said Fonso, "No payment is due till all the product arrives."

"The United States has kept their word — all of the military equipment and supplies requested have arrived. We feel it is only proper to act in a similar manner."

The men shook hands. "We also have a gift for you to remember this first trip to Pakistan." He handed Fonso an autographed picture of Dizzy Gillespie taming a cobra snake. "Since you are a lover of jazz, Leader Jinnah wanted you to have the picture he was given by Mr. Gillespie."

"Thank you very much. I will make sure to expedite your adjustment claim when the product arrives. Just call me directly, and I will arrange the details, and follow your wire transfer instructions."

Hussan stared. "I'm sorry, I don't understand what you are talking about."

Fonso realized the man wished to talk in private and might be subtly hinting about a reciprocal gift. "Ricco, would you and Fred mind waiting outside, Minister Hassan and I need to talk for a few minutes."

"I apologize for our failure to communicate. I was simply trying to say our government fully understands that you and The Leader expect to be *personally* compensated with each order. That's not a problem. Customarily, we have told decision makers to declare the proposed payment as a credit for damaged merchandise. You present us with a claim, and we send the money to a bank of your choosing anywhere in the world.

Insulted, Hussan stood stiffly. "Mr. Gravenese, I don't know what countries you deal with, but Pakistan and Pakistani officials do not lie, cheat or steal. Do I make myself abundantly clear?"

Fonso knew he had made a terrible mistake. He tried to backpedal. "Minister, my deep apologies for assuming…"

Hussan raised his hand. "No need, the Quran tells us, "Keep to forgiveness and enjoin kindness, and turn away from the ignorant.'"

"Fair enough," responded Fonso. "I guess I am ignorant in your ways."

"Uninformed," responded Hussan knowingly.

$

Fonso sat quietly in the car on the way to the airport with Ricco and Auslander. "Boss, you haven't said a word since we left that guy's office."

"Let's just say, I was totally embarrassed, and leave it at that."

Ricco's eyes lit up. He was certain he understood the issue. "No fucking way. The guy reneged on the check?"

Fonso pulled the check out of his pocket. "He delivered it to the hotel just before we left." He stared out the window, viewing the chaos of Karachi. "Strange people. Strange customs. Hussan is a straight-up guy. Go figure."

$

On the plane, Fonso's thoughts returned to squeezing more juice out of the Food for Peace orange. "I'm starting to realize we're leaving a lot of cash on the table."

Auslander thought Fonso was referring to the Federal income taxes they were about to pay on the sales commissions. "I'm working on a way around the tax due issue, but it will take some time."

Fonso laughed. "I'm talking about why it's taken us so long to get International Grain Refining approved as a Program product supplier." In his mind, the farmers who sold the surplus soybean and cottonseeds made a profit; the refiners who bought and converted the oil made a profit; the storage facilities that stored the oil made a profit; and yet, the company — his company — the one that delivered the vital sales and marketing services to open and close the deals, merely collected commissions.

"I think we should go into the refining and storage business. That way we'll have three streams of income, not just one," said Fonso, sounding like his father Dominic, many years before.

Auslander thought for a minute. "What you're proposing will require massive capital to construct the appropriate facilities, and significant operating experience in refining, which we don't have."

"How much do you estimate we have in Switzerland?"

"About four million."

"Good," said Fonso. "I estimate the first 40 tanks, the land, and the refining equipment should cost about that much."

"You would roll the dice with everything you own." said a worried Auslander.

"Fonso has a plan. International Grain puts up half, and a partner would put up the other half. The partner also comes up with the initial operating cash to hire and train the International Grain Refining staff."

"I assume you have a partner in mind?" said Auslander.

"When somebody makes a pile of money with you the first time, they're pretty fucking stupid if they don't get on the next train."

$

"Joe, this is Fonso. I think I have a new deal you and the boys might find interesting."

Lomiscolo laughed. "We were just talking about you. Everybody looks pretty sharp in their new Italian silk threads. Mickey was so pleased with his returns on our deal that he bought twenty of them for his whole family. It's now the most well-dressed family in the entire fucking Midwest."

"With this new deal, you might be able to buy forty more suits," laughed Fonso. "When and where can we talk?"

"Mickey, Anthony and me," said Lomiscolo, "was just about to meet in Tampa to discuss another thing."

"Tampa? Why Tampa?"

"Bern's Steak House. Their ain't no better prime meat anywhere. And, the wines…last time we were there, the head man told me Bern's owns the largest wine list in the world. Even gave us a private tour of the cellars." Lomiscolo paused. "When you're in town, we'll have him do likewise."

"Of course, be forewarned. Not everybody is as cultured as you and me," joked Lomiscolo. "Anthony looked at the rows and rows of great 1929 and 1945 Bordeaux, and said he loved the decor."

"What was so special to Anthony?"

"He said he could really relax during dinner. 150 tables and one small window made him feel like he was eating in Fort Knox."

Chapter 50

———

March, 1954
Tampa, Florida

Dinner at Bern's looked like something out of the gangster movie *The Public Enemy*.

Lomiscolo, Lentini and Palumbo — dressed in the finest Italian silk suits, colored shirts with white cuffs, and studded gold cufflinks — were consuming $200 bottles of wine as if they were ten-cent cokes.

"Fonso," said Lomiscolo, "You only got one suit? You look like an undertaker who hasn't slept in a week." The group roared. The more reserved Fonso was all business. "If you guys don't mind, I brought along a few business associates, so we can explain the whole International Grain Refining story, and answer all your questions."

Fonso waved to another table. Ricco and Auslander joined the foursome. Lomiscolo looked at the nattily dressed Auslander. "Who's the school teacher?"

"This is my financial advisor, Fred Auslander. I think you'll be impressed."

"And, the muscle?" pointing to Ricco.

"I'm Ricco Cicolo, head of operations."

Lomiscolo paused. "Cicolo any relation to Bartolo Cicolo?"

"He was my old man."

Lomiscolo smiled. "Fucking small world. Your father and mine were cousins. Mario Morello was my uncle." Morello was the Mafia's first New York Don.

A broad grin filled Ricco's face. They were blood family. "My uncle used to say, I save Bartolo for the tough jobs that need a little extra touch. Capische?"

Auslander, who felt he had nothing in common with the rest of the table, turned to the investment at hand. He explained the vegetable oil as two-part business: grain acquisition and storage, and oil production and refinement. "Fellas, let me take you through a few projections, which suggest an indicated a return of capital within a year, and a 50 percent return every year for as long as the Food for Peace Program exists."

"How long we talking?" asked Palumbo.

"Based on the mess the war created, rebuilding should take five to ten years."

Auslander's projections did not include the third, lucrative part of the business — International Grain's net sales commissions. In Fonso's view, his three Cosa Nostra buddies were investing in storage and refining...only.

"And if we're lucky," added Fonso after Auslander finished, "when the program ends, we may be able to sell the tank farm and the refinery to someone. Fred and I are not sure, but it's out there."

Lomiscolo smiled. "This sounds like a smart business. Different. Legit. Nice and quiet." He had one more question. "Farmer Jones, where you putting the farm?"

"I think I've found the perfect spot in Bayonne. There a huge stretch of unimproved land by the Jersey Turnpike, just across the river from the City.

"Why there?"

"It's smelly as hell, and cheap as shit. The old man who owned it died of a heart attack, and the kids want to cash out. "

"So," said Lomiscolo, "the deal is, we each put up half, and share the profits."

"Correct," said Auslander, whose interruption stunned Fonso. "Joseph, we have precisely the same skin in the game. Although there is one other potential consideration. Since we'll run the business and, I'll keep the books for both of us, we'd like you to contribute a small amount of additional working capital to identify and hire the right people."

"How much is a small amount?" responded Lomiscolo.

"About $250,000, available at the closing."

"Fonso, this guy's good. Really good. Big balls in a fancy suit."

"So what do you guys think?" asked Lomiscolo. The men looked at each other without saying a word. "Frederick, the boys just voted. We're in," said Lomiscolo.

Anthony leaned back in his chair. "How does that broad, you know, the Statue of Liberty, feel about the industrial smells in her backyard?"

$

Dinner over, a gray-haired man approached their table. "Joey," said the man, "see you brought along a few new friends. Thanks."

"Fellas, say hello to Bern Laxter, he owns the joint. "By the way, he's another Pisano from lower Manhattan."

"Laxter?" wondered Ricco out loud.

"I know, I know. Those were the days when some people thought you had to change your name to get away. Our original family name was Lazzari."

Lomiscolo pointed to the floor.

"Sure, no problem, responded Laxter. "Joey wants me to give you a tour of our wine cellar. Somewhere along the way, I decided good meat should be accompanied by good wine. The food critics tell me we have the largest wine cellar in America."

Fonso wondered, "How many bottles?"

"I think it's somewhere around 22,000."

"Isn't that a lot of money tied up in inventory?"

"Fonso, my Papa always said, life is for living, not counting. Guess I just followed his lead. But don't worry about me, we've done well enough to give each of our five kids a million-dollar home as a wedding present."

$

The money was transferred to Fonso's new Manny Hanny account. Auslander transferred a million from Switzerland, through his own channels. Fonso went to see O'Brien. After explaining the business and showing him the projections, he said, "This is pretty much a no-brainer. I'm putting up three million. I'm looking to the bank for the other million, which we are happy to secure against the value of the tanks and the inventory. So you got three-to-one loan coverage."

"Suppose things don't go as planned, and we can't get three million for the assets?"

Auslander interrupted. "With all due respect, Aemon, a blind man could liquidate those assets at an auction, and you'll get your cash back, plus all the ridiculous interest you earned on the loan."

O'Brien felt compelled to respond to the cheap shot about the high interest rate. "The rate has more to do with the character of Mr. Gravense's past dealings."

Auslander was prepared. "Let me ask you something. Was Fonso ever late on any prior bank payments? Was Mr. Gravenese ever convicted of any wrongdoing? Was Mr. Gravenese considered a prime Manny Hanny customer?"

The requested million was transferred to what would become Fonso's greatest financial masterpiece... the newly incorporated International Grain Company.

$

Next up: land acquisition.

Fonso was about as subtle as a sledgehammer with Ralph DiDomenico of Costanza & Providence, Bayonne's oldest real estate agency.

"Ralph, let's cut the crap. That shitty piece of land has been on the market for years. Nobody wants it at any price. I'm offering $200,000 in cash with absolutely no contingencies, and I'm willing to close in 30 days.

"Plus, if we sign the contracts by the close of business tomorrow, there's an extra ten grand bonus for you."

The agent's eyes popped, his entire sales commission after his office's take was $6,000.

The next day, two copies of the sales contract arrived at Fonso's office. The following morning the agent had signed agreements and a 10-percent deposit on his desk.

"Mr. Gravenese," said the agent on the phone, "I assure you I will personally handle all the closing details"— which he did.

When the closing was completed, DiDomenico asked Gravenese, for the first time, what he intended to do with the land.

"Build the biggest vegetable-oil refinery in the world," replied an understated, confident Fonso.

DiDomenico made a surprising revelation. "Christ, you should have told me. That land was the site of an old chemical plant. The soil may be contaminated."

Fonso flipped out. "You motherfucker; I'll have your ass hung on a…"

"Easy, easy," said DiDomenico, "I think I can make it right."

"What does that mean?"

"My cousin, Tom, is the head of the Bayonne City Council. He is in charge of attracting new business. He also plans to run for mayor next year, so a thriving International Grain Refining operation would be a feather in his cap."

Three weeks, and $40,000 later, Fonso had all the necessary building permits and construction approvals.

Tom DiDomenico became the Mayor of Bayonne the following year. Fonso was the major campaign supporter. He walked side by side with the mayor in the city's next four Columbus Day Parades.

$

Money and land in hand, Fonso now needed a refining plant, storage tanks, and lots of employees.

The way Fonso viewed his priorities, he figured if he didn't have working tanks, he didn't have any place to store grains or refine oil — whether he produced or purchased it. Josephine did an extensive search, and found Millbrook Waste and Storage Company in Waltham, Massachusetts. They had stored petroleum for Florio Oils, a Northeastern refiner, which had been acquired by the Esso Oil Company. Esso had no need for the massive tanks, and had no interest in moving them, Consequently, Esso transferred ownership to Millbrook for a dollar, and took the write-off.

Millbrook's owner, John Waters, was anxious to get rid of the 43 tanks, since they took up a lot of space, need periodic maintenance, and would cost a lot of money to dissemble and destroy.

"From what I can tell," said Josephine shrewdly, the owner has no cost in the tanks. So selling them at whatever price he can get is like found money."

A few days later, Ricco was sent to make sure the tanks were in working condition. "Boss," said Ricco on the phone, "the stuff is here. In fact, the guy owns tanks as far as the eye can see. But, they're petroleum tanks. I don't have any idea what it would cost to clean and reuse them for vegetable oil."

Fonso smelled a bargain basement deal. "Go tell him we misunderstood, we didn't realize the tanks had stored petroleum. That we are in the vegetable oil business. Then get the hell out of there."

The next day, Fonso called Waters. "John, this is a toughie. About the only offer that makes any sense is for me to remove the tanks and make a few bucks as scrap metal salvage."

"So how much are you willing to offer me?

"John...I should charge you to haul the shit away. Candidly, I'm only willing to take ownership risk because I have a third party who might want the scrap, assuming we crush and deliver."

Two days later, Fonso had a bill of sale. The following day he was on the phone with his old Bronx pals, Vinny & Richie Scaramuzzo, who now owned a thriving construction company that specialized in bridge construction and repair across the United States. "You guys have come a long way from building pergolas in the Bronx." Fonso explained what he was doing with International Grain and International Grain Refining.

"Bottom line, I need to hire a company who can move more than 40 tanks, steam clean the insides, and make sure they are in top working condition."

"Love to work for you Fonso," said Vince, "But, I'm not sure we are the right people. We have the large winches, trucks and the experience to dissemble and reassemble. But we're not in the steam-cleaning business, and have no experience in tank repair and maintenance."

Fonso thought of the Scaramuzzos as family. He pitched hard. "Vinny, think of tank cleaning as a new side business. My goal is to have a tank farm with 100 to 150 of these motherfuckers next to a refinery that's bubbling and percolating day and night."

Vinny laughed. "Let me talk it over with Ritchie. But, I've gotta say, you my friend, are a one-of-a-kind, genuine American original. Next day, the brothers informed Fonso they were ready to go.

$

Fonso's thoughts turned to staffing. His first call was to Donna's uncle, Sam Magro. Quickly, the men agreed on the terms of Sam's new position as Chief Operating Manager of International Grain Storage and Refining.

Sam recruited an experienced non-union crew that had worked at refineries, and added some of his old Metz colleagues that he knew would put in an honest day's work, pretty much doing whatever was asked of them. They were all loyal to Fonso, and were willing to spread the Gravenese culture to the new guys.

As the tanks were being restored, Vince Scaramuzzo explained a snag, "We've been able to clean about two-thirds of the tanks, about 15, have petroleum residue embedded so deeply that no amount of steam cleaning will ever get the stuff out completely."

Fonso imagined the smelly sidewalks around Cisco's meatpacking facility where years of fat renderings had seeped into the concrete. But he was focused on future profits; not what was edible or inedible. "I don't think that's a problem. We'll just use those tanks to store the commercial-grade oil."

But Fonso was also intuitively pragmatic. He knew somewhere down the line the question of precisely what amounts were in which tanks might arise. It was even possible a lending institution might require inventory validation via physical inspection. So he needed the kind of flexibility only a mind like his own could imagine. He saw a maze of winding pipes, backflow switches, temporary holding bays, and a central control panel, out of sight, out of mind.

"Vince, I've been thinking. Maybe you should design a return pipe network while you do the initial installation."

"Why?" asked Vince.

"Not totally sure. But think of it as a safety measure in case of fire, refinery malfunctions and the need to rebalance inventory."

Scaramuzzo understood fire and malfunctions, but he had no idea what the hell inventory rebalancing was…but who were they to question Fonso?

$

The last piece of the puzzle was buying the raw seed surplus to crush and refine into oil.

"I don't know nothing about crushing seeds," said Magro.

"So go take a trip to the heartland, see what they do in Iowa, Nebraska, go hire an experienced consultant, go hire a crop farm expert, whatever," said Fonso dismissively.

Chapter 51

June, 1954
Istanbul, Turkey

While Scaramuzzo's staff learned about chemical cleaning and plumbing, and Magro learned about soybean and cotton seeds, Fonso received an urgent call from Williamson at DOA, who knew nothing about plan to cultivate a tank farm.

"Ready for another Food for Peace adventure," joked Williamson.

"Where?

"Turkey."

"That's another one of those god-forsaken places over where?" replied Fonso. "I've dealt with you guys long enough to know there's gotta be some weird twist."

"Not important, just know unlike so many foreign governments, this one's democratic, and the President really wants our help. I'm sure they'll tell you all about it."

"Same deal?"

"Yup. As much as they need, paid for in Turkish Lira."

"Lira…Wait until I tell the *Family*. They'll crackup."

"The Family?"

Fonso registered a quick save. "Yeah, my obnoxious father-in-law, pushy mother-in-law, and my nosey wife."

$

Fonso fully expected Istanbul to be another Middle Eastern dustbowl populated by pushy Arabs in turbans, shouting unrecognizable phrases.

Turkey, steadfastly anti-communist from World War II, instituted a two-party democratic form of government in the early 50's, and elected a socialist moderate, Adnan Menderes, as its first President. Menderes promptly sold or distributed most of the wealth he had inherited to the general population shortly after his inauguration.

During Menderes' tenure, Turkey was considered vital to NATO, keeping the then Soviet puppet regimes of Egypt, Iraq and Syria contained. Turkey was eventually invited to join NATO, and permitted the U.S. to construct a multi-billion dollar, state-of-the-art, joint-use air base called Incirlik, just a few miles from the Turkish-Syrian border

In exchange for its unwavering support, Turkey received the equivalent of $2.5 billion in American military aid annually, and became a major recipient of the U.S. Food for Peace subsidies.

Economically, Menderes was staunchly pro-private enterprise. On his watch, agriculture was mechanized;

transport, energy, education, health care, insurance and banking progressed, and the economy grew at an incredible rate of 9 percent per annum. Despite this, he was universally disliked by his political peers.

A Cary Grant double, dressed in a blue pinstriped Brooks Brothers suit waved to Fonso and Ricco in the baggage-claim area.

"Good afternoon, Mr. Gravenese and Mr. Ciccolo, President Menderes is most anxious to meet you. I am his driver, Ibrahim."

A large man gathered up Fonso's and Ricco's bags. Sitting just outside the terminal door was a brand new, shiny Black Buick Roadmaster 75, surrounded by four armed guards. The front license plate read, in raised gold capital letters on a Turkish red background, ADNAN MENDERES.

"My pleasure, enter please." Ibrahim got behind the wheel. "Do you wish to hear music. It will be about 25 minutes to the Presidential Palace."

"Sure," said Fonso, prepared for Arabic wailing. Ibrahim fiddled with the radio dials. "I find a station you will like." Suddenly, Doris Day was singing the number-one song in America — *A Guy is A Guy.*

"We love America. We are good friends since the war. The President thought would be good for the people to have an American music station."

"I do have a question," said Fonso. "Is your name really Ibrahim?"

"For you, yes. For my people, I am called Dalavereci. Means Ibrahim in Turkish. Ibrahim easier. No? President has taught us many things. And life is good for most."

$

Given Ibrahim's "I love America" speech, Fonso was not surprised to find Menderes' office looked like a shrine to America. Next to the modest sitting area stood the American and Turkish flags in brass flag-holders. On the wall to the right and left of his desk were two simply framed, autographed pictures. On the right, Menderes was shaking hands in his office with President Eisenhower, and on the left with President Roosevelt at the White House.

The well-groomed Menderes was of average height with straight black hair, and dressed in a conservative business suit. His manner was easygoing, relaxed, and jocular. "I don't think our business will take long, then I want to show you around. As you say in America — the VIP tour." He laughed at his own use of the American colloquialism.

"We need American refined vegetable oil for everything. We have an aggressive modernization program underway, so that we can become economically self-sufficient in the coming decades. And we all work together. You know we are a country that is half Arabic and half Christian, and at peace with both."

"From my other stops, that is unusual," said Fonso.

Menderes seemed to have done his homework.

"Yes, I understand you have visited Madrid and Karachi...But enough about politics and religion. I have talked to my minsters, whom you will meet at dinner. We require about five million gallons of oils to begin."

Fonso gulped.

"As I said, we have strong agricultural, industrial and military needs. I have studied American pride. You win by giving people jobs and building a strong military. I will conduct myself in whatever manner necessary to achieve those same goals for my country."

"Five million gallons at a U.S. dollar per gallon is a lot of Lira, at 5,800 Lira to a dollar," said Fonso.

"Good, good, you have prepared," said Menderes. "But there is one important detail Mr. Williamson did not explain…Because of our loyalty and military commitments, DOA has approved the purchase at a substantial discount — one thousand Lira per gallon. See, I received this Telex confirmation from Mr. Standard after we spoke yesterday. By the time you leave tomorrow, we will have transferred the funds to your American banks."

Fonso wondered, would all these discounts would affect his commissions? Again, Menderes was one step ahead.

"I see you wonder. Mr. Williamson wanted me to inform you, that despite Turkey's discounts, your firm will still receive full commission on the, how do you say, published price."

Fonso couldn't even calculate the numbers in his head, but he knew if the commissions were booked as income in the United States, he would have a huge federal tax bill. Auslander wasn't present, so he asked Menderes to make the purchase order out to International Grain Refining Company. As Fonso explained, "that will allow my accountants to record our transactions correctly for government purposes."

"No problem."

True to his word, Menderes gave Fonso and Ricco the VIP. Tour. Later they were joined by the president's six most loyal ministers in a district called Beyoglu, on the European side of Istanbul, that was known for its nightlife. There the men partied well into the night, drinking glass after glass of Turkish Raki, the traditional anise-flavored alcohol that tastes like a mixture of turpentine and wood alcohol, spiked with licorice.

Despite their personal chemistry, that night in Beyoglu would be that last time Fonso would see Menderes alive.

Less than two years later, a military coup organized by 37 young officers deposed the government, and had Menderes arrested. Officially, he was charged with violating the constitution and embezzling money from state funds, although no funds were ever recovered, anywhere. Menderes was sentenced to death despite pleas for forgiveness by several world leaders, including President John F. Kennedy and Queen Elizabeth II of the UK. He was executed by the junta in the gallows on the deserted island of İmralı.

Chapter 52

June, 1954
Bayonne, NJ

"Now that is impressive." said Auslander, staring at an official government check for 43,500,000 Turkish Lira made out to International Grain.

Fonso explained the details of his Menderes' meetings.

Auslander had some suggestions based upon the fact that commissions would obviously be quite significant during the duration of the Food for Peace Program.

First, countries making subsidiary purchases needed to write commission checks directly to International Grain. Auslander knew common paper checks were virtually untraceable. Under Swiss banking law, checking deposits were considered a privileged matter between the issuing party and the bank's customer.

Checks should be deposited only by the account holder. Auslander recommended — and

Fonso agreed — that Josephine, Ricco and he should all open numbered Swiss bank accounts. And that International Grain should have bank accounts in five different countries. In that way, the parent company, International Grain, would have 25 different check deposit options, a labyrinth that the IRS and the FBI, for that matter, would never be able to unravel. (While the process seemed logical at the time, years later it would come back to haunt Fonso.)

Commission checks rendered to International Grain by DOA in the normal course of business should be deposited at Manny Hanny, and accounted for in Federal tax returns.

Payments to Lomiscolo and Company would be classified as tax-deductible operating expenses. Subsidiary income, such as storage rental fees, was neither disclosed or shared with Lomiscolo, et al.

There would be two sets of books. One for Lomiscolo & Co inspections and IRS reviews, and the other, the "official" set, for Fonso and Auslander's eyes only.

The tank farm, and its ownership structure, would be disclosed to Standard Williamson at DOA, to give the illusion of complete transparency.

Fonso explained to Williamson he was now the owner of oil refining facilities in Bayonne. "I see so many exporters making additional profits on my sales and marketing efforts, I thought I should at least have the opportunity to fill some of the purchase orders, assuming my prices are marketplace competitive."

Fonso didn't mention to Williamson that he accumulated a series of damaged storage tanks in various bankruptcy proceedings around the United States, which had been updated — to meet some of the nonedible oil health-and-safety standards. His farm now included 123 tanks in various states of operation. Other than the Scaramuzzo Brothers and Sam Magro, nobody — including Auslander and Donna — knew what was what. Fonso's latest vision saw a time when he would supply all the oil for all the international contracts he inked. But Fonso's growing greed was mixed with patience, he knew that level of production would take time.

Williamson laughed. "So now you're a tank farm owner. But, what the hell, so long as you deliver on your promises, and pay your fair share of taxes, the government doesn't care how many millions, billions and trillions you make. That's what America is all about."

$

With their new responsibilities as account holders, Josephine and Ricco got to see the extent of the wealth being accumulated for the first time. To keep them motivated, Fonso bought them a set of matching his-and-her Cadillac Coup Devilles with all the bells and whistles, and gave Josephine a Bergdorf Goodman gift certificate for $10,000. Ricco was delighted, Josephine was pissed.

"Do you realize," said Josephine, "That little bastard has made millions off your friendship, your loyalty, and what did you get...two crappy cars and a department store certificate?"

Ricco made a weak pass at defending his friend. "Jo, those gifts ain't chicken liver."

"You're right," sneered Josephine. "They're chicken feed."

Josephine continued hammering. She turned to historical analogies. "Somewhere, somehow that twisted little Napoléon is going to meet his Waterloo."

Ricco stood firm defending Fonso, which only further infuriated Josephine. Consequently, she spent her spare time, discreetly searching Fonso's office for the real books and records. The closest she came was an admonishment from Auslander when she tried to pry open a locked cabinet.

"My dear young lady," said Auslander. "What exactly are you trying to do? People have left the company for less."

$

Vince and Richie Scaramuzzo had nothing but affection and respect for Fonso. The tank farm had transformed their business into projects they only dreamed of growing up in the Bronx. Everywhere Fonso went, they were sure to follow, collecting international construction projects in developing or needy countries like Spain, Turkey, Pakistan, Argentina, and Portugal. Bridges, railroad crossings, highway roadbeds, and tunnels were all now a part of the Scaramuzzo menu of services.

As always, Fonso got a piece of every project, which was wired discretely to his Swiss account from a lending institution in the participating country. As always, Auslander kept the commission entries outside of Cosa Nostra mob profit distributions.

$

Fonso's bank deposit partner Donna Gravenese became quite the sophisticated world traveler, staying in first-class hotels in exotic locations. Her favorite destination remained Switzerland. "I love those tall mountains, small villages, and big banks."

She also liked to flirt with the handsome, refined Wilfred on her solo deposit trips, but nothing ever came of it. Not that she wasn't willing, but she figured if Fonso ever found out, he'd do everything in his power to make sure she was penniless. Money always trumped love.

$

Sam Magro became a master of salad-oil refining and storage. He trained his people on how to crush and squeeze to obtain the highest yields per bushel of raw materials. To ensure they didn't take these newly acquired skills elsewhere, Magro and Fonso made sure they were paid top dollar. It was Magro's job to reinforce how lucky they were. A story went around, planted by Fonso, that an employee had once tried to sell International's trade secrets for personal gain. The man and his family disappeared off the face of the earth.

Magro also traveled the country in search of cooperative cotton seed and soybean farmers willing to deliver product at below market rates in exchange for a guaranteed number of International Grain purchase orders annually.

It was also Magro's responsibility to work with the Scaramuzzos to insure the network of pipes and return switches were always in perfect working order. To that end, Sam introduced the concept of a "surprise guest" drill. He would have the front gate announce there were surprise visitors at the front gate to the control room. Then, the operators would time how fast they were able to move oil from 23 full tanks to the 20 empty tanks. A byproduct of this testing was that Sam became a walking computer. He could tell Fonso pretty much where every drop of oil was at any given time.

$

During this early International Grain growth spurt, Fonso made sure that his mob buddies received their profit distributions in a timely manner. Flush with cash, he also sent a check for $250,000 plus interest to Lomiscolo as a good-faith return of the capital that Joe and the boys had given Fonso for manpower, in addition to their original two million dollar investment.

Ironically, Fonso's generosity would come back to bite him. The boys were so impressed by Fonso's openness, they decided to send him a thank-you gift. A truck pulled up to the front gate of the tank farm with a case of exquisite, first vintage, 1921 Dom Pérignon.

As the guard signed the delivery receipt, the driver noticed the surrounding fields contained green and white tanks as far as the eye could see. Each contained the letters, IPG, prominently displayed in caps.

Chapter 53

President Dwight D. Eisenhower took office in January, 1953. In March, 1954, the communist dictator, Joseph Stalin died, and Nikita Khrushchev became leader of the Soviet Communist Party. In June, the Cold War became a national obsession when Senator Joseph McCarthy claimed that communists had infiltrated the CIA and the U.S. atomic weapons industry.

The Cold War continued to escalate as the allies formed various military treaties to neutralize communism, including the Southeast Asia Treaty Organization (SEATO), comprised of Australia, New Zealand, France, Thailand and the Philippines; The Baghdad Pact, comprised of Iraq, Iran, Turkey and Pakistan; and, the NATO expansion, which now included virtually every country in Western Europe.

*Eastern Europe then created the Communist **military counterpart, the Warsaw Pact, which included East***

Germany, Czechoslovakia, Poland, Hungary, Romania, Albania, Bulgaria, and the Soviet Union.

November, 1955
Belgium-Cargill, NYC

Senator Rutherman called Fonso to give him a heads-up. "I wanted to alert you. President Eisenhower is holding a press conference tomorrow to declare an end to the Food for Peace program, as we know it. He believes the generous economic subsidies Food for Peace provided our allies, combined with the signing of various military treaties, will neutralize communist advancement for decades to come."

Fonso thanked the Senator for the call. Rutherman had no idea Fonso was the sole owner of the largest vegetable oil refining plant and storage depot in the United States.

$

Fonso had heard unofficial rumors, even before the Senator's call. He knew he had to have a back-up plan that guaranteed he could undersell all of his competitors from the many contacts signed during the heyday of the Food for Peace Program.

Step One was to accelerate planned tank modifications to accommodate the virtually unlimited production of low-quality, low-cost shortening and vegetable-oil products. Because his costs for the 123 giant tanks he owned was only $4 million, half of which came from the Cosa Nostra, he could afford to invest in the highest-yield production machinery.

Step Two, at the suggestion of Fred and Wilfred Auslander, lowered product costs further by completely avoiding potential tax liabilities. They created a tax-favored subsidiary, Trans World Shortening Company, headquartered on the Island of Guernsey, part of the Channel Islands, where the Rothschild Bank, in the capital of St. Peter Port, just happened to maintain a very private correspondent relationship with Credit Suisse in Zurich.

Step Three was flat-out bribery. His international trips had given him an unparalleled knowledge of who accepted what kinds of bribes, in what currency denomination, and how they preferred payment delivery. He was confident no competitor had such a complete list.

Step Four was the use of Ricco to maintain the lowest possible cost of raw materials. If a farmer ever tried to raise their price per bushel for cottonseeds or soybeans, he sent Ricco to explain why that was not a good idea. If someone still wasn't convinced, Ricco was authorized to initiate unfortunate production-related accidents, such as a storage barn catching fire or an important piece of machinery disappearing in the middle of the night.

$

While Fonso focused on Trans World efficiency as the solution, Josephine separately concluded there had to be more.

She took the initiative to analyze Food for Peace trends such as total orders, pounds per order, and commissions paid. She discussed her findings with Donna. Shortly thereafter, they approached Fonso. "Fonso," said Donna,

"Josephine and I would like to discuss the Belgium-Cargill Company."

"The what?"

Belgium-Cargill, founded in 1813 in Belgium by Simon Fribourg, was one of the world's largest privately held family companies in the agricultural commodities business.

"According to my research, Belgium-Cargill's primary business consists of storing, selling, and shipping grains and oilseeds," said Josephine. "But, when I spoke to this very nice man at the company, he told me one of their greatest barriers to growth was the need for affordable storage facilities. And, that they were not in the business of building such facilities."

Fonso was flabbergasted. "How the hell did you find that out?"

"Simple; like Fonso, I talked to a few people, who referred me to a few people. When we got to the person who didn't want to talk to me, I knew we had reached the decision maker. I sent my husband to talk to my source. He became quite cooperative."

"You had Ricco do what?"

"Temper, temper," said Donna. "Remember, Ricco is Josephine's husband first, and then your business associate."

Belgium-Cargill relocated its corporate headquarters after World War II to Park Avenue and 46th Street in Manhattan, a short car ride from International Grain in Bayonne. Josephine even managed to convince the company to send a ranking executive to see the International Grain's tank farm, and talk to Fonso directly. The man seemed amazed he had a competitor so near.

"We're not really competitors," explained Fonso. "We're not in the storage business; we're in the refining and distribution business. We just happen to have a lot of available storage capacity because the Food for Peace program is winding down."

The Belgium-Cargill executive made what he thought was a low-ball offer on the spot. It was 30 percent more than Fonso had projected. Fonso countered. He had done his homework, "And that, according to my information, is 40 percent less than you are now paying." The man accepted the deal, but wondered how Fonso could offer such attractive storage prices, so close to New York Harbor.

Fonso responded modestly. "My father taught me to be a low-cost-of-goods supplier. Good customers always want the best price." He figured the details that made International Grain and its various subsidiaries what they were was none of Belgium-Cargill's damn business.

When the dust settled, Fonso signed a guaranteed five-year Belgium-Cargill contract with no price increases, and a Belgium-Cargill commitment to lend Fonso additional expansion capital at only 2 percent above the prevailing prime rate. The rental cash flow meant Fonso would always be profitable, and the loan terms were a lot more favorable than traditional commercial lenders.

$

The Belgium-Cargill deal got Fonso thinking. Was there another Belgium-Cargill somewhere?

Josephine went back to work. This time she found the Bunge Corporation in Buenos Aires, Argentina, a place Fonso never visited during the Food for Peace program because, as Rutherman said, the place held no Cold War military importance to the U.S.

The history of the family-run, private company was not dissimilar to Belgium-Cargill: they specialized in trading agricultural grains for profit. Johann Bunge founded the company in the Netherlands in 1818. The family moved the headquarters to Buenos Aires in 1905. By the 1950's they had a presence in over 100 countries, along with Belgium-Cargill, were considered one of the largest agribusiness suppliers in the world.

Josephine, who to Fonso's surprise spoke fluent Spanish, had no trouble getting to the top brass. After explaining her purpose, and sending them a letter of introduction and Fonso's press kit, rough as it was, CEO Juan Carlos and Fonso spoke preliminarily on the phone.

Fonso explained his low-cost storage policy, and the terms of the Belgium-Cargill deal without mentioning them by name.

Soon Carlos and his entourage visited Bayonne in person. Carlos, who looked like the handsome actor, Cesar Romero, scanned Fonso's modest office, scruffy storage grounds, squatty figure, and rumpled Robert Hall brand suit, with obvious disdain.

Fonso had handled this kind of condescension all his life. He was tired of it. "With all due respect,

Mr. Juan Carlos, do you think the grain really gives a shit what I wear or don't wear?"

By the time the group left the next day, Juan Carlos had signed the same deal as Belgium-Cargill, right down to the loan provision.

There was just one difference. Fonso took the entourage to the Rizzuto family-style restaurant on Main Street in Bayonne. He decided to make the appetizer a memorable affair.

"Richie, tell the kitchen I'd like to introduce my new friends to the off-the-menu appetizer special — you know, the fresh zeppoles and a bowl of Fra Diablo sauce."

Zeppoles were doughy Italian dessert squares, cooked in oil, and covered in powdered sugar. Lobster Fra Diablo was a spicy red sauce traditionally served over spaghetti.

"Great choice, Mr. G," smiled the waiter.

The tray arrived a few minutes later. "Gentlemen, I give you Zeppole Fra Diablo," smiled Fonso devilishly. "I guarantee you won't find them any place else but Bayonne. So when you head home, tell your friends all about 'em."

$

Fonso now had two long-term storage contracts, positive cash flow for years to come, and two favorable sources of future capital expansion and he had an unbelievably funny story about Zeppole Fra Diablo he could tell his friends for a long, long time.

$

Fonso also didn't forget Josephine's productive research initiative. He put $50,000 in $100 bills in a fancy shoe box and casually dropped it on her desk on his way out the door. "This is just a little something for you. I hope they're the right size."

Chapter 54

Christmas, 1955
Bayonne, NJ

The golden brown, stuffed 27-pound turkey was surrounded by all the trimmings, and all the people Fonso considered family: Josephine and Ricco, Donna and her mom and dad, Uncle Sam and Barbara Magro, Vince and Ritchie Scaramuzzo, and Fred Auslander.

To everyone's surprise, the normally reserved Fonso made a toast. "Thank you all for coming. The years have treated this family well. Donna and I are pleased that you could all make it. We want to wish you a blessed Christmas, and a Happy, Happy New Year. May God continue to bless and watch over us."

The crowd joked and teased each other, knives and forks clanked and scraped, the melodic sounds of Bing Crosby and Tony Bennett filled the room.

Suddenly, Josephine accidentally swallowed a piece of broken turkey bone and started to gag. She took a piece of bread and tried to wash it down with water. The damn thing was still stuck. "Are you okay?" said Ricco sitting across the table.

She nodded calmly, taking another piece of bread and more water. Suddenly, her eyes opened wide. She waved her arms then grabbed her neck. Donna screamed, "Josephine needs help." Ricco ran around from the other side of the table, grabbed his wife around the chest, and attempted the Heimlich maneuver. He pulled once, nothing. She was gasping for air, and kicking her feet. He yanked her cheek a second time. Her face turned blue.

"Somebody, call a fucking ambulance," cried out Ricco, who tried CPR by placing his mouth over hers. "Is that the right thing to do?" questioned Fonso.

"How the fuck do I know," yelled Ricco, the tears streaming down his cheeks. While he held his wife, he began speaking to her. "Hold on baby, the ambulance is coming." Her eyes rolled around her head. "Stay with me baby, stay with me," cried Ricco. Josephine's body trembled and shuttered. She stopped breathing.

The emergency medics arrived and dashed over to her. The lead medic put his hand on her pulseless neck. "I'm so sorry, the lady's dead." Everybody stood in stunned silence. Ricco was beside himself.

The autopsy ruled her death an extremely rare case of accidental suffocation. The turkey bone, surrounded by bits of food and bread had clogged her esophagus.

$

Josephine's wake was held at Hagan's Funeral Parlor. Fonso had filled the place with flowers. To Ricco's surprise, the line of mourners stretched from the viewing room into the lobby. Some were family, but most were people that had come to know and respect Josephine for good deeds Ricco knew nothing about.

"Mr. Cicolo," said a 20-something lady carrying a picture. "This is my daughter Gloria. When my husband began to abuse me, I reached out to the Samaritan House, where your wife was a counselor. She spent hours helping me regain my self-confidence, and helped me find a job. Without her, I'm not sure I would have gotten through the ordeal. She told me, she had been abused herself, and that you were her knight in shining armor." She paused, "God bless you, Mr. Cicolo"

$

The family-only burial ceremony took place under dark ominous skies at St. Raymond's cemetery in the Bronx, a few blocks from where Josephine was born.

After leading the group in prayer, Father Don gestured this was the time to approach the casket with final thoughts, perhaps a flower or a bit of memorabilia.

Fonso stood in front of Ricco, who wanted to have the last word with his wife. Fonso's lips whispered the *Hail Mary*, a prayer every Catholic child learns shortly after they can talk.

Hail Mary, full of grace,
The Lord is with thee...

Suddenly the heavens roared, and for a brief few seconds, hailstones tumbled from the sky. Fonso looked up in disbelief. A single hailstone shattered the left lens of his glasses, as others danced around the brim of his hat. Before anyone had a chance to scatter, the hailstorm stopped. Undeterred, Fonso took off his glasses, wiped them with a handkerchief, and then finished his *Hail Mary*.

$

"I've been thinking," said Donna. "Suppose Josephine's death was a message."

"From who? About what?" responded Fonso dismissively.

"From God. Maybe he wanted to get our attention. Maybe the life we lead is too much. Maybe we're supposed to do something. I don't know," continued Donna.

"That's ridiculous."

"Fonso, do you believe in God?"

Fonso removed his damaged glasses. He stared at his wife. "You want the truth?"

"After eight years, don't you think you owe me that?"

"I'm not sure... I mean, about the God thing. I've traveled a long way from St. Patrick's. Maybe you're right, maybe it's time to pause. But it's not that easy. I've got a tank farm half the size of New Jersey, employees who depend on me, and..."

"And bank accounts brimming with cash in Switzerland, which is like a Disneyland for the rich and famous."

"It's not that much, and I'm not famous," smiled Fonso trying to lighten up the conversation. "In fact today, our Swiss holdings are a few million less than yesterday. Fred told me Josephine was the sole signatory on her account. I guess we just all never imagined. We don't dare try to recapture the funds without opening a can of worms with the IRS."

"So what happens to the money?"

"I instructed Fred to have the Bank find a worthy boys charity in Europe somewhere, and make an anonymous donation. Then close the account. No paper trails."

Donna was pleasantly surprised. "That was a really nice thing to do."

"Does that mean you think your husband is a heartless, greedy bastard?"

Donna responded with a question of her own. "Fonso, how much money is enough? When do we sail off into the sunset and leave all this behind?"

Fonso's mind traveled to dark places. "Donna, don't you realize it's not about the money; it's about all the other stuff."

"I don't understand."

Fonso paused for what seemed like an eternity. "Like burying those miserable fucking grammar school nuns who told my mother I'd never amount to anything. And, that priest who…"

Donna heard disturbing "stuff" she had never heard before. She was visibly shaken.

Fonso half-heartedly attempted to return from the darkness. "I'm on a roll, now is the time to ask anything your heart desires."

She saw Fonso's forced smile. Her intuition suggested this was not right time to ask *the* question...but she threw logic to the wind.

"Fonso, I'd like to know. Do you love me, I mean really love me like Romeo loved Juliet, like Mark Antony loved Cleopatra?"

"Donna, I've always been faithful. I've never..."

"That's not what I asked you."

Romeo and Juliet, thought Fonso. What the hell do you say to a woman who talks such nonsense? His mind recalled their first date at the Rainbow Room. It was fun, it was romantic — the twinkling skyline, the cuddling, the kisses, but, would he love her for all eternity?

For Fonso, it was a question without an answer. A question that made absolutely no sense.

"I'll try harder," he responded tepidly.

Chapter 55

From 1948-58 Venezuela had been in the hands of a
group of three military dictators. In 1952, the junta
decided to hold a democratic-style presidential elections, but
the results were deemed unacceptable, and the most powerful
of the three leaders, Marcos Pérez Jiménez, assumed the
presidency. Almost immediately, the other officers conspired
to overthrow him, and, finally, with his suitcases stuffed
with dollars, Pérez Jiménez fled by private plane to
the Dominican Republic, where his colleague, Rafael
Trujillo, had ruled with an iron hand. During the Pérez
Jiménez years, the United States refused to include any of

South America in the Food for Peace program, openly stating the continent held no strategic military importance in America's quest to limit the growth of communism.

Less than 12 hours after Pérez Jiménez fled, the more powerful of the two remaining juntas, Admiral **Wolfgang** *Larrazábal, declared himself the duly elected president, and promised honest economic reform for all the people.*

Months before Fonso arrived, Vice President Richard Nixon tried to improve relations with Venezuela by meeting with the Admiral at his Palace. The meeting never took place. Angry Venezuelans halted the motorcade, and overturned many of the cars in Nixon's entourage. No shots were fired, but Nixon and his wife Pat fled to the airport under heavy security.

After Josephine's death, Donna took a more proprietary role in the affairs of International Grain, and its web of enterprises.

Now certain about Fonso's limited ability to love, she wanted to get closer to the Demigod of Greed, the one who had demoted her to second fiddle.

There were also practical considerations. Not having a co-signature on Josephine's Swiss account cost the Gravenese family big time. She wondered, did *her* Little Big Man's lack of attention to detail exist elsewhere?

$

The Belgium-Cargill and Bunge relationships meant International Grain was on the cusp of entering refined corporate air. Belgium-Cargill and seven other American blueblood institutions — Borden, General Mills, Glidden, Pillsbury, Proctor & Gamble, Ralston Purina, Spencer Kellogg, and

Swift — controlled 75 percent of the U.S. soybean storage and crushing markets.

These companies were growing fast because of middle-class America's increased consumer demand for everything from dog food to kids' cereals. Fortunately for Fonso, most had outgrown their existing storage capacity, forcing them to make a decision: invest their excess cash flow and profits in more storage facilities; or identify independent third-party storage like Fonso's 123-tank farm, located near convenient transportation and shipping hubs.

Acting as a storage agent meant he and his staff did not have to go to places like Illinois, Iowa, Indiana, and Ohio, to persuade unsophisticated farmers why they should sell and store their grains with him.

Fonso saw the blueblood storage customers as potential lending machines to expand International Grain's vegetable-oil refining capacity.

His objective was to dominate the relatively untapped international marketplace. His participation in the Food for Peace program during the past four years gave two unique advantages:

First, he knew the marketplace intimately. After all, he had exported directly or indirectly 85 percent of all the subsidy program's vegetable oil.

Second, he personally knew the decision makers in virtually every reconstructed or emerging country in Europe and Asia — from Spain and Greece to Ceylon, Burma, and Libya. He knew no two dictators and pseudo-democratic leaders were alike. Most important, he had complied a unique binder that summarized the type of bribes favored by each person. The binder sat in small safe in a fake wall behind his desk, and he was the only one who knew the combination.

$

The well-respected, 200-year-old Bunge firm fit nicely in Fonso's strategy. They controlled 50 percent of the grain earmarked for international storage, and owned an even higher share of its South American homeland.

A strong Bunge relationship would give him a presence in markets close to home — places like Chile, Argentina, Paraguay, Venezuela, and a host of other countries not part of the Food for Peace program. Fonso also believed there was only one way to build business trust — face to face, man to man.

Hammersfield Hirsch, president of Bunge, was stuffy, autocratic and honest. He was one of the descendants of a small cadre of families that owned 100 percent of the privately held commodity giant. His Buenos Aires office was as big as his ego.

At six-foot-four he towered over the five- foot-five-inch Fonso. His English was also more polished and refined. But he respected successful American businessmen. His research suggested Fonso was rough at the edges and prone to shortcuts, but he did what he said.

"Mr. Gravenese, let us respect each other's time. Bunge's ultimate business strategy is to be the world's leading vertically-integrated feed and food ingredient company. We want to supply agricultural commodities and processed products to a wide range of international customers in the animal feed, food service and bakery industries."

"Call me Fonso," said Fonso.

"Why?" Asked Hirsch. "Isn't your name Alfonso Gravenese?"

"Fonso's a nickname, given by my father."

"In Argentina, we have no nickname for Hammersfield," smiled Hirsch.

The men had broken the ice. Fonso rubbed his chin. "Well, we better figure something out. I can't call you Hammersfield every time you say Fonso."

"How about calling me Ham?" He asked Fonso for a favor. "Please, tell no one at Bunge. My managers would not accept a president named Ham."

Then Ham returned to the business at hand. "As I mentioned our strategy is not yet fully developed. So, it is not surprising Our international grain traders had neither the expertise or contacts to market or sell refined vegetable oil. We rely almost exclusively on reliable third-party refiners, like yourself, to convert the crushed seed into commercial grade vegetable oil. My friends at Belgium-Cargill tell me International Grain has an extensive storage and refining capability, and existing relationships with many international decision makers."

"All true," smiled Fonso.

They discussed the nature and the terms of their sales, storage, refining, and financing relationship. Ham agreed to draw up the agreement, and Fonso agreed to meet Ham's first referral, the newly installed Venezuelan President Admiral Wolfgang Larrazábal.

$

Caracas, Venezuela
December, 1956

Ham had not briefed Fonso about the country's distaste for America. Besides, when Ham made the meeting, the Admiral expressed no reluctance, despite the protests of influential Venezuelans in the United States.

$

Upon arrival, Fonso and Ricco were ushered into a small, modest office. Unlike other heads of state they had visited, the walls were barren. He could have been anywhere. There was a small coffee pot and a small covered plate on the table. A cautious, gray-haired man of average build and height, in unadorned military dress, entered the room. Fonso thought the man was the polar opposite of Generalissimo Franco in Madrid.

The man uncovered the small dish. "Venezuelan plantain. Taste it."

Fonso did.

"Delicious, no? This is a food of our people, but they are hungry. They have no oil to cook. At the moment, the bolívar is not an attractive currency. But, the more my countrymen eat, the more they work to develop our resources. Then Venezuela will be healthy. Do you know how plantains grow?"

Fonso was getting impatient with all the talk of plantains. "Admiral, your time is valuable. I am here to discuss business possibilities."

"Yes, yes, you sell oil for the people," said the Admiral. "Why you help others, ignore Venezuela?" in a clipped version of English.

Fonso had no idea what the Admiral was talking about. The Admiral climbed on his imaginary soapbox, waving and strutting. "You tell us, no food, just guns. You demand we fight some imaginary devil. You disrespect our dignity. Not for one year, not two, but ten. You help devious Arabs who lie — you leave peace-loving Christians to starve. That is America to me."

"Sir," said Fonso, playing it straight, "I am a businessman, not a politician. I have no power over those decisions."

"No such thing in Venezuela. Business means money. Money means power."

Two gun shots echoed from the street outside the palace walls. The Admiral kept talking as if nothing had happened. "Just gunshots. Always somebody wants to be the president."

Fonso walked over to the window. He saw "Yankee Go Home" signs carried by men with rifles circling the Palace. "Ricco, take a look." Two more gun shots echoed. Ricco saw one soldier fall. Others returned the fire.

"What the fuck," yelled Ricco, pulling his gun out.

The Admiral calmly raised his hand. "No worries, we are secure. My soldiers shoot to kill. No second chances."

"Admiral, with all due respect. You're full of it. Get us out of here, now." screeched Fonso.

The Admiral ignored the need for urgency, one last time. "What do you expect? My people see your wealth, your greed, your blindness. They don't understand. Do you blame them?"

318

There was the sound of scuffling and shouting in the hall. The Admiral's door shook and rattled. Finally, the Admiral made a call, and led them to a small hidden passageway behind a bookshelf which led to a garage, where they hustled into a waiting bulletproof car. "Down," said the driver. Ricco instinctively pushed Fonso on the floor and covered him like a human shield. As the driver sped away, a single gunshot shattered the rear window. Ricco was ready to exchange the gunfire. "No," said the driver. "Problem past. Airport is secure. You take the president's plane."

$

On the flight back, a subdued Fonso said little, other than they had made their last sales call to South America on behalf of Bunge. Fonso thought he'd be happy to lease storage space in Bayonne, and borrow lots of *their* cash to refine and ship *his* oil to Europe and Asia. But that was it.

As Fonso recalled, Ricco took a picture of Josephine from his wallet. A tear formed in the big man's eye, and rolled down his cheek. Ricco was more than a man in love with a memory. He was a man who was willing to take a bullet for his friend. Fonso wanted to thank him, something he had never done before. He began awkwardly, "Ricco, I just wanted to thank you for…"

Ricco interrupted. He knew how hard it was for Fonso. "Got it boss, no need to say more." He quickly changed the subject. "That Venezuela joint's got some crazy people."

Then Ricco surprised Fonso with some insights about the world's political and economic systems.

"Our travels had got me to thinking about the differences between communism, socialism, social democracy, and American capitalism. You know, there are some good things in all those systems," he said.

"But no system is good for everybody. The commies want everybody to have a little taste, so nobody complains. The socialist Venezuelan nutbags think the government's supposed to provide free everything, all the time. They don't know nothing about tax rates and tax exemptions. Then there are the snooty Europeans. They think they invented social democracy. Nobody's gotta worry about anything and you can still make a lot of money in business."

Ricco wasn't quite finished. "That's why I like us. You can make as much as you want, have the best that money can buy, and not give a fuck about the rest, if you don't want to."

Fonso chuckled. He found Ricco insights accurate and humorous.

$

When Donna asked how the trip went, all Fonso would say was, "the Venezuelans are a tough sale. I'm not sure they're worth the effort."

A day later, Donna walked into Fonso's office waving a piece of paper on official Venezuelan letterhead. "If those Venezuelans were such a tough sale, why did they fly you back on the president's plane? Do you have any idea how much your extravagant ego cost us?"

Part Six
The Great Swindle

Chapter 56

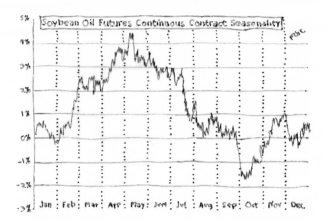

The organized buying and selling of agriculture commodities through a licensed U.S. Commodity Exchange has existed in the United States since the end of World War I. Its original purpose was to provide farmers an incentive to grow large quantities of basic food commodities, such as soybeans and cotton seeds.

By 1950, the New York and Chicago Commodity exchanges cleared almost 95 percent of all U.S. commodity transactions. These exchanges allow buyers to purchase cotton seed and soybean futures contracts with as little as 5 to 10 percent down. This sum, called the initial margin amount, allows buyers to control large amounts of commodities with small amounts of money. However, because these futures contracts are so highly leveraged, a small drop in the price of a contract could quickly translate into a huge loss. When this happens, a brokerage house asks the investor to deposit additional cash to restore the initial margin amount.

322

January, 1958
La Cote Basque, NYC

Bertrand, the snotty head sommelier at Manhattan's trendiest new gastronomic temple, poured the pricey 1929 Chateau Bordeaux into Auslander's glass. He inhaled, tasted, and nodded his approval.

Auslander raised his glass to Donna, Ricco and Fonso. "Thank you for having allowed me to join you." His toast assumed the end of the Food for Peace program.

Fonso's magic carpet ride through exotic ports of call had left him in a place that few businessmen ever reach. He was a man of wealth, who had millions of tax-free dollars stashed in Switzerland. He was a man of influence, who owned political connections at the local, national and international level. He was a philanthropist, who had given to the Catholic Church, the Boys Club of America, and to those who had his back. He was a man of strategic vision who had taken full advantage of the Free Lunch Act, The Emergency Price Control Act, and Food for Peace.

The meaning of Auslander's toast finally registered. "Fred, what do you mean 'having allowed me?'"

"I think the world we knew has just changed," said Auslander. "Our international customer base knows the Food for Peace subsidiary program is history. From now on, they have to buy refined oil at full market price. Bottom line, they're going to buy almost exclusively on price...that's never been our strength."

"Why can't we compete?"

"It would mean watching watch every dollar. Making rock-bottom commodity purchases. Creating detailed inventory management systems. Producing every gallon cost-efficiently."

Fonso dug in. "We can do that."

"It would also mean tight cash controls, such as insisting on letters of credit from customers before we ship product."

$

Donna had heard enough. She agreed with Auslander. None of the new requirements fit *his* skill sets or *her* personal interests.

"Fonso, maybe Fred's right. This could be time for all of us to head off into the sunset. As he said, we've got a ton of money in Switzerland, and a whole life ahead of us to enjoy it. And Ricco and Fred can split Ricco's account, as a lifetime bonus for a job well done."

Ricco nodded approvingly, while Josephine's conscience danced on his shoulder. Auslander remained characteristically noncommittal.

$

Fonso was a man who believed his past accomplishments were merely a prelude to the construction of his ultimate financial masterpiece. Michelangelo had the Sistine Chapel, Beethoven had his Fifth Symphony, Da Vinci had the Mona Lisa. Fonso would orchestrate the greatest financial scam the world had ever known.

Quite simply, he would go on a buying spree to control the world market price of cottonseed and soybeans. Then he would manipulate the wholesale price of refined vegetable oil by becoming the world's largest producer and exporter.

He would become the Salad Oil King.

Chapter 57

———

March, 1958
Bayonne, NJ

Fonso tried to win over Donna with practical logic. In her mind, enough was enough. She had an answer to every issue Fonso raised.

"What do we do with the tank farm?" asked Fonso as they sat in his office.

"Sell it," snapped Donna.

"A Bayonne tank farm. Buyers will smell fire sale."

"Who cares, we have no cost of goods," responded Donna with the confidence of a person who had graduated with honors from Columbia University.

"What about Joe, Mickey and Anthony?"

"You've already returned their initial investment, plus a hell of a lot more."

"Dumping a vegetable-oil farm is not exactly like selling a truckload of Rheingold beer. Do you realize what it could cost to maintain a bare-bones staff until the right buyer comes along?

"Fine then, burn the damn place down. At least we'll get the insurance."

"You mean like mini-arson? That's illegal." Donna laughed. Fonso suddenly wanted to do things by the book. She chose the course of least humiliation. "Fine. Just declare bankruptcy. Businesses do it all the time."

Auslander overheard the debate as he passed. He began to smile.

"What the hell are you smiling about?" grumbled Fonso.

"She's right," replied Auslander, tapping his cigarette in the ashtray.

Fonso began to stomp around like a spoiled brat. "I've made you a rich man. You're supposed to be on my damn side."

"Fonso, honey...stop with the intimidation. This is Donna. You know...your loving, faithful wife of ten years."

"What about *my* boys? We got fifty or so people who depend on us for their livelihood... including *your* dear uncle. Do we just say goodbye?"

Donna countered. "*our* boys have been paid twice the going salary to keep their mouths shut. Then there are the house payments, the Cadillac's.

"As for my uncle Sam...did you conveniently forget what he said just last night. Thanks to *your* husband, Barbara and I never have to worry about money again."

$

"The discussion is over," declared Fonso. "We are going to control the price of cottonseed and soybeans by buying up all the futures contracts we can get our hands on. We'll take delivery of some product at contract expiration, and roll the remaining contracts over and over. This way, we can control the final price of refined oil with international customers. When somebody tries to bid lower, we can lose a little, then make it up when the competitors are gone."

Now Auslander raised objections. "I'm not sure that's possible. There are numerous non-controllable supply and demand fluctuations, and other variables."

"Would you feel any better if we controlled 85 percent of the product supply and we controlled 85 percent of the refined vegetable oil production?"

"Certainly," responded Auslander. "But absorbing that many futures contracts could require a massive international sales program."

"Fred, has anybody got a better book of vegetable oil customers? Just a matter of adding some sales guys we can train. Plus, when it comes to closing the tough ones, we pretty much know every decision maker's hot button"

Auslander was leaning, but still skeptical. "We're also going to need an enormous amount of capital on demand. Manny Hanny has already said, no more. I'm guessing the other banks will probably follow suit."

"We don't need those stuffy old banks," replied Fonso. "I've got two gigantic commodity firms storing their grain with us, and seven more to come. To a person, they've said they're happy to lend against inventories."

"At what interest rate?"

"It doesn't matter. So long as we control the supply of raw materials, keep manufacturing costs down, take a few gallons out of each order for the house, and set the selling prices, they'll always be profits. The only adjustment might be a smaller margin on larger volume. No matter how you slice it, we'll still net millions a month."

"Let's assume I buy your arguments," said Auslander. "How the hell are we going to corner product supply?

"Just a matter of lining up a friendly brokerage with clout and a staff of experienced commodity traders."

"Why the hell would someone want to risk their reputation?"

"Oldest reason in the world…greed."

For perhaps the first time, Auslander realized Fonso now personified greed gone mad.

April, 1958
Washington D.C.

IRS Chief Langston Kiel sat at the end of a large, government-issue, mahogany conference table. He stared at the seven senior agents who had just finished their report.

"So, John, let me get this straight. Mr. Gravenese owns a series of companies engaged in vegetable oil refining that had over half billion dollars in sales in each of the last two tax years, and he got paid $30,000 a year?"

"Correct, Sir, said the wavy-haired gentleman with granny glasses.

"And, because they had so many business deductions, International Grain, Transworld Refining, and whatever, paid absolutely no federal income taxes."

John nodded. A second, deep-toned, agent spoke. "Mr. Kiel, when we did our audit, we were also struck by the fact that five key employees — the same five — in all the companies, accumulated huge, deductible travel bills."

"Do we have enough to request an audit?"

The second agent leaned back in his chair. "In my opinion, no. Their documentation meets every requirement. There's not even a mathematical error."

"Do it anyway. Maybe the audit demand will send a message."

A frustrated Kiel got up and walked over to the window, and stared at the Capitol Building down Constitution Avenue. "I wonder what President Lincoln would have thought about citizen Gravenese?"

May, 1958
Little Italy, NYC

While Kiel stewed in Washington, Anthony Palumbo fumed at the Ravenite Social Club in Little Italy.

"Two years, and you don't say nothing?" screamed Palumbo at a quivering man. The man was the driver who had delivered the mob's gift of Dom Pérignon to Fonso for paying back their investment ahead of schedule in late 1956.

The driver cowered. "I didn't know nothing. The place just looked like a bunch of tanks with smoke. I just happened to see the story about income-tax evasion yesterday in the *Daily News*. I said to myself, how many tank farms are there in Bayonne? Maybe you should know."

Chapter 58

In 1792, 24 of New York's most powerful financial brokers created the Buttonwood Agreement, which codified an ethical, organized process to generate wealth through the purchase and sale of company securities based upon a fixed commission schedule.

This loosely organized group evolved into the New York Stock Exchange. Over time, brokers paid to become NYSE members. The high costs of commission trading were purposely designed to discouraged broad public participation. The Exchange members maintained a clubby, elite behavior for almost 150 years. The growth of the middle class after World War II caused security trading to explode. Brokerage back rooms that processed trades were fraught with errors, as computers did not become common place until 1968.

To protect customer holdings, and meet all of their financial obligations, New York Stock Exchange members are required to maintain a net capital reserve fund based on an industry-standard process. Securities are valued *at market prices, less a discount, based on each security's risk characteristics. This discounted value is considered the minimum liquidation value of the securities.*

The member is expected to maintain that value, plus a reasonable cushion, as a net capital reserve in the event of a liquidation demand. Should a member's reserve fall below that minimum, he must report its status to the Exchange within the same business day, or, in the case of weekends, prior to the next trading day.

June, 1958
Wall Street, NYC

Donna's research identified that there were two New York Stock Exchange members who might have the appetite and capacity to wheel and deal large amounts of futures contracts.

Fonso decided to focus on the respected firm of Ira Upton & Company, located near the corner of Trinity and Board Streets in the heart of Wall Street. They were rumored to be less risk-averse than other NYSE members.

The firm was founded by the elitist Ira Upton. In 1936, Upton had married Enid Annenberg, the sister of one America's wealthiest media moguls, Walter Annenberg, who owned a number of ultra-successful media properties including the *Philadelphia Inquirer*, the *New York Racing Form* and *TV Guide*, among others.

By 1938, Enid had convinced most of her brother's equally wealthy circle of friends to grow their fortunes at Upton & Company. By 1950, Upton had become one of the largest brokerage firms on Wall Street. They had an impressive book of 30,000 high-net-worth customers. Many had successfully used margin loans to buy and sell additional stock at a profit. Upton was also known to have a strong capital reserve that met all NYSE requirements in case of client default.

Despite the firm's success, Ira Upton struggled with a variety of ailments, and was forced to retire in 1956. He appointed the uninspired, bespectacled, fiscally conservative Morton Edgars to replace him. Edgars, a third-generation Harvard Business School graduate, did an adequate job of growing the firm, but, when he was introduced to Fonso, he was still searching to place his own imprint on the firm.

$

Fonso's relationship with Upton & Company started uneventfully. Donna called their general number to ask for Mr. Edgars. She was transferred to his secretary, Gloria Day.

"My husband and I are seeking a company with interested in trading commodities." Gloria assumed Edgars had little interest in the unglamorous world of commodity contracts. "Mrs. Gravenese, I'm not sure you are in the right place," said Gloria condescendingly. "We do have account minimums."

"Is $500,000 minimum enough?" responded the feisty Donna.

Gloria's tone softened. "Mrs. Gravenese, can you hold on for a minute while I locate Mr. Edgars?" She interrupted Edgars's weekly staff meeting. She whispered in his ear. Edgars knew nothing about commodities, other than they had something to do with animals, farmers, and a bunch of lowlives he wouldn't be seen dead around. But $500,000!

A smiling Edgars picked up the phone. "Mrs. Gravenese, so nice of you to think of Upton & Company. I'm sure our services can accommodate you and your husband. I suggest you stop by at your convenience, take a tour of the place, and meet the account person we'll assign to you. At Upton, clients are like family."

Edgars told Gloria to schedule a time right away. "Get Thompson Pierce to run the meeting and the tour. I think he knows something about commodities."

Soon Pierce was standing in front of Edgars. "Mort, why me? I don't know shit about commodities."

"Neither do I, but who cares? A 5 percent commission on a half a million dollars, churned four or five times a year, should keep that daughter of yours at Smith."

$

Two days later, Fonso showed up in his usual crumpled black suit and horned rimmed glasses. Pierce got three traders and two support staff to volunteer as Upton's commodity trading division. He'd done his research on Fonso, the good, the bad, and the ugly. He knew Fonso was not the typical Upton customer, that Fonso had built one of the largest refinery tanks fields in America just across the Hudson River. He looked past the government irregularities, and the rumored mob associations.

Pierce began to describe trends and process, Fonso interrupted. "One thing you guys gotta learn is I have the attention span of a gnat," he said. "Bottom line, I've got oil orders to fill around the world, right now. So, I need to purchase some short-term commodity contracts. Are you up for it?"

"Of course," said Pierce. "We just need to open an account, and..."

Fonso again interrupted, "I know, I know, and make sure the funds clear."

"Nothing personal, sir."

Fonso pulled a Manny Hanny cashier's check out of his pocket, and flipped it across the table "You guys good with a cashier's check from Manny Hanny?"

"Good as gold," smiled Pierce.

"Let's start with 75,000 bushels of soybeans, and a 125,000 bushels of cottonseeds. Last time I looked, they're both selling around a buck a bushel. Offer 90 cents."

Pierce looked down at the check. It was for $500,000.

$

While Fonso was wheeling and dealing at Upton, two IRS auditors paid Auslander a visit at the Bayonne facility. They hand delivered a highly unusual demand for a three-year audit of all 12 Gravenese-related companies.

"Gentlemen, you're making a time-consuming mistake. Every audit has shown no change. This request borders on harassment. What you're asking will take weeks to pull together. To say nothing of the expense," said Auslander.

The taller agent said, "That's why the audit date is 28 days away." The two men then turned and left.

Fonso arrived not long after. Auslander explained the IRS demand. Fonso circled his office like a caged lion. "Sons of a bitches. They've got nothing else to fucking do. They should focus on murders and drug dealers, not a bunch of businessmen in Bayonne. Call Riperton. Tell him to fuck these guys up in court so bad that they can't tie their own shoes. Nobody pulls this shit on Fonso, and gets away with it."

$

About the same time, Lomiscolo and Lentini were getting a report about Fonso's brokerage activities from Palumbo at Gene and Georgetti's steak house on Franklin Street in Chicago. According to Palumbo, a cousin who worked in the Upton mailroom had seen a note detailing the size and importance of their new client.

"Since we don't know anything about it, I assume Fonso wanted it to keep it private."

Lomiscolo was furious. He stabbed his knife into the thick, rare New York strip steak sitting in front of him. "That wasn't our deal. That little bowling ball has disrespected all of us."

The men talked about punitive options. Lomiscolo didn't like any of them. "Let me think about it. We need something really creative to catch this greedy fu... attention." Lomiscolo caught him about to curse. "Now Joey. Watch your language. Anthony and I don't want you to sound like one of those common criminals."

$

Soon after the market opened, Pierce was on the phone to Fonso. "How's my new favorite client this morning? Just wanted to tell you we executed your first Upton & Co trade. Got your seeds at 80 cents a bushel. I think we saved you about thirty grand."

Chapter 59

August, 1958
Global Express Headquarters, NYC

Though he just didn't realize it at the time, the next call to Fonso would change his life forever.

His new assistant explained there was someone on the phone trying to raise contributions for a political campaign. She proudly announced, "But I got rid of him." Fonso realized Senator Rutherman had called.

"Where did you get that broad?" roared Rutherman, "She's one hell of a step down from Josephine."

Rutherman explained the events of his past few weeks. He had been named made chairman of the Senate's new Economic Revival Committee. The goal of the committee was to maintain America's favorable balance of trade by stimulating exports. As such, he had been meeting with relevant corporate leaders. The day before he had met with Archie Paulson, Chairman & CEO of one of America's best-known international corporations, the GLOBEX Company. Most people traveling overseas used GLOBEX traveler's checks as currency, and the prestigious GLOBEX credit card was heavily used by affluent business travelers. But despite its prestigious brand name, GLOBEX was losing money.

Rutherman explained that GLOBEX had created a new subsidiary that was a perfect fit with the committee's mandate.

Paulson knew the elimination of the Food for Peace program left numerous regimes — Egypt, Poland, Spain, Pakistan — with a gapping need for farm commodities, which America continued to produce in abundance. These leaders knew maintaining their power and personal wealth was directly related to their citizens having full stomachs. And refined multi-use vegetable oil, the kind Fonso specialized in, was on everybody's shopping list...at the right price.

Paulson concluded a commodity field warehousing subsidiary under the GLOBEX name could be a lucrative operation, if structured and operated correctly.

Historically, banks acted as lenders to the commodities growers and processors, with the goods acting as collateral. To protect themselves, banks insisted that independent specialist storage companies safeguard the goods from pilferage, and issue certified receipts to banks and other lenders that acted as security on customer loans.

It was common for a storage company to establish a field warehouse on the property of the borrowing company by simply placing its name on designated area and to co-opt certain customer employees onto their own payroll.

There were glaring security defects in this system. Fraudulent warehouse receipts, and lax oversight by the lenders themselves, were certainly around before Fonso. But the pudgy, homely, bespeckled Fonso brought these fraudulent practices to unimagined heights.

Paulson hired an experienced white-collar banking executive, Braxton Fields, to transform his vision into a profitable operating company. Fields had a long and successful career in transactional lending — but he knew little else.

Fields' first marketing efforts focused on signing up private companies typically classified as higher-risk. Their lower credit rating would allow GLOBEX to make loans at higher rates, and thus generate higher profits than traditional lenders.

GLOBEX operating profits — the spread between the cost of money and the customer interest rate — would be shared equally between the GLOBEX Bank and GLOBEX Warehousing.

Paulson structured Field's compensation to be 10 percent of the subsidiary's operating profits. The more the subsidiary earned, the more Fields could earn. There were no income ceilings. The 53-year-old Fields saw his position as an opportunity to maintain his lavish lifestyle, and fully fund a cushy retirement.

"When I heard about the GLOBEX plans, I said to myself this is tailor made for Fonso, and his companies," said Fonso.

The sound of cash registers rang in his ears. Thanks to GLOBEX, he would now be able to buy unlimited amounts of soybean and cotton seed oil futures, and make money on contract spreads. He could also borrow money to add more storage tanks, which would allow him to refine more oil, and complete more deals with his corrupt network of international decision makers. Thanks to his participation in Food for Peace, he knew precisely how to steal a few bucks on every gallon shipped.

"What's the next step?" Fonso asked Rutherman.

"*I'll* organize meeting Fields at your farm," replied Rutherman....and I hope *You'll* remember I'm about to run for a second term."

$

Donna did some more discreet research and found that GLOBEX warehousing was already hemorrhaging money, and Fields's job was in peril. The subsidiary had built overheads without one client.

Fonso turned the charm on the desperate executive. As they walked through the tank field, Fonso banged his hand on the metal exterior. "Hear that?'" he said. "That's the sound of lost opportunity. I've got all these tanks that could be filled with refined oil, ready to ship to open purchase orders."

Fields bit. "What do you mean, "open purchase orders?"

Fonso talked about the contacts made during the Food for Peace days. "I don't want to sound like I'm blowing smoke"— which was exactly what he was doing — "but I don't think there is a vegetable-oil processor anywhere in the world with the combination of storage assets, refining capacity, and decision-maker contacts we have."

He led Fields through a maze of refining pipes and holding areas, belching refined oil that workmen were pouring into 55-gallon drums.

Fonso waved to a man to come over. "Hey Sam, say hi to Braxton Fields from GLOBEX. Braxton, this is my refinery foreman, Sam Magro. We've been together for a decade. There is no one that knows more about the operations side of International Grain than Sam."

"Fonso, stop with the compliments," teased Sam. "It's unbecoming. Besides, it could cost you a big raise." The men laughed.

On the way back to his office, Fonso continued his performance. "You know the best part of this business? These guys are like family. They know I've taken my savings and built this state of the art facility. We don't owe anybody anything." In Fonso's mind, the mob's investment was in the distant past.

Fields thought he had discovered the goose that laid the golden egg. "So, what do you need?"

"Well…we need more working capital to buy and crush more soybeans and cottonseeds. And more working capital to the refine the vegetable oil we need to fill the orders sitting on my desk."

Fields saw dollar signs. He began his own pitch. "That kind of lending is pretty unconventional. We might have to charge a few points more."

Fonso knew exactly how to play the game with someone with Fields's ego. "Understood. Just try not to kill a good customer."

"We'll also need to periodically audit inventories so that we can justify our secured lending."

"Not a problem," smiled Fonso, pointing at the tank field. "International Grain is an open book."

$

Fonso's employees demonstrated their new inventory management system to the GLOBEX auditors. The chubby men, who looked like they hadn't missed a meal in weeks, were led to several different preselected tanks in specific areas of the farm.

"To save you guys some time," said Sam casually, "I've randomly selected some tanks around the farm. There are faucets at the base with large holding drums. Open those, and you can see, feel, and taste, the quality of the oil in our storage tanks."

Sam pointed to a long winding ladder affixed to each tank in the farm. "John," said Sam, pointing to a man in a soiled tee shirt with muscles bulging from both arms, "will escort you to the top. He'll also show you how to use the measuring apparatus to identify how much oil is in each 500,000-gallon tank."

The two inspectors looked up. "How many of these do you want us to do?"

"As many as you want. It's your audit."

The men huffed and puffed their way to the top of the first tank. Their equipment indicated the tank was at 98.3 percent of capacity. They each made a few notes, and carefully began their descent. About midway, the first man slipped on an oily step, and painfully bounced down the remaining steps on his back.

"Christ, you guys need to be more careful," said Sam at the bottom. "At least your papers are still in intact."

The men nodded as they dusted themselves off.

"Just four to go," smiled John. "Ready."

The senior auditor spoke. "I think we're seen enough."

$

Fields and Fonso each received reports of the day's activity.

The GLOBEX auditors told Fields they had never seen such quantities and such organization.

Sam told Fonso that filling the tanks with hundreds of thousands of gallons of saltwater, topped and bottomed with premium oil, worked like a charm.

Fonso asked how the specially rigged measuring rods had worked, and how many tanks the GLOBEX men actually audited.

"The rods worked fine at the one tank they inspected," smiled Sam. "As did the oil we poured on the steps — one of the dumb fuckers bounced down 45 steps on his fat butt."

Chapter 60

Gamal Abdul Nasser Hussein became president of Egypt in 1956 by overthrowing the monarchy. He was pro-nationalization, pro-socialism, and cultural modernization. Despite ruling with an iron hand, there was little corruption by the standards of the day.

Nasser-Hussein's winning blend of populism and dictatorial tendencies was criticized by detractors for numerous human-right violations. But he was revered by ordinary citizens, who applauded major projects like the ground-breaking Aswan Dam, and his belief in revolutionary freedoms for women. He dreamed his vision for the true modern Egypt would make him the defacto leader of a chaotic Arab world, embroiled in territorial disputes and religious wars for centuries.

Nasser Hussein appointed the popular, light-skinned moderate, Anwar Sadat, his trusted Secretary of State. The men shared the same views, and a proud Sadat rapidly became the second most powerful figure in Egypt. He also held a number of other influential positions in the National Assembly.

January, 1960
Cairo, Egypt

Fonso pitched the idea of increasing the amount he could borrow on his margin account to his new best friend at Upton, Thompson Pierce.

"Fonso, we love your business. But there isn't much history yet."

"Didn't you make a nice commission on the trade?"

"Yes, but…"

"Suppose I told you I already had a huge guaranteed customer order waiting for my refined vegetable oil?"

"Where?"

"Spain and Pakistan."

"You gotta be kidding. You want me to ask Mort to extend your credit because you've got orders from a bunch of bullfighters and turban tops," said Pierce, showcasing his white Anglo-Saxon prejudices.

"Suppose I told you all the inventory we acquire and refine would be certified by GLOBEX. Would that provide Upton & Co some comfort?" Fonso was starting to use some Wall Street lingo. If he was going to be a major securities player, he needed to sound like one of them.

$

At first, Edgars was reluctant. "We've got 30,000 customers, and we've only given margin accounts to a handful. This guy walks in the door two weeks ago…and you're talking about giving him a million dollars in credit."

Pierce explained calmly about the commissions they already made, and those to come.

"I really don't get the commodities market," said Edgars. "If it rains too much, or gets too hot, prices go up. If we have a normal growing season, prices decline — and the guy who holds the contract to buy the stuff can lose his shirt."

Unlike Edgars, Pierce was actually starting to understand the subtleties of commodity trading. "Gravenese is buying futures contracts, so if things look like they are going to turn to shit, he cuts his losses by selling the contract before delivery.

"Let me put it this way. GLOBEX certifies his inventories, he's already got orders for the refined product, and our commissions during the next year can double our prior year's income."

$

Pierce called to inform Fonso he was now a privileged Upton client with a 55 percent margin account and a low interest rate.

It was now Fonso's turn to perform. Those imaginary guaranteed contracts now needed to become reality. His first planned stop was Spain, where he had done substantial business during Food for Peace. Circumstances had changed. Some of Franco's social programs had started to take hold and unemployment was down.

Fonso discovered Minister Aiza was no longer easy prey. "We thank you for past efforts," said Aiza, 'but, we now supply our own needs, and our currency is recognized." Aiza said. "Nevertheless, we never forget our friends. That is why I would like introduce you to the Egyptian President, Colonel Gamal Abdel Nassar. He has a new Minster of State, Anwar Sadat, who might have a need for your services."

Having never traveled to the heart of the Arab world, Fonso wasn't sure. "Minister Aiza, thanks, but would you be offended if I said no thanks?"

"You made money in Spain… Correct? Lots of money…Correct? I promise you can do the same in Egypt. My friend is easy to deal with."

$

Even Ricco had objections.

"Egypt? We're going to sell vegetable oil to a bunch of Bedouins. They'll probably leave us out in the middle of the Sahara Dessert. Isn't there any other fucking place we can sell our shit?"

"Ricco," I'm not sure," said Fonso calmly, "I think Aiza was trying to say Egypt may be an untapped gold mine."

"Tell you what," said Ricco. "One trip. There is a limit to how far I'll go for money." Fonso felt differently.

$

All Fonso knew about Egypt was that the country needed refined vegetable oil because farming was a low-yield cottage industry due to the harsh desert climate. Fonso and Ricco's first clue that Cairo was not Caracas was the billboard of a

349

schoolboy kissing a school girl on the way in from the airport."

The government driver looked in the rearview mirror. He saw Fonso and Ricco with open mouths.

"You understand? asked the driver.

"No, not really," said Fonso.

"That is a toy ad for our famous department store, Omar Effendi. It says each child is very happy they received a present from the other, thanks to Effendi."

Fonso's meeting with Sadat was pleasant and businesslike. Quickly, Fonso learned Sadat was a straight shooter.

"Egypt occupies a unique place in Arab history. We are an important *center of learning and intellect*. A place where the Western and Eastern way of life meet."

As the men lunched, Ricco got up to look out the window, hand inside his jacket, finger on the trigger. To his surprise there was no chaos, no chanting crowds. It was just a warm, sunny day in Cairo, with people walking to and fro.

Sadat laughed. "Mr. Cicolo, there are no guns. This is not Caracas."

Fonso appeared surprised. "How did you..."

"Americans are funny. They do not realize leaders talk. Your South American adventure was a humorous story in our newspapers."

Fonso didn't know what to say. The gracious Sadat came to the rescue.

"Our needs are quite substantial. We will do much business if you treat us fairly, and with respect. We ask nothing more. You will learn

Egypt can be an International Grain customer, and a friend."

By the time dessert arrived, Fonso had closed his largest sale ever — 500,000 gallons of oil for 12 months at the current world market price. Consequently, Fonso had an honest two-dollar a gallon profit, and Egypt had a predictable cost. No additional payments were hinted and none were offered.

Sadat, recognizing the weakness of the Egyptian pound, volunteered a final price adjustment. "How much do need to add to the price to cover the currency disparity?"

Fonso didn't have a clue. Sadat had a reasonable suggestion. "The pound is currently trading at a 25 percent discount to the U.S. dollar. Shall we use that figure?"

Fonso nodded. The men shook hands and departed. Fonso was ecstatic.

On their return to Bayonne, their flights were interrupted by two different storm fronts that required unscheduled stops in Rome and Dublin before crossing the Atlantic. The exhausted men arrived home 36 hours late. After a short nap, Fonso went to the office. His new secretary said the bank had called, and that there was a wire transfer from Egypt awaiting his acceptance.

$

Fonso called Auslander to talk about what had just transpired in Egypt.

"This stuff is amazing," said Auslander. "You couldn't make it up."

The two men did some quick calculations. "I guessing about a million dollars in profit a month, after all costs," said Auslander.

"I think that covers about another 24 million in futures contracts," replied Fonso, thinking about controlling the world's marketplace.

When the money cleared, Fonso instructed Pierce to buy even more futures contracts. Pierce became a bit concerned. This was the largest single customer transaction in the history of Upton & Co.

Before committing, Pierce reviewed the customer order with Edgars. Despite Edgars' lack of commodity knowledge, he drooled at the prospect of the enormous commissions. He approved the transaction. As Pierce readied to go back to the trading desk, Edgars smiled and said, "It's going to be one hell of a Christmas around here.

Chapter 61

January, 1960
Bayonne, NJ

Futures financing had become a game of Monopoly. Fonso owned GLOBEX, Upton, Belgium-Cargill, Bunge, and several of America's iconic corporations with names like Pillsbury and Proctor & Gamble. Could he add banks with names like Manufacturers and Chase?

The phone rang. It was Aemon O'Brien at Manufacturers Hanover. "Just thought I'd call to say hello. The Senator tells me you guys are bursting at the seams."

Fonso smelled it was a business-development call. People don't just call to say hello. He decided to go fishing.

"He's kind. But I must say, things are going pretty well, particularly since we cut the deal with GLOBEX and Belgium-Cargill."

"GLOBEX? He didn't mention that."

Fonso went on about financing, futures, and most of all, his unique international niche. "All that hard work servicing the Government in the Free Lunch Program and Food for Peace has given us an understanding of emerging international markets that is rather unique," he said. "Plus, you wouldn't recognize the tank farm. We have something like 125 storage tanks."

"What kind of inventory can you handle?"

"My head operations guy — you remember Sam Magro, Donna's uncle, been with me a long time — I think he calculated something like 65 million gallons."

"Christ!" exclaimed O'Brien. "What the hell does a vegetable oil refinery do with that kind of space?"

"You sell a lot of shit to places like Egypt, Pakistan, and Turkey."

O'Brien paused. "Maybe we should get together?"

Fonso went for the close.

"No disrespect, Aemon, but for what purpose. I'm on the road quite a bit. You understand business development?"

"Did the Senator mention my new role at the bank?" He did, but Fonso played dumb. "He did mention something about you working at another branch. Just don't remember the particulars."

"It's a little more than just another branch. Thanks to a business like yours I'm now head of commercial business development at our headquarters on Park Avenue."

"Congrats," smiled Fonso. "Boy from New Jersey makes it big."

O'Brien invited Fonso to lunch in the executive dining suite. He suggested he'd bring along a few colleagues. That maybe Manny Hanny could syndicate a secured lending facility. Fonso played dumb.

"What do you mean syndicate?"

O'Brien explained. "These days all the U.S. banks want to get a piece of the growing international segment. At the same time, it's new territory, so we all want to hedge our risk. That's why we work together on the larger credit deals."

"What kind of line are you thinking?"

"Depends on your cash flow and revenues. What are your projected revenues for this year?"

"I'm not sure. Fred's got those numbers. Something like $400 million." Fonso actually knew to the penny.

"Holy cow, I had no idea."

"So, like I said, what kind of credit facility are we talking about?"

"I'm guessing if we syndicate with Barclay's in London and Deutsche Bank in Frankfurt, we could create a $50 million revolver. Would that work?"

Fonso projected calm, although his pulse pounded. "Hang on, Aemon, let me check my schedule over the next few weeks."

After he confirmed a date, Fonso leaned back in his chair and looked out at his vegetable-oil empire. He wondered incredulously...is it possible a kid from the Bronx with little formal education has stumbled into the financial scheme of a lifetime?

$

March, 1960
IRS Offices, NYC

A Request-For-Audit letter from the IRS had become commonplace around International Grain. But this one was different. For one thing, it was addressed to Auslander, as the tax preparer. Secondly, it did not detail the typical areas under audit. Rather, it requested copies of the last three years of operating income calculations for International Grain, and all of its related companies. Last, and perhaps most unusual, the letter requested Auslander to report to Room 1526 at IRS regional headquarters at 290 Foley Square in lower Manhattan, to discuss his calculations.

$

Room 1526 was unremarkable, with gray enamel walls, dated furniture, and four faces with pained expressions at the end of a conference table.

After formal introductions, the meeting became a question-and-answer attack and counter-attack. The ranking IRS agent spoke first. The others then chimed in.

Q. "Mr. Auslander, we understand you have been preparing Mr. Gravense's business returns for the past ten years."

A. "Yes."

Q. "How many times have you been audited?"

A. "Ten."

Q. "Does that strike you odd?"

A. "Should it?"

Q. "What were Mr. Gravense's approximate gross sales last year?"

A. "$ 472 million."

Q. "And, the year before?"

A. "382 million."

Q. "And the year before that?"

A. "Perhaps, $280 million."

Q. "And how much did he pay in federal income tax during that three-year period?"

A. "I'm not sure, I'd have to look that up."

Q. "Would $7,300 sound about right?"

A. "Possibly."

Q. "You do realize that is a tax rate of less than one-tenth of 1 percent?"

A. "His company is in an early growth phase. He is reinvesting most of his capital for growth."

Q. "Then how is it that Mr. Joseph Lomiscolo and his friends in Chicago have declared on their tax returns, and under oath, that Mr. Gravenese paid them almost $5 million out of partner profit distributions?"

A. "They misunderstood, they were never partners. There is no partnership agreement."

Q. "Than what were these gentlemen, and I use that termly lightly?"

A. "They were investors who received an early return of capital, and accrued interest on their loan to Mr. Gravenese."

Q. "There were no additional profit distributions… on or off the books?"

A. 'Have you found any? Because if they did, and didn't report it, that would be fraud."

There was a pause. The men huddled.

Q. "We'd like to turn to another matter. We understand you are a dual American and Swiss citizen. Is that correct?"

A. "Yes."

Q. "According to the company's own travel records, Mr. Gravenese, his wife, and a few other company executives took multiple trips to Switzerland during the last few years. Do you have any comments on that observation?"

A. "Am I supposed to?"

Q. "Doesn't it seem odd that everybody went to the same country? A country known for its private banking abuses."

A. "I believe the word is client confidentiality."

Q. "Again, doesn't it strike you odd that all these people, including yourself, visited the same city, Zurich, on multiple occasions?"

A. "Are you trying to imply something? Are you making an accusation? What are we doing exactly?"

Q. "Needless to say, our hands are partially tied by Swiss Banking laws. But it seems to us that somehow, there has been a gross understatement of taxes due."

A. "Are you saying, Mr. Gravenese is guilty of willfully evading income taxes?"

Q. "No. That would be defamation of character."

A. "Precisely."

Q. "Last question! On the numerous occasions that you and the Gravenese family visited your brother at Credit Suisse, did you make any deposits above the legal limits of $10,000 U.S?"

A. "Did I say we visited my brother?"

Q. "You realize you are being most un-cooperative?"

A. "Is that a question?"

"Mr. Auslander, you are free to go," said the group spokesman. "But let us state for the record, that we believe you and Mr. Gravenese have willfully, and, I might add, skillfully, evaded many laws. But be forewarned, this department will not rest until justice is served."

$

Auslander concluded it was time to flee America.

Two days later, bags packed, he called Fonso's secretary to inform her he had caught a flu, and would be bedridden for a few days. Four hours later he was on a plane to Zurich. His first stop was to see brother Wilfred at the bank. Wilfred pulled a Fendi suitcase out of his closet. "I believe this is yours. Here's the withdrawal slip for your records."

Auslander looked at the slip. It was for $5 million. "Did you leave anything in the account for Ricco?"

"Ten dollars," smiled Wilfred devilishly. "In case they want to replenish the account, they don't have to redo all the paperwork."

Auslander chuckled. "Fair enough. Ricco earned every dollar."

Auslander fumbled as he tried to pick up all his bags. "Brother, why fuss with those other bags? Fendi is really all you need."

Chapter 62

August, 1960
Wall Street, NYC

"He has no balls..." screamed Fonso.

The man he had made rich disrespected him by leaving him to spar with those peckerheads at the IRS. But that was easy. The real issue was International Grain's complex corporate structure. It was filled with tax-avoidance subtleties only Auslander could decipher. And he hadn't been gracious enough to leave the operating manual.

Fonso had no idea that Auslander had cleaned out the account in Zurich. Fonso called Wilfred in Zurich, looking for Auslander. Wilfred played dumb. Yes, Fred had been by. Yes, he took a withdrawal. But he had no idea how much. Fonso asked Wilfred to check the balance. Wilfred put Fonso on hold to simulate a delay.

"There's only $10 left."

"How much did the fucker take?"

"About 5 million."

"How did *you* let all this happen?"

"I'm not my brother's keeper. I was in a board meeting when he came and went."

"Lomiscolo and his boys will find him."

Wilfred knew about the IRS threats, and the Lomiscolo deposition. "I'm not sure they'll be receptive to your overtures. From what I hear, they were really upset with the IRS audit results."

"What are you talking about?"

Wilfred made believe there was a connection problem. "Fonso, can you hear me? Fonso, are you there?" Then he hung up.

$

After the Egyptian deal became public knowledge, the international orders started to roll in. To maintain momentum, Fonso made sure prospective customers knew he was willing to deal in local currencies and apply market-rate U.S. dollar adjustments.

As usual, Fonso's initial focus was on increasing profit margins of product sold and delivered. He came up with two new ideas. First, he had Sam ship the oil in used barrels, rather than quality leak-proof containers. Since he owned the shipping company, he thought final inspections by shipping-line personnel would pass with flying colors.

His second profit enhancement was to ship 10 percent less on each order. Then, split the projected revenue equally with the buyer's own personnel, who transported the product to their storage facilities.

All worked smoothly until a greedy manager from Karachi appeared at Fonso's office unannounced. "You cheated me on the rebate. I checked the selling price of oil. Instead of 5 percent, you paid only 3 percent."

Fonso called Accounting. It turned out the man was correct. He wanted to maintain the man's good will. "Mohammed, I'm so sorry. Accounting says you are right. They estimate the difference is about $80,000 U.S."

"Similar to my calculation," said the well-dressed turban-topped man.

"Why don't we have some lunch, while they make transfer arrangements with our banks."

"I say yes to lunch, but no to transfer. I prefer cash."

"Cash it is," smiled Fonso. "But, that may take a little longer."

"Then, let us make lunch longer," replied the man.

Fonso's assistant ordered a car to take the men to the El Morocco Club in Manhattan. Mohammed and Fonso dined and drank until almost 4 pm. On the way back, the man commented, "You spend more on one lunch than we spend for a week of dinners in my country."

Mohammed wanted to subtly send an additional message. "Maybe you might also want to tell the owner, zebras are not just black and white, some are gray and white."

When they returned to Fonso's office, most people had left for the day. He reached into his office drawer and pulled out a manila envelope with a clasp. "Mohammed, I believe this is yours."

Mohammed took the envelope. "Don't you count to make sure?"

Fonso shook his head. "In business, I've learned you've got to trust people."

The man put the unopened envelope in his attaché. "Then, I will do the same. I wish to learn the American way."

$

As the orders rolled in, Fonso became fiscally irrational. Some said he personified, "Greed Gone Mad."

To finance his madness, he created his own pyramid scheme. Fonso would buy huge numbers of futures contracts with secured loans — at above-market interest rates — from his now willing pool of 51 lenders with high-profile names like Chase Manhattan and Bank of America. When the loans came due, Fonso would simply borrow from another lender to pay the prior lender. Before long, his debt service — the amounts he allocated to paying loan interest — exploded exponentially. But lenders were reluctant to raise solvency issues because they were collecting millions in interest. They also took comfort in the fact that 100 percent the vegetable oil inventory was secured by good-as-gold GLOBEX Company warehouse receipts.

In less than two years, Fonso controlled 90 percent of all the futures contracts on the two major exchanges.

$

Fields became a hero at GLOBEX. His subsidiary's income from product inspections and issuing accredited inventory receipts increased from tens of thousands to tens of millions. The more fees he created, the larger his personal compensation grew, and the less carefully his staff measured the inventory in Fonso's tanks.

At one point, GLOBEX top management expressed concern about the subsidiary's rapid growth. So Fields, concerned about his credibility and his compensation, ordered a surprise inspection of the tank farm, which lasted an entire week. On the first day, a Saturday, his inspectors found water in the first five tanks they checked. However, when they returned to continue after the weekend break, they found nothing suspicious in the next 65 tanks. But to be thorough, the inspectors took samples from five random tanks for a detailed chemical analysis.

One of Fonso's faithful lieutenants overheard the inspectors talking, and immediately told Fonso. By the time the inspectors finished sampling, Fonso had convinced Fields to use International Grain's chief chemist, Mario Manzatti, to analysis the liquids. Fonso explained, "Mario and his staff are probably the most qualified lab technicians in the entire New York Tri-State area." Fields readily accepted Fonso's seemingly persuasive rationale. An official report was issued, stating the initial liquids found findings in the first five tanks was attributed to steam that had condensed into water because of a section of broken steam pipes.

To forestall potential future rumors, Fields hired the well-respected CPA of Williams, James & Sells to complete an operational audit. Again, Fonso got wind of the plan from one of his loyal

IGC employees that had also been hired by GLOBEX to work for them.

Fonso made sure all the handpicked International Grain employees were properly briefed and incentivized before the actual audit. He hired a team of educators who spent five days and nights teaching key employees how to discuss International Grain's everyday use of industry-standard operating practices.

The CPA's official opinion stated that the International Grain organization plan provided for "the usual segregation of functional responsibilities, the application of reasonable accounting controls, and the assignment of qualified personnel for commensurate tasks."

Fonso rewarded each employee who attended the training sessions a $5,000 bonus, almost 15 percent of their annual base salary, for working overtime.

$

Unknowingly, Upton traders also played their part well. At first they remained curiously silent about Fonso's blatant disregard for commodity price fluctuations. About three months into their relationship, Upton Managing Director Morton Edgars insisted that Pierce challenge Fonso's trading resolve and financial acumen.

Pierce called Fonso. "Mort and I appreciate your business, but we also know commodity trading is not for the faint of heart. So we felt we should check in. We all realize the inexplicable spike in commodity futures has cost you guys tens of thousands of dollars over the last four trades."

Fonso always had a plausible answer. "First of all Thompson, I appreciate the call. It's good to know the pros are watching our back. I guess it's appropriate to explain the International Grain's business philosophy. God knows, we are not your traditional traders... make a buck here and there, then vanish."

Thompson laughed. Fonso poured it on. "As you know, our core business is refining and selling vegetable oil in the international marketplace. Our trading strategy is to make sure we have constant supply of raw materials, at a reasonable price. We make our profit on refining and shipping, so if from time to time our raw costs spike a bit, that's okay. We more than make up for those increased costs on the product sale side."

Since Fonso always seemed to have the money to cover his margins when due, Thompson just let it go. He never realized that Fonso was borrowing at a high rate of interest from his other sources to keep Upton & Co whole.

Over time, Pierce and his boss, Edgars, became blinded by the unprecedented commissions they were earning. So they were foolishly willing to join International Grain's growing list of lenders.

Also, Upton Partners were so confident about credibility of GLOBEX's warehouse receipts, they waived International Grain's obligation to make additional cash deposits to cover margin calls. Instead, they met the New York Stock Exchange reserve capital requirements themselves by borrowing the money from its own bankers.

When that source ran dry, they expanded the margin accounts of thousands of their own customers. The Upton broker pitch was simple — get a piece of the commodities pie before it's all gobbled up.

Chapter 63

November 1961
Bayonne, NJ

Fonso was sitting alone in his office when he heard a knock on the door.

Joe Lomiscolo, Mickey Lentini and Joe Palumbo stood in the doorway. They weren't happy. "You little motherfucker, what is all this?" asked Lomiscolo, pointing out the window toward the endless rows of tanks.

"It's *our* investment," said Fonso

"Never try to con a con man. This place is worth a shit pile more than $4 million plus a little interest," said Lomiscolo, referring to the mob's 50 percent silent-partner agreement.

"On paper it is, Joe. But that's only if and when we sell the farm." Palumbo pushed Fonso into a chair. "You little scumbag, I oughta…"

Ricco, who was walking the halls, heard the commotion. He pulled his gun and entered.

"Put that gun down, you idiot," urged Fonso, not wanting to risk a shootout. Fonso turned to Lomiscolo. "Joe, nothing's changed — a deal's a deal. The problem is that Auslander bolted after he met with the IRS, and I can't make heads or tails out of the numbers."

Lomiscolo paused. He knew the IRS met with Auslander, but he wasn't sure what to believe.

"Let's assume some of this is true. We want our share in 48 hours, with a reconciliation report — signed by you."

"No problem," replied Fonso, who turned to Ricco. "Go find Sam and our financial manager. The three of you prepare Joe's reconciliation for Monday morning."

"What time?" growled Lomiscolo.

"How about nine? We can agree the numbers, have a cup of espresso, and get the bank to issue a cashier's check.

$

Ricco exploded shortly after the boys left. "What the fuck did you just do? Magro and I don't know shit about accounting."

"Go hire a temp, put Sam's numbers into some kind of report," responded Fonso dismissively.

"It's Friday night. Where do you expect us to find an accountant and have something ready for Monday morning?"

"Just figure it out."

Ricco had daggers in his eyes. "One more thing. Don't ever fucking call me an idiot again. Understand?"

$

Ricco explained the urgency of the matter to Sam. "I told Fonso and Fred we were playing with fire," said Magro.

"Doesn't matter now." said Ricco.

Sam Magro's first cousin, Mario Esposito had a son named Johnny, who was an accounting major at nearby Hofstra University.

After a brief negotiation, they agreed to pay Johnny $1,000 to prepare a report over the weekend that met generally accepted accounting principles, and had the appropriate back-up documentation.

At 8 a.m. Monday morning, Johnny explained the projections to Fonso. "Best I can tell, you owe your partners about $262,000."

The number sounded way low to Fonso. "Did you reverse the inflated expenses?"

"How am I supposed to know what that is and how much they are?" asked Johnny.

Sam supported Johnny. "Fonso, the kid's right. The only guy who could possible know that is Auslander. And the information is probably all in his head."

Fonso turned to Ricco. "What about the second set of books and records in my closet?"

"Christ, I thought those were just the old Metz books."

"We've gotta go get them, and rework the numbers," said Fonso.

Johnny said he was exhausted.

"Will another thousand dollars give you some fucking energy?"

At 9 a.m., Lomiscolo walked in. "So."

"Jesus, Joe," said Fonso calmly. "We just discovered we missed adding back some inflated expenses we used with the IRS."

"How much?" glared Lomiscolo.

"We don't know for sure. Johnny has to get the information, and add it back to your report," said Fonso, waving the paper in front of Lomiscolo.

"Let me see that," snapped Lomiscolo, as he pulled the paper out of Fonso's hand. "$262,000!" said an outraged Lomiscolo. "Do you know who the fuck you are playing games with?"

"Tomorrow," said Fonso, getting nervous. "Tomorrow. Promise."

"No second chances." said Lomiscolo, slamming the door.

$

Victor Magro's funeral parlor had a full house.

Senator Rutherman was a popular figure throughout the state. His sudden heart attack on the way home from the Senate's winter session stunned everybody who knew him. He was in great shape, and seemed not to have a care in the world.

Father Don's tender homily included recollections of family moments, his patriotic service as a pilot during World War II, and his tireless efforts to help the Catholic Charities Boys Club.

The prayers and condolences lasted long after the usual closing time. Victor told Mary and Donna to head home. That he and Father would chat for a few more minutes, then he would close the place up and head home.

Father Don gently protested. "Victor, we can talk some other time. You should be with your wife and daughter."

"Father, we're all so busy these days, who knows when I'll see you again."

"Besides," joked Mary, "My husband needs to go to confession. He missed a Sunday Mass about seven years ago."

"I agree," said the priest, "Your husband is a kind, generous man. By the way, speaking of men, where is Fonso? He and the Senator were longtime friends."

"To be honest with you." said Donna, "I'm not sure. He just said he had something very important to deal with. But he said he'd definitely join us at the cemetery rites tomorrow."

"Good, good. I always liked your husband. Like the Senator, he's always been generous with our boys."

$

At 9:30 p.m., only Victor and Father Don remained.

Three masked men with semi-automatic weapons walked into the Senator's prayer room, and began shooting everywhere. Victor and Father headed for cover.

In the reign of bullets that followed, Father Don was hit several times in the back. He lifeless, bloody body slumped over the closed casket.

"Jesus Christ," said one of the gunmen, "We killed a fucking priest. We're going to hell."

"Ain't no such place," said another.

The men were distracted just long enough for Frank to pull out a gun out of his safe to defend himself. The three men started to exchange fire. The two men ran out of ammunition. Frank realized his good fortune, smiled, walked calmly up to the men, and pumped them full of lead until they were virtually unrecognizable, and he was out of ammunition.

The third man returned. It was his turn. He started

firing. "Die, you motherfucker, die." The police arrived and busted down the back door. The man made a beeline for the front door. Another hail of bullets. The shiny white funeral parlor porch was bathed in crimson.

$

While events at the funeral parlor raged, Fonso and Ricco were taking care of their own business.

They knew Lomiscolo comment about "no second chances" didn't bode well. Ricco called in two carloads of violent hoods brandishing machine guns to act as security reinforcements.

Ricco, Fonso, Sam, and Johnny stopped at Fonso's house to get the real books. Fonso knew they might be his lifeline. The entourage then dropped Sam and Johnny at Sam's house, and placed two armed guards in the shadows of the front porch. "See you guys at seven," said Fonso. "Be ready."

Fonso decided to stay at Ricco's for the evening. He thought that would be safer for him and Donna. Shortly, Donna's car violently crashed into Ricco's front porch. Bloodied and dazed, she got out and ran up the walk, screaming at the top of her lungs.

"You miserable bastard. "You slime of the earth. "You sick sack of shit."

Several neighbors heard the commotion and came running. Ricco called the local hospital to send an ambulance, which arrived in minutes. They tried to minister to the hysterical Donna. She took a swing at the paramedics.

"Sir," said one to Ricco. "We've got to restrain her, otherwise she's going to bleed out." Ricco pointed to Fonso. "That's the husband."

"I understand," said Fonso. "Do what you have to do."

One medic held the weakening Donna around the chest, and while the other placed a restraint around her arms. She stood kicking and screaming until she was tied down to the gurney and sedated.

"We'll meet you at the emergency room," said one of the medics. "We've got to get her stitched up quickly." Fonso jumped in the truck with them. Ricco followed in his car.

An hour later, she was stitched and resting comfortably. She regained consciousness. She looked around the hospital room, and noticed bandages on her arms and legs.

"Where am I?" she asked the attending nurse. Donna didn't seem to recall anything. The nurse wondered if the accident had caused post-traumatic amnesia. She tried to ask her a few questions. Donna's responses made no sense. She said she was on the way to meet her mother and father for dinner, when a truck pushed her off the road.

She looked at her bandages again, then looked at Fonso, who she thought was the doctor. "Doctor, how am I?"

The medical team had a consultation with Fonso. The decision was to sedate her so she could get a good night's sleep. Then they would perform some tests in the morning to better understand her status.

"Mr. Gravenese, why don't you go home. I'd say, we'll have some results by noon or so." Fonso thanked them. He and Ricco headed back to Ricco's.

$

By 10 a.m., Fonso had a detailed financial report for the mob, and a cashier's check for $8,330,000. He called Lomiscolo. A tall man in a stylish Burberry trench coat and wide brimmed felt hat arrived shortly thereafter. The man picked up the check. Not a word was spoken.

Fonso headed back to the hospital.

Part Seven
Days of Reckoning

Chapter 64

November, 196
Overlook Asylum, Essex, NJ

Fonso went straight to Donna's hospital room. The bed was empty. He assumed they were still doing the tests. A nurse entered. "And, sir, you are...?"

"I'm Mr. Gravenese. The patient's husband."

"I'm so sorry. They tried to call you right away, but nobody answered."

"Called me about what?" said a now shaken Fonso.

The nurse explained sometime during the evening, Donna had awoken, and tried to leave the hospital in her medical gown. When the nurses tried to calm her down, Donna pulled a surgical scissor out of one of the nurses' pockets and stabbed her several times.

"We had no choice but to restrain her. The doctor then ordered her sent to Overlook Asylum in Essex County."

"What does that mean?" asked Fonso.

"I think it best you talk to the doctor."

Ten minutes later, a tall friendly man in a white coat approached Fonso in the waiting room. "Mr. Gravenese. There is good news and some difficult news. Medically, your wife will be fine, in time. She had a broken leg, a few broken ribs, and required about 48 stitches in her scalp and forehead. Emotionally, there seem to be multiple problems. She definitely has a case of post-traumatic amnesia. Sometimes patients snap out of it by themselves, other times the amnesia is complicated by other feelings. I can't comment on that because I don't know her past psychological profile."

"So now what?"

"She needs to undergo psychiatric counseling, group therapy, and such. They can fill you in at Overbrook on their specific recommendations."

"Is there any time frame in which I can expect my wife to get better?" asked Fonso.

"Not really. Every case is different. But more than 90 percent of post-traumatic patients regain their memory."

"Well, if that's the difficult news," said a relieved Fonso, "we'll just have to deal with it."

The doctor paused. "Actually, that's only part of the bad news." The doctor explained that Donna exhibited strong suicidal tendencies, in addition to her having uncontrolled rage. "That's the main reason she was admitted to the

Overbrook Asylum. Conventional medicine is simply not equipped to manage such cases."

$

Overbook was on Route 78 about 40 minutes west of Bayonne. It was a poorly kept, meandering red brick structure that looked part-prison, part-mental asylum.

The doctor was professional and matter-of-fact. "Our prelims suggest she is a difficult case. It may be a while before the rage within will even allow her to participate in the Asylum's normal activities."

Fonso wondered what all that meant. He didn't have to wait long. "We've started her on an anti-depressive drug called Librium. As you'll see, it has a strong calming agent, but like all mood-enhancing drugs, it has certain side-effects that vary from patient to patient."

"I've also prescribed some electroshock therapy."

"The drugs sound dreadful, but that electro thing sounds even worse."

"I'd be less than honest if I told you the treatments were pleasant. We do have to secure her before administering the electric current. But, if we don't shake her out of her current mood state quickly, she is likely to try to kill herself, or one of our staff."

"Suppose I don't authorize your recommendations?"

The doctor stared at Fonso. "Mr. Gravenese, I don't think we understand each other. Your wife has committed attempted murder on two separate occasions. Legally, those actions combined with her psychological state make her property of the state, until we determine she is no longer a menace to society."

The doctor instructed a nurse to take Fonso to Donna's room.

They walked down a long dimly lit hall dotted with thick dark doors. Each door had a tiny observation window. Strange sounds came from some of them.

They reached Room 177. "This is your wife's room," said the nurse. Fonso saw a narrow room with barred windows, a small sink and a toilet. Next to the sink sat a single bed. The ceilings and walls were covered with peeled white paint. There was also a tiny fan bolted to the wall over the bed.

Fonso stared at the unrecognizable woman on the bed. She had deep circles around her eyes. A face etched with pain. Disheveled, dirty hair. Soiled clothes, and filthy hands.

He backed away in horror. What happened to the beautiful woman he asked to marry him at the Rainbow Room?

Fonso cried all the way back to Ricco's. For one of the few times in his life, Fonso felt genuine guilt.

$

Life was not about to get any easier.

Ricco told him his mother-in-law wanted a quick, private funeral. She didn't want her neighbors to see some patched, embalmed version of her handsome husband.

Fonso wondered if he should attend. Ricco quickly resolved that issue. "She made it clear — we weren't invited."

Separately, Ricco told Fonso about Father Don's final arrangements at the cemetery. "There were just too many people for a funeral parlor." Ricco explained the Archdiocese decided to have last rites at St. Raymond's Cemetery in the Bronx, not far from where Father Don grew up.

Fonso recalled their good times together, and how deeply he cared for this man. He felt compelled to pay his final respects in person. Fonso and Ricco drove to the cemetery. Cars lined the streets surrounding the burial site. It was almost time to begin the service. Ricco volunteered to stay with the car, while Fonso attended the ceremony.

Minutes later, Fonso stood quietly in the rear of the church, ready to offer a few prayers. Father Don's colleague and boss, Cardinal Coogan, spotted Fonso and walked towards him.

Fonso began to offer condolences. The tall priest stared down at Fonso. "My son, I ask you to leave. You are not wanted here." Fonso tried to respond, but the Cardinal put his hand over Fonso's lips. "Even God sometimes finds forgiveness difficult."

Chapter 65

September, 1963
Brugg, Switzerland

By the summer of 1963, the wheels were coming off. Despite strenuous efforts of Fonso's overseas sales team and his network of connections from past deals, few international orders were coming in.

The political landscape had begun to change. While corruption remained prevalent, many of the new leaders distanced themselves from it. They believed they worked for the common good. And they were appointing ministers and mid-level managers who felt similarly.

Fonso's reputation for shortchanging contracts and shipping sending inferior product in cheap packaging made some of those leaders weary.

"God damn it, we service our ass off for years and nobody says a thing. But, if we make a few honest mistakes, the whole world knows," was Fonso's response.

$

But Fonso's corner-the-market price strategy was still working.

He owned for about 90 percent of all soybean and cottonseed futures on the two largest exchanges in New York and Chicago. He had masked the purchases so they appeared to be coming from a variety of sources, although Fonso owned all the companies.

But Fonso's success drove the price of futures up, not down. He had to borrow more and more money to pay for the contracts. This increased his cost of goods and refined-oil per gallon sales price, at precisely the time that international refiners in places like Italy and Spain were popping up and producing quality product for less.

He was left with two equally unattractive options:

Don't produce the oil, and let cash flow crash. Or, sell the refined product at a loss to maintain cash flow, and cover the losses with more loans.

He chose the latter. At his high point, Fonso would owe money to more than 51 lending institutions around the world. Nobody blew the whistle.

Some didn't want the brokerage commission and loan interest gravy train to stop; others feared customer backlash should word get out they had mismanaged their fiduciary responsibilities.

$

GLOBEX remained Fonso's temporary savior. Every lending institution predicated their irresponsible lending activity on GLOBEX warehouse receipts. They actually believed their loans were 100 percent secured, even in a worst-case scenario. This despite some amazing facts —

The supposed oil stored in Bayonne, supported by warehouse receipts, totaled *twice as much as all the oil in the United States*, according to DOA's own annual reports.

Fonso's physical inventory holdings never made any sense. On paper they amounted to an astounding 2 billion pounds, *more than the total ever exported from the United States in a single year.*

The actual inventory tank farm inventory was represented as approximately 937 million pounds. But, when finally, and accurately measured, oil tonnage was less than 10 percent of that figure.

When the end was near, the FBI finally completed an unsupervised audit. No Fonso, no employees, no friends and family. They needed to go no further than the primary GLOBEX tank number 6006. Company receipts indicated the tank contained $4 million worth of soybean oil. But in reality, the tank contained less than 200 gallons of oil worth $2,000. The rest of the tank was sea water, which poured out for 12 days.

They also discovered Fonso and his team had stolen a book of GLOBEX receipts and made copies. The copies were so good, nobody including GLOBEX ever realized they were counterfeit. Fonso had been issuing them like popcorn.

$

As one piece of bad news after another arrived at Fonso's desk, he knew the end was near. There would certainly be indictments for fraud, income-tax evasion, market manipulation, theft and whatever else.

The only saving grace was that International Grain was a private company. So Fonso had no public disclosure requirements, which meant he had a few days before the media, the FBI, and all the rest would come knocking on his door. Time to allow him to take two actions.

First, he quietly rehired Walter Riperton, considered the best corporate defense attorney money could buy.

Second, Fonso and Riperton developed both personal and corporate bankruptcy declarations. Personally, Fonso declared $210,000 in assets and $5,300,00 in liabilities. On the corporate side, Fonso's asset-to-liability ratio was even more lopsided. The company estimated it had at least $10,000 in liabilities for every dollar in assets. When the certified audit was complete, International Grain's balance sheets assets would disclose about $210 million in assets and almost $2 billion in liabilities. This would be the largest bankruptcy scandal in American history up until then.

As Fonso sarcastically joked with Riperton just prior to the actual filing, "I guess I'll be known as The Salad Oil King."

$

Fonso explained the good, bad and ugly to Ricco.

"Do what you want, but I would make myself scarce. They might be so focused on me, that you've got a bit more time to disappear somewhere."

Ricco decided "the somewhere" was Switzerland. He would go get his money, and disappear somewhere in Europe or Asia. With $5 million, he could live like a king. In two hours he was on a plane with a ticket charged on his GLOBEX card, which was still active. He also converted $500 into Swiss francs at the airport, so he would have some weekend spending money. Sunday, he checked into a nondescript local hotel under an assumed named. First thing Monday morning he asked Wilfred Auslander for a withdrawal. Auslander leaned back in his chair. "You aren't aware?"

"Aware of what?" asked Ricco.

That was how Ricco learned his savings had shrunk to ten dollars. He called Fonso. The operator said he had a collect call from Ricco in Switzerland. Fonso knew what it was about, but he had too many of his own problems to deal with. He refused the call.

$

A despondent Ricco walked the street of old Zurich for hours searching for a solution. He saw a local church and walked in. He lit a candle, and said a few prayers to Josephine, who he missed more than words could ever say.

He then walked to the center of town and boarded one of the charming tour boats that plied the Limmat River. About an hour later, the boat reached the town of Brugg which was dotted with 13th and 14th century houses, and pedestrian foot bridges. He thought he'd never seen such natural beauty, such tranquility.

As the boat neared one of the footbridges, Ricco's mind recalled another time...

He saw a young lady dropping red rose pedals into the water. Their eyes met. Josephine smiled and waved. When the boat passed under, Ricco looked back. Josephine was gone.

The rear of the boat was devoid of passengers. Ricco walked to the back, took one more look around. A barge coming the other way honked. The people on both boats waved to each other. Ricco smiled. Then slowly removed his gun from his holster, put the cold barrel to his temple, and pulled the trigger. His lifeless body fell into the canal...and nobody noticed.

Chapter 66

**Ask Not What
Your Country Can Do For You...
Ask What
You Can Do For Your Country**

November, 1963
Dallas, TX

Fonso decided to file for bankruptcy on Friday, the day usually reserved for bad news, which can get lost over the weekend.

Earlier that week, the cottonseed and soybean futures markets took a nosedive. Rumors of International Grain's disappointing sales, hints of bribes and short-changing customer orders ricocheted up and down the canyons of Wall Street.

Because International Grain held so many cottonseed and soybean contracts, small fluctuations in price significantly altered the total value of IG's brokerage account. By the close of business on Tuesday, prices had dropped three cents per pound. An alarmed Thompson Pierce demanded that Fonso deposit an additional $15 million to keep his Upton account current. Pierce didn't realize the price drop had wiped out much of International Grain's value.

Fonso ignored Upton's demands. He went on the offensive. Fonso accused them of leaking false rumors so *they* could profit by short selling the futures contracts.

In short-selling, the investor bets a contract will decline in value. The short-seller usually borrows the money to sell the contract to another investor, who is willing to buy that contract at the current price. The short-seller takes his profits when the price of the contract declines.

$

By close of business Wednesday, November 20th, soybean futures dropped another 20 cents, which meant another $360 million in value had vanished. Upton was now about $200,000 below minimum capital requirements. Edgars promptly reported the shortfall to the NYSE's member-firm department. A midlevel department official didn't think it significant enough to even report the infraction. They merely made a notation for the file.

Upton's individual account holders didn't know that the partners had convinced themselves that Fonso had cornered the market on vegetable oil supply, demand and pricing. They concluded, as the firm's lead broker, they were entitled to share in International Grain's gravy train. So they voted to invest the majority of the firm's capital reserve fund — $9 million, and another $37 million borrowed from willing lenders — to finance what amounted to insider trading in vegetable oil speculations.

$

The price of both cottonseed and soybean futures dropped another dollar. Upton was tens of millions of dollars below the reserve. Thousands of individual Upton accounts were in jeopardy. The entire value of Fonso's holdings, and all of Fonso's loans were worthless.

The NYSE froze Upton trading activity as it pondered damage control. When it opened on the following Monday the Exchange knew it had to have a solution to keep investors whole. Otherwise, the Exchange itself risked a complete loss of confidence on a scale never before seen.

$

At 1:41 pm, the next day, word that President John F. Kennedy had been shot flashed across the floor of the New York Stock Exchange.

Over the next seven minutes, panic selling ensued. Trading was halted at 2:07 pm. On Sunday, Kennedy's body was taken to the rotunda of the Capitol for public viewing. Monday became a day of national mourning. The stock market reopened on Tuesday, November 26th.

From the Exchange's point of view, this terrible tragedy gave officials approximately 48 hours to clean up Fonso's mess. The main priority was the clients, second were the injured lenders, and last, what to do with Upton.

Exchange officers, a sea of attorneys, and Upton management met over the weekend at NYSE headquarters. According to Edgars's calculations, the firm needed $10 million to make its clients whole, thereby avoiding legal action.

The Exchange disagreed. Their number was twice that — not including an estimated $50 million owed several domestic and international banks.

Their resolution was swift and decisive. The NYSE would take money out of their own reserves to reimburse all damaged Upton account holders, and suspend Upton forever. It would take the lead in negotiating a settlement with secured and unsecured lenders on both sides of the Atlantic.

By Sunday night, client plans, Upton's fate, and American bank agreements were in place. One obstacle remained. Would the European banks, which had no particular concern about the viability of the New York Stock Exchange, agree to a heavily discounted return of capital?

As part of their negotiating tactic, NYSE officials implied the millions buried somewhere in Fonso's twisted world would be identified and redistributed to the lending institutions. By Monday night, after another series of whirlwind meetings in London, all the international creditors had agreed to the terms.

When the market opened on Tuesday, the confusion caused by the Kennedy assassination still overshadowed the massive fraud. Privately, Fonso concluded the assassination of the President was one of the best things that ever happened to International Grain.

$

Wednesday morning, the FBI slapped Fonso with a Federal indictment that detailed a mountain of charges which translated to a lot of years behind bars. Bail was set at a million dollars, and his passport was confiscated. Fonso wanted to pay the bail immediately. Riperton strongly disagreed. "You're supposed to be bankrupt, remember?"

Riperton posted the bail four days later, after things quieted down. The four days Fonso sat in jail gave Riperton time to prepare a defense strategy. He knew the courts would ask about the source of the money, so he didn't ask Fonso. The truth was, Riperton didn't want to know.

"What about your wife? Technically, I'm guessing she can still cause a lot of trouble if she testifies."

"She won't be testifying." Fonso explained what happened at the funeral parlor and Donna's subsequent incarceration. Fonso was expecting a sympathetic reaction. Instead Riperton was surprising dismissive. "Sounds like that's one thing we don't have to worry about." Riperton paused. "Are you absolutely sure she's incoherent?"

Fonso nodded.

"Good," said Riperton. "I can work with that. Might take years off your sentence."

Chapter 67

February, 1964
Federal Court House, NYC

Riperton reviewed the modified indictment without saying a word. Fonso sat nervously clicking his pen. The silence caused the clicking to sound like a mission bell clacking in his Riperton's head. "Stop with that goddam pen. With what you're paying me per hour, you don't want me distracted."

"Looks like they upped the charges since last week. Now we've got 19 counts — plus three charges of conspiring to circulate $200 million worth of forged warehouse receipts via interstate commerce from 1961 to 1963. If we go to trial, and lose, you could be looking at a maximum jail term of 185 years."

Fonso was stunned. Never in his wildest imagination!

"Look, let's get real. You're going to jail. The question is for how long?" said Riperton. "We've also got another little complication. Upton is suing you for misrepresentation."

"They know there's no money, so what do they expect to achieve?"

"Keep their good name. They were duped. Not a bad strategy. Could allow them to remain an entity. Maybe take some pressure off the partner fines."

Riperton seemed calm as he explained the defense strategy. Fonso would plead guilty to only three charges; forging warehouse receipts, underpaying personal incomes taxes, and creating a conflict of interest with an International Grain employee that also worked for GLOBEX by offering him a bribe.

The rest of the charges he'd blame on Auslander. He needed to reinforce that he was an uneducated butcher from the Bronx who got involved in matters way over his head. That he was the one who was duped by sophisticated charlatans who got his confidence. That he and Donna signed numerous tax returns that they didn't understand, but believed to be correct.

Fonso and Riperton knew Auslander would never come out of hiding to defend himself. He had money and anonymity. Wilfred was certainly not going to put his cushy president's_job in jeopardy for something as silly as truth and justice.

As for the mob, it was unlikely they would step forward because they would have to disclose names or exercise their Fifth-Amendment rights.

Beyond that, anybody who knew something —
Ricco, Josephine, Donna, Victor, et al, were either
dead, missing or legally gagged.

Riverton challenged Upton. "Is there any
paper anywhere that says you coerced Upton into
buying stock on their behalf?

"Never," responded Fonso.

"Are you absolutely, positively sure?"

"I fucking told you. The answer is no," said
Fonso indignantly.

"Is there anything else I should know?" asked
Riperton.

"Not that I can think of," said Fonso
convincingly. He decided that Riperton had no
need to know about the millions he discretely
tucked away in places like the Isle of Man and
Lichtenstein.

$

It was showtime. The clock read 10:10 a.m.,
and there was still no defendant. Judge Rupert
Warner raised his bushy gray eyebrows. Fonso's
lawyers fidgeted. Fonso walked in, apologized
profusely, then sat down and whispered in
Riperton's ear. He nodded.

"Mr. Gravenese wants the court to know that
he just came from a session with his psychologist,
since he's trying to deal with his feelings of despair
over the prospect of jail time."

The prosecutor sneered. Riperton surprised
the prosecution by deposing Fonso first. They had
agreed Fonso should conjure an image of himself
as the generous benefactor to a close-knit family of
employees. Varying his tone and intensity, Fonso
explained the responsibility he felt for his

employees. "I am very proud of the fact that all our employees are good family men, all living in the same Jersey community."

"Is there any truth to prosecution claims that you willingly doled out bribes when the need suited you?" asked Riperton.

"If you mean did I advance money to my employees, the answer is absolutely yes."

"Can you give us an example or two?"

The prosecution objected on the grounds the information was irrelevant. Riperton disagreed on the grounds that much of the indictment rested on hearsay testimony, so the accused's credibility was critical. The judge overruled the prosecution.

Fonso detailed a $35,000 loan he gave an employee to purchase a home. When asked if the loan was paid back, he stated his deceased secretary, Josephine, handled those matters. He also testified that he had taken $10,000 out of his own pocket and given it to an employee named Thomas Clark because they were expecting a baby. The prosecutor asked if gifts of $3,000 or more appeared on his income-tax statements. Fonso said you'd have to ask his accountant, Fred Auslander.

Riperton then subtly went after GLOBEX credibility.

"Did you know Mr. Clark was also an employee of GLOBEX warehousing?"

"Not originally. I just heard he worked two jobs to make ends meet. So I thought we should help him out."

"Did you know he has testified that you asked him to falsify inventory levels?"

"I'm disappointed that he would say such a thing," said Fonso despondently.

$

"I think the show went well today," said Riperton. "I saw it in the judge's eyes. Tomorrow we'll crush Upton's bankruptcy allegations."

Riperton's day two strategy was to continue portraying Fonso as part charlatan-part benefactor. Fonso openly admitted he'd made some grievous mistakes, but he was not a monster who should rot in jail for the rest of his natural life.

Q. Did Upton handle all your future contracts?

A. Yes.

Q. How much of the existing supply of cotton-seeds and soybeans did you control at your high point?

A. Somewhere around 80 percent.

Q. During that period, did Upton ever protest the amount of contacts you held?

A. No.

Q. Do you know if they bought any contracts for their own account?

A. Yes.

Q. How did you know that?

A. They told me.

Q. Did you at any time suggest they do so?

A. No.

Q. Did they ever tell you they bought contracts using their customers' margins accounts?

A. No.

Q. Did they willingly accept GLOBEX receipts?

A. Yes.

Q. Did they use those receipts to borrow money to buy more contracts for Upton?

A. They never said anything to me.

$

Two weeks later Fonso pleaded guilty.

The clerk announced the entrance of Judge Wagner and opened with the statement that "the United States of America versus Anthony Gravenese" was the first case to be deposed. Riperton read the charges. Fonso chewed his lower lip.

After the reading, the Judge said, "Let him stand before the lectern." He asked Fonso if he understood the charges.

"I do, your honor," said Fonso.

The Judge asked if he was pleading of his own free will. Fonso replied, "absolutely."

After the court session ended, Riperton gave reporters a prepared four-page statement. It noted the government was still looking into some phases of the International Grain activities, which had driven many companies into liquidation. Fonso stated, "Officials have asked for my cooperation. I intend to give it to them fully and truthfully, just as I have been all along."

Two weeks later Fonso was sentenced to seven years at Sing-Sing prison in nearby Ossining, New York. His tiny room had views of the Hudson River. He was also fined $25,000.

$

The Judge later ruled that Upton knew full well he had engaged in unethical behavior. The firm was dissolved as a going concern, and all its partners were banned from trading securities for life.

Chapter 68

September, 1964
Sing-Sing Prison, Ossining, NY

Prison was not something Fonso had spent his life preparing for. He never once had asked the many ex-cons he knew how life was behind bars.

When he got on the bus to be transferred to Sing-Sing, he stood out from the rest of the inmates. A potbellied middle-aged man among a strident group of ten macho men with bodies and violent egos to match. Physically, he was a boy among men. Intellectually, he was a man among boys. He could see people looking in the metal caged windows, partially out of fear for their community, and partially out of curiosity.

Sing-Sing was at the end of a steep tree-lined road in the bustling commuter town of Ossining, New York. The wealthy upscale town was a mere 40-minute train ride from Times Square.

$

Fonso's urine-scented gray prison bus pulled up to two big dark wooden doors. The bus honked, the doors swung open. Armed guards formed a lane.

Chained in shackles, they walked slowly into a holding area where they were meet by a small man with a mustache who strutted like a peacock.

"I'm Warden Jenkins. You are now official residents of hell. Let me tell you the rules. Do what I say, anytime, all the time. Those are the rules. Protest or drag your ass, and you'll find yourself in solitary. Protest or drag your ass a second time, and I promise you'll wind up in hell forever."

The men were stripped and searched, while their clothes and other belongings were put in bags and labeled. They each were given prison work clothes and shoes and led to their cells down a long corridor. The warden pointed to the common showers, the mess hall, and then stopped at a black metal door. "Since we're doing the tour, I thought you might want to see this," said the warden. He pulled the door open. There on a stone pedestal sat Sing-Sing's infamous electric chair, a heavy dark wood structure with thick leather straps at the areas where arms, legs, and chest were placed. "From the records I got, none of you have made a reservation here. But there's always next time," he said with a curious sense of disappointment. "We've had some real pieces of shit here." Just like in the movies.

$

Fonso also quickly came to dread exercise time. He had to walk the yard with the other prisoners, who taunted, mocked and laughed at him. If he said something, anything, he knew he'd get pummeled. In the first week he incurred a few bumps and bruises but didn't complain. After all, who was listening?

At the end of the first week a chaplain arrived for his monthly stop. Sometimes an inmate would say something to him in private, and other times he just delivered a little sermon about virtues and values. At least you got to sit in a chair in an assembly room without bars for 60 minutes, as armed guards stood at the ready perched on a walkway above the floor.

Fonso decided he wanted to talk to the Chaplain, mostly just to hear a voice that didn't shout or mock. "Father," said Fonso. "This is a terrible place. I'm not like the others. Why am I here?"

"My son, those are questions for God and the warden."

"Aren't they one and the same?"

Fonso talked about the wanton greed that landed him where he was. The Chaplain absolved him, and gave him a wooden crucifix. "Perhaps this will give you comfort." Fonso thanked the Chaplain, then tore a small strip of cloth from his bedsheet and hung the artifact from one of his cell bars. That first night would be Fonso's best night of sleep.

The next day when he returned from lunch the crucifix was gone. He assumed the guards took it. He said nothing, since he had learned quickly that prisoners had no rights. Later, as he walked by himself, circling the exercise yard, an ornery looking man sneered and taunted. "There walks Jesus Christ, our man of the cross."

Fonso tried to ignore him. Two other prisoners joined the taunting session. Fonso stopped and tried to calmly reason — big mistake. "Fellas, please give me a break, I haven't…"

The largest of the three men pulled the crucifix out of his pocket, while the other two dragged him over into a corner, barely visible by the guards. The man wielded the crucifix like a knife, slashing Fonso's face, again and again. Blood oozed everywhere as he fell to the ground moaning.

"Joe, Mickey, and Anthony just wanted you to know they're still real pissed," said the large man.

Finally, the guards saw Fonso lying by himself in a pool of blood. They dashed down and brought him to the infirmary. Nothing was said about the incident, nor was anyone reprimanded.

A few days later, he had healed enough to be brought to the warden's office. The warden looked at the bandaged man. "Fonso, I've got some good news," said the warden sarcastically. "Your lawyer must be fucking connected. He made a case with the courts to get you moved to our low-security prison resort in Arizona. Apparently, your financial schemes didn't warrant seven years at my establishment."

$

Fonso was transferred – first by train, then bus — to Lewis prison in Arizona, escorted by a Federal Marshall.

Best Fonso could tell, Lewis was about 50 miles outside Phoenix. It was dark when they arrived, so he had no idea what the place looked like or how things were organized. He was told he'd meet the warden in the morning. As things turned out, Lewis was more about rehabilitation than merely punishment. The black warden, James John Jones, was quite well read. He had followed Fonso's exploits in the press. In time, he suggested that Fonso might want to contact *Life* Magazine, and tell his side of the story.

To both men's surprise, *Life* was interested. They sent a staff reporter and photographer. Some months later, a nine-page feature story entitled *The Great Soybean Scandal* appeared in its pages. While the story didn't make Fonso out to be a saint, it did marvel at how he duped so many people for so long. As Fonso complained privately, it was only half the story. They hardly mentioned the good things he did under The Free Lunch Act and Food for Peace.

$

Fonso was told he had a visitor — his first in three years. It could only be Ricco, who had finally come out of hiding.

As he walked into the visiting room, there sat his now 69-year-old mother at a table behind a thick glass. Philomena still lived in the Bayonne house Fonso bought her when he and Donna first married. Over the past 30 years, Fonso occasionally had visited, but mostly he sent money every month. He took care of all the house expenses. The bills went directly to his office and were paid out of one of his accounts by whoever handled corporate receivables.

"Mama!"

She pulled out a copy of *Life* magazine, and waved it at the window. "Is it true what they say?"

Fonso tried to explain. "Mama, you need to understand about business…"

She interrupted, repeating the question with fire in her eyes. "Is it?"

"Some is, and some isn't."

She was disappointed. Fonso changed the subject.

"Mama, I will be free before you know it. Things will be different. We will be able to talk, spend some time together."

Philomena shook her head and got up to walk out.

"There is nothing to talk about. You are a stranger. My son died a long, long time ago."

Chapter 69

Luke 15:11-32
Holy Bible, New Version

Jesus continued: "There was a man who had two sons. The younger one said to his father, 'Father, give me my share of the estate.' So he divided his property between them.

"Not long after that, the younger son got together all he had, set off for a distant country and there squandered his wealth in wild living. After he had spent everything, there was a severe famine in that whole country, and he began to be in need. So he went and hired himself out to a citizen of that country, who sent him to his fields to feed pigs. He

longed to fill his stomach with the pods that the pigs were eating, but no one gave him anything.

"When he came to his senses, he said, 'How many of my father's hired servants have food to spare, and here I am starving to death! I will set out and go back to my father and say to him: Father, I have sinned against heaven and against you. I am no longer worthy to be called your son; make me like one of your hired servants.' So he got up and went to his father.

"But while he was still a long way off, his father saw him and was filled with compassion for him; he ran to his son, threw his arms around him and kissed him.

"The son said to him, 'Father, I have sinned against heaven and against you. I am no longer worthy to be called your son.'

"But the father said to his servants, 'Quick! Bring the best robe and put it on him. Put a ring on his finger and sandals on his feet. Bring the fattened calf and kill it. Let's have a feast and celebrate. For this son of mine was dead and is alive again; he was lost and is found.' So they began to celebrate.

"Meanwhile, the older son was in the field. When he came near the house, he heard music and dancing. So he called one of the servants and asked him what was going on. 'Your brother has come,' he replied, 'and your father has killed the fattened calf because he has him back safe and sound.'

"The older brother became angry and refused to go in. So his father went out and pleaded with him. But he answered his father, 'Look! All these years I've been slaving for you and never disobeyed your orders. Yet you never gave me even a young goat so I could celebrate with my friends. But when this son of yours who has squandered

*your property with prostitutes comes home, you kill the
fattened calf for him!'*

*"'My son,' the father said, 'you are always with me,
and everything I have is yours. But we had to celebrate and
be glad, because this brother of yours was dead and is alive
again; he was lost and is found.'"*

Warden Jones saw the *Life* Magazine article
differently than Philomena. He saw a potential
rehabilitation opportunity in Fonso's entrepreneurial
skills.

"Fonso, have you ever thought about teaching
a class on how to start a business? The fact is most
ex-convicts when they get released have a hard
time re-entering the real world. The way I look at it
is that they made their mistake and paid their debt
to society. They just need a little jump start."

"Warden, I don't have experience in teaching
anything," responded Fonso.

"Suppose I told you, if the program worked,
I'd support time off for good behavior with the
parole board?"

That caught Fonso's attention. He desperately
wanted to make peace with his mother. "How
would this work?" asked Fonso.

"You tell me. You're the corporate genius. I
know I can get the men there. They'll do anything
to trade working in the damn desert sun for a few
hours in an air-conditioned classroom."

Fonso spent weeks preparing a course that
would be informative and understandable. He
showed his progress to the warden who was so
impressed he gave extra time in the prison reading
room to work under better conditions. Fonso

surprised himself. His knowledge, both good and bad, was now a six-week course, including practical team-building exercises.

The warden kept his side of the deal. The first day was a full house — 36 bored convicts.

Fonso began with a question. "How many of you are here to get out of the heat?" No hands raised. "How many of you want to stay out of Lewis?"

Hands raised.

"How do you expect to do that? You're a goddamn ex-con. Somebody might give you a job as a dishwasher or a janitor. But do you really think somebody is going to hire you for a good job?"

He had their attention. "There is only one sure way out of here. Start a business that allows you to make a fair wage."

"That takes money," mocked the prison bully, Bull James. "You lending?"

"Not as far-fetched as you might think," said Fonso. "Suppose I told you I've got millions waiting for me when I get out?"

The class hooted and howled.

"Laugh all you want, but when was the last time a millionaire businessman offered to share his secrets with you?" Fonso paused. "That's what this is all about. So either give me your attention or get out." Nobody moved. Fonso summarized his forthcoming curriculum in convict-speak:

What am I trying to sell? A product or a service?

How do I know anybody wants to buy it?

Where am I going to get the money to make it?

How am I going to price it?

Where am I going to start my business?
How are people going to learn about it?
Suppose I need help, what do I do?
How do I keep records for loans and taxes?
How do I treat employees?

Over the next several years, the Warden gave Fonso an overhead projector, and the course was committed to a series of overhead acetates which Fonso wrote himself. From time to time, he would add, update, and edit the course as he recalled the details of his business life.

Warden Jones decided to award certificates of accomplishment to program graduates. The local, and ultimately national press ran stories about the one-of-a-kind rehabilitation program. During the numerous press interviews that followed, the Warden proudly proclaimed, "Not one of our business school graduates has been re-incarcerated."

$

Mama never again visited or responded to his letters. One day he received an attorney's letter notifying him that his mother had died of heart failure in a local nursing home. The lawyer said he was the executor of his mother's estate and that she had left some $500,000 to charity.

From time to time, he'd write to the Overbrook Asylum to inquire about Donna. Nobody ever replied. One day he was reading a dated newspaper in the reading room, which contained a syndicated story about abuses in mental institutions and the horrible consequences. The investigative reporter talked about a 30-something female patient admitted to a New Jersey asylum five years earlier after witnessing the violent death of her father. The story detailed the experimental treatments that she had undergone without regard for potential side-effects, and that the patient had broken free from her restraints and hung herself in the middle of the night. Fonso knew it was Donna.

Guilt-ridden and depressed, Fonso was alone with no one to turn to. He thought about his Catholic roots and how far he had strayed. He recalled the words of the Cardinal at Father Don's burial, "Even God sometimes finds forgiveness difficult."

The prison chaplain made his monthly visit. Fonso went to his first church service in many years and spoke to the chaplain afterward. Fonso explained much of what he had done. The chaplain passed no judgment, instead suggesting Fonso might find some solace in reading the Bible.

Fonso soon received a Bible in the mail. Each evening before lights out, he'd read a few passages, say a few prayers, and ask himself some tough questions.

Was his soul lifeless? Had he done the terrible things people say he did? How many lives had he ruined in the process? Was there any possibility of redemption? Was there even a partial road back?

Naively, he hoped for a sign from God. Something to light his future path. None came. Two more weeks later a crucifix arrived in the mail. He hung it on the rear wall of his cell over the bed. Fonso thanked the chaplain for the Bible and the crucifix on his next prison visit. The two men sat in Fonso's cell; the chaplain told him, "I didn't send either."

$

Years passed. Fonso was summoned to the warden's office. "Like I said way back," said Jones. "You do for me; I do for you. The parole board has agreed to give you time off for good behavior."

Fonso smiled. "How much."

"Two years." (Fonso had already served five of the seven). Fonso wondered out loud. "So that means…" The warden interrupted. "Yup, that means you're out of here next week."

The two men shook hands. Fonso started to leave. "One thing, I've been meaning to ask you for years," said the warden. "Do you really have millions waiting for you?"

Fonso smiled. "You should keep my program materials."

$

The day Fonso dressed to leave, he noticed his seven-year-old business suit hung loosely like a potato sack. He had lost almost 30 pounds…

Chapter 70

September, 1970
Phoenix, AZ

At dawn, the doors of Lewis prison slowly creaked opened. Fonso stepped into the world a free man for the first time in almost six years. He eyes scanned a no man's land — a few prickly tumbleweeds wandered across the parched, barren, windswept landscape.

Fonso had arrived in darkness, so this was his first genuine view of the prison complex. It was dreary — rows of tiny, single-story boxes with bars connected by windowless black concrete tunnels.

But on this day, the glumness was majestically overshadowed by a vibrant purple, orange and yellow Arizona sunrise.

He looked around for the car the warden said would be waiting. In the employee parking lot sat a shiny black stretch limousine. A tanned, smiling man in a uniform got out and waved. "Fonso, over here."

The man looked familiar, but after seven years, his memory had dulled. Fonso's blank expression told the man he didn't remember.

"Fonso, it's me. Sam Magro."

Fonso smiled. "Sam…I'm so sorry, I just didn't recognize you." Sam had lost 40 pounds, and sported a glowing Arizona tan under a head of retouched jet black hair.

"I could say the same about you. Looks like you went to one of those fat farms while you were away. How much did you lose in there?"

Fonso laughed. "Sam, to tell you the truth, I never even noticed until this morning."

Sam smiled. "If it wasn't for the fact that you're still wearing that same crumpled black suit, and those same horned-rimmed glasses, I might not have recognized you either." He didn't mention that Fonso's hair was now mostly gray.

"Please…get in. We can talk as I drive."

The plush limousine interior reminded Fonso of the good old days.

"So… where do we start?" offered Sam. "About five years ago, Barbara and I decided we had enough of the New York winters. Thanks to you, I had a little bar and grill in Bayonne. It became a popular watering hole for a lot of the old crowd. Barbara and I did a little research, and decided to move to the land of the sun. We thought the dry desert air would be good for Barbara's asthma, and my arthritis. So we sold the place and the house on 22nd Street in Bayonne, and never looked back."

"She still a shopping machine?" smiled Fonso.

"Not really. But she's developed a new obsession."

Sam proudly pulled two pictures out of his wallet as he drove down the highway. "Meet our granddaughters. Holly is 17 and Jessica is 16. "Great kids. Sweet and smart as hell. Probably my only regret, we don't see them as much as we'd like. Now, they're getting ready for college. Time flies."

Sam asked Fonso about himself. Fonso summarized prison. "It's like going on vacation to a half-star resort. Bad food, bad people, bad accommodations." The men laughed. It had the feel of the good old days.

Sam turned serious. "You gotta be one of the luckiest people on earth. All the shit you pulled and you get off with five years.

"Fonso, while you never did wrong by me, you really fucked up my niece. She still in that looney bin. Barbara and I tried to see her a few years back. The doctor's say she has no idea who she is, doesn't remember her childhood, nothing."

Fonso didn't know how to respond.

$

Sam reached over on the seat, and picked up an envelope, and handed it to Fonso.

"Almost forgot, this came for you. It was on the front porch of my house. Fonso stared. It said "To be opened only by Alfonso Gravenese." "There was a second envelope with $300 and instructions when and where to pick you up."

"I wonder why you?"

"Got me," smiled Sam. "Barbara and I always thought you got a bum deal. The way those bastards all bailed on you. That's what I told the Feds when I got deposed. Guess they didn't want anybody to know the good stuff."

"Thanks, Sam. Been quite a while since I've heard a compliment."

Fonso opened the envelope. It contained a single, handwritten card. "Welcome back. I guess we're now even." It was signed Joe, Mickey and Anthony.

Sam pulled off at Glendale, exit 133. "Barbara and I were talking. We figured you didn't make reservations at the new Camelback Resort, so why not come stay with us for a few days."

Fonso smiled gratefully.

"You know, there's no rush. We can have a few laughs, and you can think about what you want to do."

Fonso stayed three days. He learned Sam and Barbara had made a lot of new friends and incurred a lot of medical expenses for Barbara's asthma. "Nothing to complain about," said Sam. "My little limo business keeps me out of trouble, and lets me earn some extra money to help pay for the grandkids' college tuition."

"It's what grandparents do," said Barbara.

The couple asked Fonso if he had any plans. Fonso laughed. "Maybe I'll start another business… far, far away."

Sam asked awkwardly. "Fonso, I hope you don't get insulted. But Barbara and I were wondering…do you have any money?"

Fonso smiled mischievously. "Well, I have a few safety deposit boxes in Switzerland and Lichtenstein. I've just gotta round up a little money for the airfare."

Sam looked at Barbara. She nodded. "Barbara and I thought that might be the case, so we wanted you to have this. It's not a lot, but maybe it can help you get back on your feet."

Fonso opened the envelope. There were twenty $100 bills. A tiny tear formed in the corner of Fonso's eye. "You're such good people. Promise I'll pay you back."

Sam explained the money was not a loan. It was a gift. A belated thank you for what Fonso had done for him, and so many of his former employees.

Sam smiled. Tell you what, when you pay me back, just add a million dollars in interest. We'll call it even."

$

The morning before Fonso left Barbara opened the front door with a big smile. "Someone has traveled a long way to say hello."

A tall, handsome, broad-shouldered young man with dark wavy hair stood in the doorway. He had a smile that could light up a room. His features had a distant familiarity.

"Fonso, I'd like you to meet your godson, Alfonso Cicola. I don't believe you've seen him in a long, long time."

"Hello, Godfather."

Fonso's eyes welled with tears. Barbara was right. He had not seen the young man since his baptism in Little Italy 16 years ago.

The men hugged and wept.

"Godfather, I have so many questions only you can answer."

Fonso learned that when Josephine died and Ricco disappeared, Sam and Barbara volunteered to raise Alfonso. He was an excellent student, and had earned a scholarship to prestigious Exeter Academy prep school in New Hampshire.

"When did you get here?" asked Fonso.

"Just now. When Aunt Barbara opened the door. Uncle Sam called me last night to say you were in town. I wanted so much to meet you, I flew through the night."

"Thank you," said Fonso still brimming with emotion, "Thank you very much...really."

"Alfonso is very mature for his age. He's planning on going to Harvard University, then, hopefully on to Harvard Business School."

There were no easy questions at dinner.

"Was my mother as beautiful as her pictures?"

"Perhaps even more so."

"Did she really choke to death."

Fonso nodded as the memories flooded his mind. The screaming. The suddenness. The finality of it all.

"Alfonso, it was just one of those freak accidents."

"How did my father take it."

"Your father loved that woman like no man has ever loved a woman. He felt that way from the first moment he saw her at the office, to the last breath she took."

"If you don't mind me asking what ever happened to Aunt Donna?"

Barbara jumped in. "I don't think Fonso wants to go there."

Fonso leaned forward. "No, it's okay. I owe my Godson the truth. The truth is I ruined her life. The lies. The mistakes. The greed. It all feels like the unimaginable dream. I wouldn't even know where to begin."

"Godfather, would you mind. I have one last question." Alfonso paused and looked directly in Fonso's eyes. "What happened to my father?"

Fonso took his horn-rimmed glasses off. His hand brushed against his chin. He gently shook his head. More tears. "He was my best friend in the whole world, and I don't know the answer to that question."

$

The next morning, Sam and Alfonso drove Fonso to the airport for a flight to New York. This time, his clothes fit. The men hugged affectionately for what Fonso knew would be the last time.

As Fonso flew across the country, he thought about his first 55 years. If he had to do it all over again, what would he do anything differently? How did the chaos he created get so out of control? Why do bad things happen to good people, like Father Don?

How would he fill the void created by the loss of those he loved most — his mother and Donna? Is there such a thing as redemption?

Most important, where did he go from here?

$

Sam waited to deposit a few checks into his Sun Valley Bank branch. Instead, he opened a new account specifically earmarked for the grandkids' education.

The teller spotted a notification. "Mr. Magro, our branch manager would like to speak with you.

"About what?" Sam's first thought was...his checking balance fell below the latest account minimums. The Valley had grown quite a bit since they first arrived. Most of the newbies seemed to be wealthy retirees.

"Mr. Magro," said the smiling manager. "What a coincidence. I was just about to call you."

"Why?"

"It's not every day we get wire transfers like this."

"Wire transfer? From who?"

"I'm not privy to that information.

"Where's it from?"

"Sorry, sir. I'm not authorized to disclose the name of the banking institution."

Sam thought there had to be some mistake. "I'm Samuel J. Magro. Are you sure you have the right Sam Magro?"

"I think so." The bank manager confirmed Sam and Barbara's address and social security numbers. Then he showed Sam a transfer. It read $1,002,000. The notation was simple. "The funds are for loan repayment...plus interest."

"How would you like the funds deposited?"

"Why don't you open an account for my grandchildren, Jessica and Holly Magro" replied Sam without hesitation.

Sam started toward the door. The banker called out. "Mr. Magro. We're not quite finished."

Sam assumed there was some paper he had neglected to sign.

"Mr. Magro. There is a second transfer from the same transferee. It is for the benefit of your nephew, Alfonso."

"How much?"

"Five million dollars."

As Sam walked outside, a low-flying Swiss Airways jet passed directly overhead...He looked up and waved goodbye.

Epilogue

The little boy named Fonso was born on Spring Street in Manhattan's Little Italy. Occasionally, his parents hired a baby sitter, a little neighborhood girl by the name of Frances. As they grew, Fonso and his family moved to the Bronx, and he became a butcher.

Frances' family also moved to the Bronx. They didn't see each other much, but remained friends with a note here, and a call there. They mostly shared memories of growing up in Little Italy.

Frances eventually married a nice young man named Matty. He also was a butcher. She introduced him to Fonso. Matty and Fonso became friends.

Fonso always had big ideas, and so he went into business for himself. Matty and Frances invested a few dollars of their savings in Fonso's business. Fonso paid them back every cent, plus interest.

As the years rolled by, Fonso became a big success. Frances kept in touch. Matty died suddenly at the age of 60. Fonso paid his respects to Frances by phone. Their first communication in 20 years.

Ten years later, Frances read Fonso had gone to jail for things she never imagined that little boy could do.

She tried to pay him a surprise visit in prison. He was too embarrassed to see her. Several years later he was released from jail, and disappeared.

Frances, who lived alone, was sitting in her living room, just passing the time, as people in their seventies do. The phone rang. It was Fonso. He said he just wanted to hear her friendly voice. That he never forgot her. That he was fine, and living in upstate New York. He told Frances that was the last time they would speak, for more reasons than he cared to discuss. He gave no address.

They never spoke or wrote again. Frances died some years later at the age of 93. There are no records of where and when Fonso passed, because if he were alive today, he would be 101 years old.

I know this story to be true — because Frances was my mother.

References

Con Artists Hall of Infamy.
http://bit.ly/1QwaC4t

Lehman Brothers Collection
http://hbs.me/1WSCgZh

School Lunch Act.
http://bit.ly/1Lb5sUy

School Lunch History. 1930's
http://bit.ly/1Y79wyo

School Lunch History. 1940's
http://bit.ly/1Y79wyo

Pictorial History of the World of Crime
http://bit.ly/1QAZljx

Hog Killing Day on the Farm
http://bit.ly/1H0Nycg

How War Changed the What America Eats
http://huff.to/1H1qMRn

Foundation for Economic Advancement: WWII Two-Tier Pricing
http://bit.ly/1iZX2bZ

Investment Company Act of 1940
http://1.usa.gov/1SwYEWX

Buying a Bankrupt Business
http://1.usa.gov/1HTFQLX

History of Kansas City Meatpacking
http://bit.ly/1H4KKuA

International Tax Havens
http://bit.ly/20XcyI0

Surplus Marketing Administration
http://1.usa.gov/1PCbKo6

Asset Based Financing
http://bit.ly/1XlQ6DP

Food Prices: 1940's
http://bit.ly/1LwqWv8

The Meatpacking Jungle
http://to.pbs.org/1OoCsgN

Jimmy Hoffa and the Teamsters Union
http://bit.ly/1YqluDs

Salad Oil Swindle
http://bit.ly/1PebZWq

The Great Salad Oil Scandal
http://read.bi/1NrZSyA New Empire

Mob Attorneys: Portrait of Scoundrel
http://bit.ly/1PSnSS1

The Brown Derby
http://bit.ly/1NyHQRu

About Exeter Academy
http://bit.ly/1oZ5ITE

Depositions
http://bit.ly/1TcuJn6

Food for Peace
http://bit.ly/1NCqlgb

Spain after World War 2
http://bit.ly/1U4EFQ2

Economic History of Spain
http://bit.ly/1Thrw6b

Vegetable Oils
http://bit.ly/1mBbWb9

Fundamentals of Cottonseed Oil
http://bit.ly/1mgNewe

Soybean Oils: The Facts
http://bit.ly/1U5OflU

History of Soybeans
http://bit.ly/1ObspNq

Spanish Civil War
http://bit.ly/1mCmLtB

Economic History of Spain
http://bit.ly/1Oq6tjI

American Military in Spain
http://bit.ly/1SfCY3V

Naval Station @ Rota
http://bit.ly/1Jz6n1W

American Air Presence in Spain
http://abt.cm/1mDKJ9o

History of Spanish Pesetas
http://bit.ly/1MzprNn

Personality of General Francisco Franco
http://bit.ly/1QSDjKg

Karachi: City in Turmoil
http://bit.ly/1JaHqyP

History of Karachi
http://bit.ly/1mkMZAm

Gillespie Charms Karachi
http://bit.ly/1QUcsxI

Pakistan Governmental Ministries
http://bit.ly/1ZvNpCD

Ahmed Hossain
http://bit.ly/1QUABUG

Middle Eastern Garments
http://bit.ly/22tP260

The Religion of Islam
http://bit.ly/1JdH7mS

History: Bern's Steak House
http://bit.ly/1YLNm8O

Turkish – US Relationships
http://bit.ly/1R1qE8p

Incirlik Air Base, Turkey
http://bit.ly/22ABE07

Post War Economic Expansion
http://bit.ly/1JTNQ0o

Post War Communism
http://bit.ly/1mw6xCw

Eisenhower and the Cold War
http://bit.ly/1ZKMTAG

History of Continental Grain Company
http://bit.ly/1VCI7TB

History of Bunge Limited
http://bit.ly/1OHYTej

Global Oil Seed and Soybean Trading
http://bit.ly/1O7MO4N

History of Soybeans
http://bit.ly/1ZdD5SR

Economics of Commodity Trading
http://bit.ly/1n7WYtl

Venezuelan Politics
http://bit.ly/1N3pykt

Venezuelan Food
http://bit.ly/1IZ6Q2F

Financial History of the United States
http://bit.ly/1Spfcn8

New Encyclopedia of American Scandals
http://bit.ly/1Qe6tmf

Bankruptcy Proceedings: Ira Haupt & Company
http://bit.ly/238tiwN

Twelve Classic Wall Street Tales by John Brooks
http://bit.ly/208eo7A

Egyptian Life – 1960s
http://bit.ly/1Pg0RZQ

Life and Times of Abdul Nassar Hussein
http://bit.ly/1Pg0RZQ

Life and Times of Anwar Sadat
http://bit.ly/1nyE2Eu

Net Capital Rule
http://bit.ly/23oEsh9

Sort Selling the Market
http://bit.ly/20pghgh

Bergen County History
http://bit.ly/1VMDqWC

Historical Currency Conversions
http://bit.ly/1R2Ebvk

History of Hijabs
http://bit.ly/1S3TDsu

Trading Commodities
bit.ly/20h05LX

Overbrook Asylum, Essex County
http://bit.ly/1V3JJoE

Introduction to Cynar
http://bit.ly/21dU9G4

Parable of the Lost Son, Holy Bible
http://bit.ly/1Y56Tg6

Link sourcing: Bitly.com

CPSIA information can be obtained at www.ICGtesting.com
Printed in the USA
LVOW08*2142280716

498209LV00002B/2/P

9 780991 477357